Multinationals, Global Value Chains and Governance

This book uses the examples of local supply firms in China and Brazil and their connections to the global automotive industry to explore the nature of current global value chains. It argues that lead firms make use of product architecture to globalize their procurement and supply chain management and that they effectively restructure the global supply base by internationalizing the most capable supply firms, thereby creating oligopolies controlled by the lead firm. The book goes on to contend that some firms have gained such powerful positions that they have gained a degree of control over other firms without the necessity of ownership – altering the mechanics of governance. Also, it shows how, although some supply firms from emerging markets have utilized their business ties with western assembly firms to upgrade themselves within the global value chain, most are squeezed out through increased global competition. Overall, the book makes a major new contribution to the economic theory of governance.

Peter Hertenstein, who completed his doctorate at the University of Cambridge, is a guest lecturer in International Management at the University of Antwerp and works in strategy consulting at Roland Berger.

Routledge Studies on the Chinese Economy

Series Editor

Peter Nolan, Director, Centre of Development Studies; Chong Hua Professor in Chinese Development; and Director of the Chinese Executive Leadership Programme (CELP), University of Cambridge

Founding Series Editors

Peter Nolan, University of Cambridge

Dong Fureng, Beijing University

The aim of this series is to publish original, high-quality, research-level work by both new and established scholars in the West and the East, on all aspects of the Chinese economy, including studies of business and economic history.

The Political Economy of Banking Governance in China
Xuming Yang

Reforming China's Healthcare System
China Development Research Foundation

Chinese Private Manufacturing Firms
The Challenges of Global Competition
Xiao Chen

The Silk Road and the Political Economy of the Mongol Empire
Prajakti Kalra

The Evolution of China's Banking System, 1993–2017
Guy Williams

China and the West
Crossroads of Civilisation
Peter Nolan

Wind Power in China
Ambiguous Winds of Change in China's Energy Market
Julia Kirch Kirkegaard

Multinationals, Global Value Chains and Governance
The Mechanics of Power in Inter-firm Relations
Peter Hertenstein

For more information about this series, please visit: www.routledge.com

Multinationals, Global Value Chains and Governance

The Mechanics of Power in Inter-firm Relations

Peter Hertenstein

Routledge
Taylor & Francis Group
LONDON AND NEW YORK

First published 2020 by Routledge

2 Park Square, Milton Park, Abingdon, Oxon, OX14 4RN
605 Third Avenue, New York, NY 10017

Routledge is an imprint of the Taylor & Francis Group, an informa business

First issued in paperback 2020

British Library Cataloguing-in-Publication Data
A catalogue record for this book is available from the British Library

Library of Congress Cataloging-in-Publication Data
A catalog record for this book has been requested

ISBN: 978-1-138-39199-4 (hbk)
ISBN: 978-0-367-78442-3 (pbk)

Typeset in Times New Roman
by Apex CoVantage, LLC

To My Wife and Children

Contents

Figures

Tables

Author biography

Peter Hertenstein (Ph.D., University of Cambridge) is a guest lecturer in International Management at the University of Antwerp and works in M&A and strategy consulting at Roland Berger. His research interests include strategic management, internationalization of the firm, global value chains, and the catch-up strategies of firms from the emerging markets. His research has been published in major international management journals, such as the *Management International Review*, *Asia Pacific Journal of Management* and *Technovation*. He has been a visiting scholar at the Haas School of Business at the University of California–Berkeley and the China Europe International Business School (CEIBS).

Preface

This book is based on a research project that I conducted for my Ph.D. in Development Studies at the University of Cambridge, England. The project started off with the objective to explore the role large western multinationals play for the development of the local industries in the two emerging markets of Brazil and China. Over the time of the research I realized that the global automotive value chain has undergone significant and deep structural changes over the past decades. The assembly firms have shifted their approach to orchestrate their supply base to control the processes outside the firm. It became obvious that some of the largest and most powerful firms in the industry have gained a high degree of control over some of the other firms in the industry and extended their orchestrating activities even beyond the first tier of suppliers. As a consequence, the attention of the research project shifted to explore the power asymmetries that determine the inter-firm dynamics in the global value chain. At center stage was the modern lead firm, a powerful and large multinational corporation, spanning across national borders and multiple continents, which governs and orchestrates trade and capital flows of entire industries. Less powerful firms participating in global value chains are increasingly becoming dependent on the leading multinational corporation and have to follow the strategic direction set by the lead firm. New forms of governance emerged that are based on power differences between the firms. Through the research I explored the mechanics of governance within several layers of participating firms in the global value chain of the automotive industry. By using the global value chain framework, the changing inter-firm dynamics between buyer and supplier were analyzed. The results highlight the role of product architecture in defining the value chain governance approach. Through the evolution of product architecture, the lead firms can globalize their approaches to procurement and supply chain management. Moreover, the globally harmonized products allow the lead firm to effectively restructure the global supply base to establish a globally harmonized components supply industry by internationalizing the most capable supply firms. Oligopolies along the entire global value chain are consciously created by the lead firm. The dynamics of competition between supply firms are changing, as the market for integral components with high asset-specificity is merging into one global market with oligopolistic and oligopsonistic features. Returning to the original question, I explored how the new forms of governance pose new challenges for the integration of developing markets into the world economy. In particular, firms from the emerging markets face a new set of challenges through increased globalization of markets, concentration of power, and new requirements for participation set by the lead firms in the value chain. While some supply firms from the emerging markets have been able to utilize their business ties with western assembly firms to upgrade within the global value chain, most are under pressure to be squeezed out of the global value chain through increased global competition.

The research project is based on the automotive industry, as the automotive industry played a key role in the development of Brazil and China, yet it is dominated by western firms. Moreover, the automotive industry has consistently been at the forefront of changes and innovation of manufacturing systems, supply chain organization, globalization, and consolidation processes in the past decades. Insights gleaned from it may be relevant to other industries, particularly for the manufacturing sector involving complex supply chains entailing numerous discrete inputs. Brazil and China were selected as the two emerging economies for this research, as both national industries have evolved to become major production hubs in the global automotive industry and have become central in the global strategies of the leading multinationals in the industry. Several firms were selected for the case study. The objective was to study a discrete value chain of a leading German assembly firm and multiple participants. The Volkswagen group was selected as the core lead firm because it is one of the largest and leading assemblers in the global automotive industry and because it has a particularly long history in Brazil and China. In addition to the lead firm, several supply firms along the value chain were selected for the research. The aim was to analyze a sufficient number of firms to be fairly confident that the results had some general applicability, while limiting the sample to enable in-depth interviews within a tractable timescale. All the selected supply firms along the value chain are participants in the value chain of the lead firm and were selected in a way that firms from all different positions in the value chain are represented, including firms with high tech and with relatively undifferentiated products. It is important to note that all data collection was finished before the news of "diesel gate" broke out.

During the time of this research project, technologies have emerged at a rapid pace through digitalization, again revolutionizing the automotive industry through disruptive innovations. These include the electrification of the powertrain, new production processes of additive manufacturing and industry 4.0, and advances in automated driving and connected vehicles through the use of Internet of the Things applications and algorithms that enable self-learning systems through artificial intelligence. This has led to a convergence of industries, as new technologies like semi-conductors and enhanced software engineering become increasingly important. New firms from other industries enter the automotive industry to capture dominant positions in the value chain for key technologies of the future. The new entrants to the industry include powerful firms such as Tesla, who developed vehicles based on a different technology, or Apple, Google, or Uber, who want to play a key role in the technology for automated driving. Other established supply firms, such as Qualcomm, play an increased role as their products (semi-conductors) become more relevant in the industry. Incumbent firms need to rapidly adapt their business models and technologies in order to maintain their position in the automotive industry. This requires them to develop dynamic capabilities to adapt to the fast paced changes in the industry. The rapid introduction of new technologies was unforeseen at the beginning of this project, and the trajectory and changes they will bring are unclear and still open. Therefore, even though these changes dominate current discussions on the automotive industry, they are not at the core of this research. While the framework used and developed in this book may help to understand how the advances in technology shape the structure of the industry, it has not been developed for this purpose.

The book is structured as follows: The first chapter explores the context of the changes, with a short review of the literature on globalization and the globalization of the automotive industry. This is followed by an introduction to the global value chain framework and a short method section. The third chapter describes Volkswagen as the lead firm in this study, exploring how its value chain orchestrating activities have evolved over time. The fourth chapter summarizes the role of supply firms from Germany within the value chain of Volkswagen. Chapter five examines the possibilities of supply firms from the emerging markets of Brazil and China for entering and upgrading within the value chain of Volkswagen. Chapters six and seven draw the conclusions for economic theory of governance and for development of emerging markets, respectively.

I want to thank the various people that supported me during my research. Special thanks to Peter Nolan, who supervised my dissertation and made himself available for numerous discussions about my ideas and the direction of the research. Further, I want to thank Klaus Meyer for inviting me to visit CEIBS for several months in China, and David Teece, for the opportunity to spend one year at UC–Berkeley as visiting scholar. Peter Williamson, John Anderson, and Dylan Sutherland deserve my thanks, for the ability to jointly work on research projects and publications. Finally, I want to thank my family for their unconditional support throughout the years.

Abbreviations

EUR	"Euro," the European currency
FAW	First Automotive Words, a Chinese automotive assembler
FDI	Foreign Direct Investments
GDP	Gross Domestic Product
GM	General Motors
GVC	Global Value Chain
ICT	Information and Communication Technologies
MNC	Multinational Corporations
MQB, MLB, MSB	Name for modular platforms by Volkswagen
M&A	Merger and Acquisition
NAFTA	North American Free Trade Agreement
OECD	Organization for Economic Cooperation and Development
OEM	Original Equipment Manufacturer
OICA	International Organization of Motor Vehicle Manufacturers
PQ	Name for modular platform by Volkswagen
R&D	Research and Development
SAIC	SAIC Motor, a Chinese automotive assembler
SME	Small and Medium Enterprise
UNCTAD	United Nations Conference on Trade and Development
USSR	Union of Soviet Socialist Republics
WTO	World Trade Organization

1 The dynamic process of globalization

The world economy has changed. The past three decades saw an unprecedented industrial restructuring worldwide, ushering in a new phase of globalization. The new phase of globalization through accelerated internationalization of firms, vertical disintegration, and dominance of large multinational corporations (MNCs) has changed the competitive landscape in the world economy (Cassis 1999; Chandler 1994; Dembinski 2009; Nolan 2001b). Enabled by technology advances in transportation and more importantly telecommunication, the firms' refocused on their 'core business.' Through the subsequent outsourcing of manufacturing processes, the leading firms have triggered an unprecedented restructuring of global manufacturing (Dicken 2011; Milberg and Winkler 2013; Nolan, Zhang, and Chunhang 2007; Ruigrok and van Tulder 1995; Sturgeon, Van Biesebroeck, and Gereffi 2008; Womack, Jones, and Roos 1990). The large and focused firms that emerged as lead firms in their respective industries take on an orchestrating role for the extended value chain through new forms of governance. At center stage is the modern lead firm, a powerful and large multinational corporation, spanning across national borders and multiple continents, which governs and orchestrates trade and capital flows of entire industries in structured global value chains (GVC) (Dembinski 2008; OECD 2012). Less powerful firms participating in such global value chains are increasingly becoming dependent on the leading MNCs and have to follow the strategic direction set by the lead firm. Thus the boundaries of the firm become increasingly blurred (Cantwell 2013; Coase 1937). The globalization of entire industries is steered by the firm at the top. Globalization accelerates as the lead firms restructure their production network and value chains globally.

Despite the widespread discussions about globalization, there is no unified theory or understanding of its dynamic process, its mechanics, and its drivers. This chapter lays out the context for the book by exploring globalization through a simple mechanism: the reduction of existing barriers to the flow of information and physical objects. Globalization is thereby defined as the process of reducing the barriers to exchange information and objects between separated territorialities. Through the reduction of barriers, the 'distance' between formerly separated and isolated territorialities is reduced to make their particular set of resources, goods, markets, knowledge, culture, and social activity accessible to one another (Ghemawat 2001). Existing barriers are factors that increase the cost for or slow the process of the flow of information or objects. Such barriers range from national barriers and trade barriers, to natural obstacles such as mountain ranges, large streams, or oceans. Barriers can be reduced by lowering the cost and increasing the speed for exchange, often achieved by establishing an infrastructure to build networks that accelerate the exchange.

In the proposed model of globalization, the multi-faceted factors of globalization are dissected in two overarching processes: shaping processes and reactionary processes. The two processes in turn are made up of four different factors. The first two factors are (1) *enabling factors*, in particular innovations and politics that lower cost and increased speed of transportation, and (2) *driving factors*, in particular the economy. The latter two factors are part of the reactionary process, describing the impact globalization has: (3) *increasing optionality*, available at the connected territorialities, which (4) allows a *new bundling of information* and goods, which feeds back to the enabling factors (Figure 1.1).

Enabling factors lay the foundation for a potential globalization but are not driving the process of globalization. For instance, lowering trade barriers enables globalization – but it is the increase of transnational economic trade that utilizes

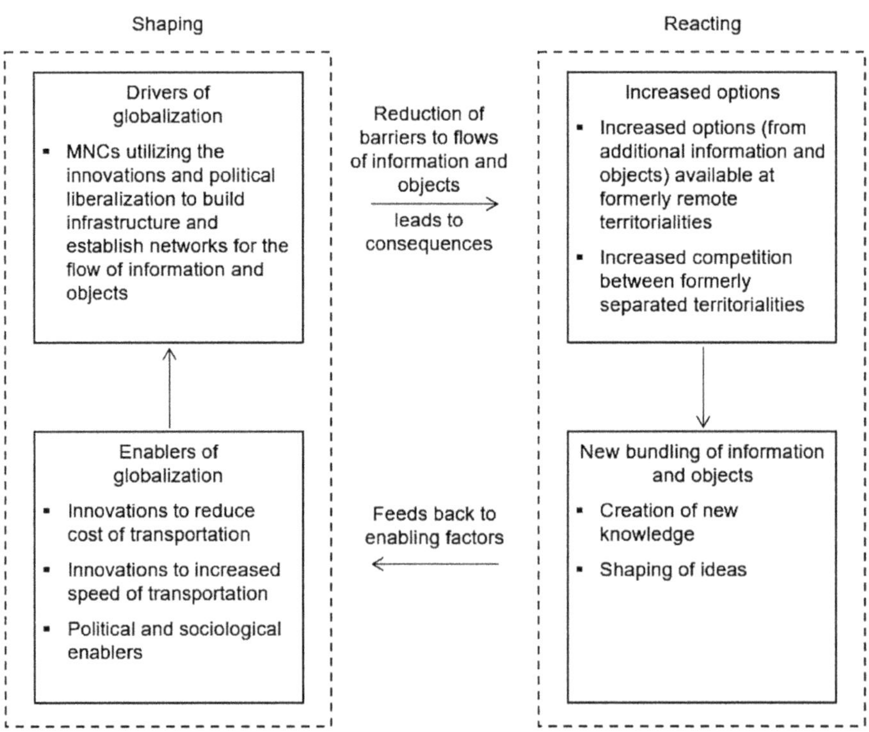

Figure 1.1 The dynamic globalization process model

Source: Author's own figure.

the enablers to drive globalization. Through the increased flow of information and goods, additional and new options become available at the connected territoriality, like resources, goods, information, cultural, or social activity. Through the new options, new information can be bundled and combined in new ways to create new knowledge that leads to innovations but also reactions on the changes in society.

By viewing the process of globalization as an interplay between shaping and reacting factors which feedback into the shaping factors, the overall process is not deterministic. This enables us to understand phases in which globalization is in retreat. After decades of social and economic integration and globalization since the 1960s, social movements started to empower governments in the 2010s that erected barriers rather than further reducing them. The model allows such developments through different results from the reactionary process. As research has shown, globalization does not benefit all individuals equally and can have a negative impact on individuals, societies, economics, or the environment in particular territorialities (Fisher 2009). This can lead to a reaction that influences the enabling factors to increase barriers rather than decrease them.

In the attempt to explore the economic globalization witnessed in the past decades, the shaping dimensions of the process are described (left side of the figure), together with some consequences of globalization that are clearly linked to economic globalization and the role of the firm in globalization. This limits the scope of this chapter to economic globalization, not regarding sociological or political aspects. While the broad impact of globalization is a fascinating topic worth studying, it would exceed the purpose of this chapter and is better explored by other social sciences.

Enablers of globalization

The core enablers of globalization are innovations that enable the transnational economic activity to be managed and operated effectively, and political enablers that reduce barriers. The innovations can be distinguished between (1) innovations that increase the degree of digitalization of information, i.e. the speed of information transportation, and lower the cost of information transportation; (2) innovations that lower the cost and accelerate the transportation of physical goods; and (3) innovations in the management capabilities as a moderating enabler, which expands the limits of the organizational size. The political enablers are the liberalization of trade and capital flows, the privatization of business, and historic catalysts accelerating the integration of national economies into the world economy.

Innovations in transportation of goods

Key innovations to lower the barriers for the transportation of physical objects were made in the past decades through continuous innovations for large transport ships that revolutionized sea transportation and economized transcontinental transportation of physical goods. The cost of sea transportation dropped by more than half from 1974 to 2004 (Bank 2009). A key innovation was the standardization of containers in the 1960s that decreased the lead-times for transition between vessels and between sea, rail, and road transportation. For air transportation, innovations were made in the aircraft industry, most notably the invention of the jet engine to allow flying long distances and at high altitude to be independent from weather conditions. Through the continuous building of infrastructure, the inventions mentioned earlier are utilized to decrease the barriers of transportation of goods. By building new roads, rails, ports, or airports, or by expanding existing canals, crucial links between countries are built, the distance between countries and continents are bridged, and globalization of trade is enabled.

Innovations in transportation of information

The transportation of (digitized) information has been transformed most radically in the past decades. Since the invention of transmitters in 1947 and the integrated circuit in 1958, the rise of the semiconductor industry has transformed the world economy. Through innovations like personal computers, the internet, and mobile devices, the technology for fast transportation of information was created. Communication and information exchange has vastly improved and become faster and more cost-efficient. The revolution in the telecommunications sector has facilitated a revolution in the globalized financial system and capital markets, in the marketing strategies and development of globally recognized brands, and in the organization of research and development (R&D) and product design (Nolan 2001b).

Equally important were key innovations that helped to codify information so that the information can be digitized and thereby become detached from physical objects and be transmitted through the communications network. Through broadband internet, advanced sensors, or camera systems, additional information can be digitized, such as gestures or facial expressions during long-distance conversations using IP video phones. Through further inventions, such as precise capturing and digitizing of movements and the re-production of these, a deeper spectrum of information can be transported.

Innovations in the organization and management of increasingly complex systems

While the innovations in transportation of goods and information mentioned earlier lay the groundwork for globalization, the increase in transnational operations increased the complexity for organizing and managing the complex systems. Innovations in the management capabilities enabled the globalization of operations. Key innovations include the reorganization of work, the focusing on core business activities, innovations in the management of complex systems, and the establishment of systems integrators.

Reorganization of work and the fine-slicing of activities

The most profound organizational change that occurred was the fine-slicing of activities that enabled business to focus on their core activities and outsource much of the non-core activities previously performed in-house (Chandler 1977; Milberg and Winkler 2013; Ruigrok and van Tulder 1995). The specialization and division of tasks decreases complexity and enables simple, repetitive tasks to be performed in a shorter time span (Pavitt 2003). In the early 1900s, the automotive industry revolutionized manufacturing processes through the organized division of tasks into a value chain in what later became known as 'Fordism.' However, the process required a high degree of product standardization and led to the simplification of products towards few options for the customer. In the 1980s, the automotive industry again revolutionized manufacturing processes, this time in Japan in what has been coined 'Toyotism.' The lean manufacturing principles allowed companies to increase the handling of complexity to allow more product variety. While the core change in Fordism was the change towards strictly divided tasks, 'Toyotism' is the move from strictly divided tasks towards a more flexible specialization (Ruigrok and van Tulder 1995).

Refocusing on core business activities

In the post-Fordism era, the theatre for the fine-slicing of tasks changed. In the Fordism-era, the division of labor occurred within in the factory. In the past decades, the process of dividing tasks has been elevated to a new level, from tasks performed by individuals to dividing tasks performed by organizations or businesses (Gereffi and Korzeniewicz 1994; Milberg and Winkler 2013; Nolan 2001b; UNCTAD 2013). Vertically integrated firms started disintegration in order to focus on their 'core business.' The global economy therefore witnessed a "widespread narrowing of the range of business activity undertaken by the individual large firm" after the 1970s (Nolan 2001b: 33f), as large firms sold their assets in 'non-core' business segments. The separation of tasks allowed the firms to specialize in their core activities, decreasing the overall complexity to compensate for the increase of complexity from globalized operations (Ruigrok and van Tulder 1995; Womack et al. 1990). Increasingly, the restructuring of the value chain happens at a global level (Nolan 2001b; Nolan et al. 2007). In the ongoing restructuring of activities, firms globalized their value chains (Kaplinsky 2004; OECD 2013; WTO 2013) and outsourced many of their activities to new countries (Chandler 1977; Milberg and Winkler 2013).

Innovation in management systems

Linked to the reorganization of activities are innovations in management capabilities and manufacturing systems. The evolution of manufacturing systems, like the introduction of lean manufacturing principles such as zero stock, just-in-time and just-in-sequence delivery, enabled the lead firms to orchestrate the growingly complex network of economic activities within and outside the boundaries of the firm (Womack et al. 1990). Innovations in management capabilities and manufacturing systems are thereby a key element to enable globalization (Fujimoto 2012; Hill 1989; Sturgeon 2002; Womack et al. 1990). Some of the key innovations of the past decades include the development of efficient organizational structures for the internal management of large enterprises (Chandler 1977). This has been further strengthened through IT-systems and the internal training of employees. Additionally, new manufacturing techniques have enabled large companies to combine economies of scale with increasing demand for flexible production. In particular lean manufacturing techniques enabled firms to cope with increasing complexity. The adaptation of supply chain management enables the firms to effectively manage complex supply chains across national borders (Bertrand and Mol 2013; Contractor et al. 2010; Milberg and Winkler 2013; Sturgeon et al. 2008).

The role of systems integrators

In order to minimize the organizational efforts across the value chain, large corporations can select capable supply firms to hand over some of the orchestration and organization tasks (Johnson 2003). This is made possible through an increased modular approach to product development and manufacturing. The supply firms, called systems integrators, have an important role in the value chain. 'Systems integrators' integrate different components into a sub-system or into the final product. The systems integrator has to coordinate and orchestrate different component supply firms. This is a particularly difficult process for products with complex systems, comprised of highly interdependent components (Dembinski 2008). As an engineering concept, 'systems integration' refers to the testing and verifying of components' performance and the integration of these into the system (Johnson 2003: 36).

Organizing cross-organizational activities via systems integrators became necessary as systems grew in complexity so that knowledge was distributed among the increasing number of people and firms involved in the research and development process and as responsibilities were spread among departments or different firms. In large, transnational operating firms, systems integration has become an important management system to control the value chain and to ensure smooth production processes of products with increased complexity. According to Tell, a

> systematic shift in innovation patterns took place, from an emphasis on individual human creativity, ingenuity, entrepreneurship, and vision in an initial system building phase to more collective and organized patterns of corporate led innovation in components, subsystems, architectures, and their integration in maturing systems.
>
> (Tell 2003: 56)

One of the most important capabilities of a firm is, therefore, its ability to design components and sub-systems in collaboration with its suppliers in such a way that they are not only compatible with one another but also complementing each other and are "optimized for overall systems performance" (Sapolsky 2003: 24).

The reduction of political barriers

Liberalization of trade and capital flows

A central political enabler to globalization is the liberalization of trade flows. The triumph of neoclassic economics since the 1990s paved the way for international trade treaties and the liberalization of transnational investment flows, leading to the globalization of the capitalist economy (Nolan 2012). The liberalization of trade flows led to a sharp increase in transnational trade since the 1990s. The share of business that is done internationally vis-à-vis domestic has almost doubled between 1990 and 2009, as it rose from 27% of world GDP to 53% (Nolan 2012). At the same time, the liberalization of capital flows enabled firms to go international and develop into large multinational corporations.

Privatization of businesses

Equally important to globalization was a wave of privatization of business that unleashed market forces and the drive of firms for profit maximization. The liberalization of trade and capital flows coincided with a wave of privatization around the world. Following neoclassic economic models, entire industry sectors that were previously state owned in most countries were privatized (Nolan 2001b). This includes some assets that were considered strategic, like infrastructure such as rail networks, highways, airports, and shipping ports, as well as energy producers, electric network companies, telecommunication providers, and large service providers like railway companies. While not a direct contributor to reduce distance, such privatization facilitated the role of firms as drivers for economic globalization.

Historic events catalyzing globalization

Historic catalysts accelerated the process of globalization, such as the dissolution of the USSR and previous East Bloc countries (Nolan 2001a), the rise of the East Asian Tiger economies (Amsden 1989), and the economic opening of China and India, two of the largest economies in the world (Nolan 2001b). After the collapse of the USSR, great endeavors took place to integrate the former east bloc countries into transnational treaties, which further accelerated the process of economic globalization. These catalysts have led to immense efforts to integrate the emerging markets into the world economy. In addition, the opening of the 'rest of the world,' comprised of former 'inward-looking' developing countries of the non-communist bloc, forged a truly *global* economy that reaches into every corner of the world. Furthermore, it has led to a global shift in production to cheaper locations, 'unbundling' production and consumption from one another (Baldwin 2014;

Dicken 2011) and rapidly increasing international trade at a rate outpacing the growth of the world economy (OECD 2012; UNCTAD 2013). Nations became interdependent on one another and moreover became dependent on large transnational firms with a global footprint and a strong presence in almost every economy.

The drivers of globalization

The rise of big business and the multinational corporation

The emergence of big business as a predecessor of the multinational corporation plays a central role in globalization and the development of global value chains (Dembinski 2009). Early research on business as an organization proposed that the maximum size of business is constrained by the growing complexity of conscious organization (Cassis 1999). The margin for the maximal size of the firm has continuously risen as technological advances enabled more effective ways of management and effective organization of economic activities (Chandler 1977). One of the key propositions brought forward by Chandler is that the emergence of large firms altered the basic structure of entire industries, as it enabled efficient coordination of large quantities of highly complex activities required for the manufacturing and distribution of the final product (Chandler 1977). The rise of the big business has been a triumph for the world economy and is responsible for the majority of economic activity today. In a study on the largest listed companies, Dembinski finds that big businesses contribute disproportionately more to the economic growth compared to SMEs. He further shows that these big businesses are more productive, showing 'extraordinary performance' (Dembinski 2009: 114).

The MNC, in its search for markets, resources, and other locational advantages, is the driving force behind globalization. While some international corporations, like the Dutch East India Company, existed as early as 1602, most firms started internationalizing after the Second World War, setting of a new wave of economic globalization. In the 1960s, scholars started to analyze the trend, and Hymer developed the ground work towards a theory of the MNC (Hymer 1960). Since the 1990s, firms have internationalized at an unprecedented pace and the market share of MNCs has grown rapidly. The rise of a globalized economy is further reflected in the growing importance of foreign markets for such MNCs, measured in the proportion of foreign assets to domestic assets and foreign sales to domestic sales. By 2010, the foreign assets of the 100 largest MNCs had risen to 57% of their total assets, and their foreign sales to 61% vis-à-vis 39% domestic sales (UNCTAD 2010). The search for profits of business that drives the globalization has become global as the barriers for trade and capital flows were reduces. Over the decades, the modern large and powerful MNCs emerged spanning across national borders and multiple continents. Such MNCs are found to be responsible for the majority of transnational trade and capital flows, steering and orchestrating entire industries in structured global value chains.

Some economic consequences of globalization

The consolidation of industries

On the industry level, the emergence of big business and the MNC shaped whole industries. Large corporations merged and expanded their market share via mergers and acquisitions (M&A), and entire industries were consolidated and transformed into oligopolies. The trend has been observed in a wide variety of different industries, from the commercial aircraft over most segments in the information technology industry to pharmaceuticals or beverages, just to name a few (for a list of industrial sectors, see Nolan 2012: 18–20). In this "trend towards increased concentration," large firms are able to capture significant market share that enable them to dominate the entire industry (Dicken 2011: 315). As a consequence from the rise of the MNC, many industries are consolidated not just on a national level but on a global level, with few large MNCs dominating the world economy in their sector (Gibbon, Bair, and Ponte 2008).

The industrial consolidation not only happened at the level of the lead firms. Instead, the newly formed large corporations exerted pressure for growth and consolidation onto their suppliers (Nolan 2001a; Nolan, Zhang, and Liu 2007). The "process of concentration through the simultaneous de-merger of non-core businesses and merger of core businesses is cascading across the value chain" (Nolan et al. 2007: 43), which inevitably led to large first tier suppliers to position themselves as globally leading firms. These turn-key suppliers in turn exert pressure for consolidation on their suppliers, setting in motion a cascade effect to pass the pressure on along the entire value chain.

The rapid emergence of large MNCs was accelerated by aggressive M&A growth strategies. M&A allow firms rapid growth and internationalization, albeit more drastic and associated with higher risks (Haspelslagh and Jemison 1991). Several waves of M&A have accelerated the consolidation of industries. The first wave of large M&A occurred during the late 1960s. From 1965 to 1969, the numbers of mergers and acquisitions tripled from 2,000 to over 6,000, leading to what Chandler called a 'mania' for growth via M&A (1994: 315). Most of the M&A activities, however, were aiming for diversification rather than horizontal or vertical integration. Often, target firms were not in the same industry as the host company, a trend that has dramatically changed since then (Chandler 1994: 622). Since the 1990s, a second wave of M&A took place. This time, a large proportion of M&A activities were transnational, with cross-border M&A surging from a mere US$ 156 billion in 1992 to US$ 1100 billion in 1997, almost doubling in the next year to over US$ 2 trillion in 1998 and rose to over US$ 3.3 trillion before the turn of the century (Nolan 2001a: 38). Since then international M&A activities have been steadily grown in value, volume, and deal-size, with the two financial crises in 2000 and 2008, only making dents to the trend.

The explosion of M&A since the 1990s led to a shift in power in the global economy and prepared the path for the dominance of a few MNCs. With the resulting large firms, many industries have developed oligopolistic features (Nolan 2012).

Thus the decade of M&A had a deep impact on the global economy and transformed whole industries. With the parallel vertical disintegration described earlier, and the globally liberalized trade flows, the diversion of value-adding processes in industrial value chains spread spatially across the world, leading to value chains that are truly global in scope and governed by a handful of lead firms with immense power (Gereffi, Humphrey, and Sturgeon 2005; Sturgeon et al. 2008).

The shift of production and unbundling of activities

Driven by the economic growth in the emerging markets and catalyzed by the state policies to localize economic activities and attract inward FDI for job creation and economic development, a tremendous geographic shift of production to the east took place since the 1990s (Dicken 2011). Production of goods moved from the old triad region of the USA, Europe, and Japan towards East Asia and to some extent towards South America (Dicken 2011: 334). Both Brazil and China benefited greatly from this shift (Van Biesenbroeck and Sturgeon 2010; Shapiro 1994; Thun 2006).

Through the fine-slicing of activities, the MNC benefited from cost advantages in foreign countries by separating production from consumption and localizing production in advantageous locations (Baldwin 2014). The geographic separation was driven by the MNC's ability to separate production from marketing, as managerial competencies increased and barriers for transportation decreased. In its search for markets, resources, and localization advantages, the MNC divided its activities and localized each activity to an advantageous location across the globe (Menz, Kunisch, and Collis 2013; OECD 2012).

The globalization of the automotive industry

The global automotive industry has undergone a tremendous consolidation since 1985, as the leading firms attempted to increase economies of scale, reduce R&D costs, and realize synergies. The industry is highly consolidated and has developed oligopolistic features (Nolan 2012). Competition is fierce, and only a few global players occupy large shares of the global industry (Datamonitor 2011; Sutherland 2003). In 2015, the top four largest assemblers accounted for 40% of the global passenger car production. The next ten largest assemblers accounted for another 41%, leaving just 19% for all other assemblers (OICA 2016; see Figure 1.2).

Every traditional major automotive nation is represented in the group of the top four largest producers: Japan, Germany, the USA, and South Korea (with Toyota, Volkswagen, General Motors, and Hyundai respectively). The same four countries are also the nations of origin for all of the next ten largest car producers, with the exception of SAIC, the largest Chinese assembler. Even without considering alliances among the leading producers, the industry appears highly consolidated and features oligopolistic traits.

The consolidation not only pertains to the assemblers but, as importantly, tier-1 and tier-2 component suppliers, as pressure for economies of scale and lean

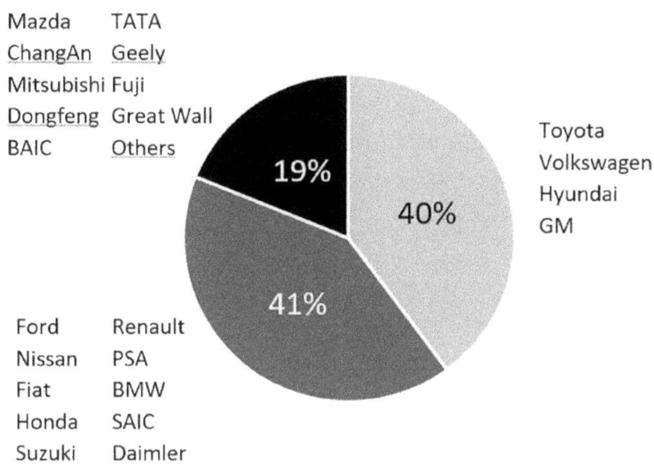

Figure 1.2 Market share of the automotive industry

Source: Author's calculation based on OICA (2016).

production have been passed on down the value chain (Nolan 2001b). The global tier-1 supplier base, for example, has rapidly consolidated and consists of a relatively small number of very large, highly competitive, globally active players. Assembly MNCs have intensified their business network relationships and have established long-term strategic partnerships with component makers to lower development costs for new platforms and vehicles (Womack et al. 1990). Suppliers are forced to be able to supply globally, while having their R&D centers close to that of the assembler: "Increasingly, lead firms demand that their largest suppliers have a global presence and system design capabilities as a precondition to being considered as a source for a complex part or subsystem" (Van Biesenbroeck and Sturgeon 2010: 209).

Shifts in global production

In the past 25 years, the geography of production underwent tremendous shifts from the old triad regions of the USA, Europe, and Japan towards emerging markets in East Asia and South America (Dicken 2011: 334). A key driver for the shift in production is the market growth in these regions. Unlike most consumer products, vehicles are typically produced or assembled in close proximity to the final consumer, which results in low numbers of exports for wholly assembled vehicles due to political forces constraining and limiting imports. Policy makers try to attract inward FDI to localize vehicle production and establish production plants through import taxes and tax reductions (Van Biesenbroeck and Sturgeon 2010). Because of the large scale of one production plant (a standardized plant of VW produces 150,000 vehicles annually), the high upfront investments required and

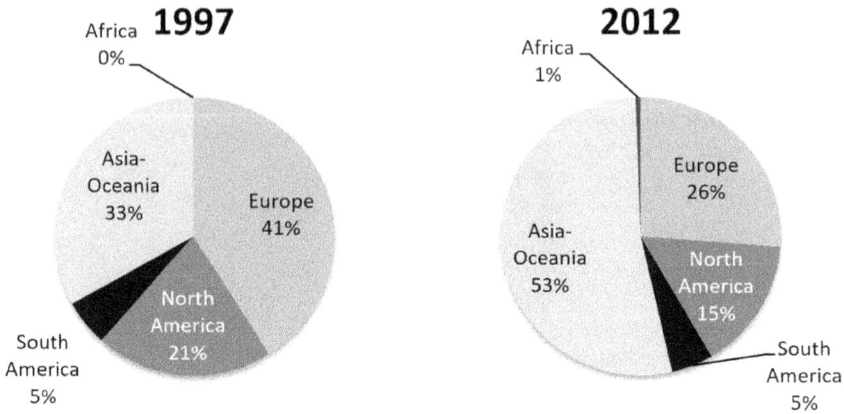

Figure 1.3 Geographic shift of automotive production

Source: Author's calculations based on OICA (1998, 2013).

the large upstream supply base needed for production, production typically clusters around the initial locations for investments. This is especially the case for relatively young production sites in the developing world.

While the traditional two regions of Europe and North America accounted for a combined 62% of global production in 1997, their share decreased over just 15 years to a mere 41% in 2012 (OICA 1998, 2013). The main benefiter has been not only the Asian region, which increased its share of production from 33% to 53% over the same time span (ibid.; Figure 1.3) but also Latin America, which sustained its share at 5%.

Germany in the global automotive industry

Germany sees itself as the birthplace of the automobile, and to this day Germany is most famous for its automobiles. The automotive industry has played a central role in the German economy. With innovations like the combustion engine, Germany has a strong tradition in automobiles. The auto industry is one of Germany's largest and certainly its most important industry. With a turnover of 351 billion EUR, the automotive industry accounted for about 20% of Germanys total industry revenue (GTAI 2013). The industry makes more than 3% of the nation's GDP and contributes more than 2.5% for direct employment. The automotive industry is also a driver for the successful export model of the economy, as some 77% of the vehicles produced in Germany are destined for foreign markets. The 19.6 billion EUR of investments into R&D in the auto industry make about one third of the nation's R&D expenditure (GTAI 2013). Moreover, Germany is the home for global players like Daimler, BMW, and Volkswagen that are widely renowned for the highest quality standards, innovation, and enjoyable drivers' experience. With the founding of the Volkswagen AG in 1938, Germany brought forth an assembler that was able to claim a spot at the table of the largest assemblers worldwide and that fought to become number one in terms of vehicle production numbers (Lupa 2008; OICA 2013).

The Brazilian automotive industry

The automotive industry is arguably the most important industry for the Brazilian economy. Chosen for its close linkages with steel and oil, the automotive industry received special attention from policy makers since its inception in the 1950s (Shapiro 1994; Wolfe 2010), and it was to become the spearhead of Brazil's development. The auto industry was to create a large domestic market for the local steel and oil industries to grow upon. Furthermore, the Brazilian government chose trucks as the primary means for transportation to bring together the vast landmasses of the country and unite the fragmented economy. The industrial development of Brazil's automotive industry took off in the 1950s when president Juscelino Kubitschek (1956–1961) included the automotive industry in his Target Plan (Wolfe 2010: 113). Establishing indigenous assemblers, or 'national champions,' was discarded early on by politicians, as the potential market was considered too small to allow such a path, and financial and technological requirements were too high (Shapiro 1994). Instead of establishing indigenous assemblers, Brazil relied heavily on investments from international firms of the western developed world (Wolfe 2010). By attracting foreign firms to invest in Brazil, the government hoped for a localization of their production that would provide jobs and create a highly skilled workforce. Localizing the production was incentivized through a combination of financial incentives for localizing production and penalties for imports.

Unlike on the assembly level, it was the plan to develop a strong supply base of indigenous Brazilian firms. The local content rate of components for passenger cars was set to increase to 80% by weight and 70% by value in 1960 (Abreu et al. 1999; Ramalho and Francisco 2008). However, even though the supply industry was not very consolidated at that time, foreign supply firms entered the Brazilian market and soon dominated the industry. In particular capital- and technology-intensive sectors of the value chain were dominated by foreign firms, while local firms produced standardized components and replacement parts with low profit margins (Kim and Lee 1994; Shapiro 1994).

By 1972, the Brazilian government created a policy framework that would allow the local industry to become more integrated into the global industry. The Brazilian government encouraged exports of whole vehicles as a means to fight international trade deficits, and exports increased dramatically from under US$ 100 million in 1973 to US$ 1.57 billion by 1981 (Lee and Cason 1994: 234). The policy framework was a success, and today Brazil plays an important role in the global automotive industry as one of the major production hubs in the world, ranked in a respectable 7th place, with a 3.5% share of global passenger vehicle production (following China, Japan, Germany, the USA, South Korea, and India) (OICA 2013).

In the 1990s, the government introduced deregulation policies to open the market (Ramalho and Francisco 2008). Prior to 1990, the Brazilian market was dominated by just four assembly firms: Volkswagen, Fiat, Ford, and General Motors. When the market opened, new firms entered the market, such as Toyota, Hyundai, Nissan, Renault, and Peugeot, introducing new technologies and vehicle models to the market. In the relatively closed market prior to 1990, the incumbent assembly groups had little interest to upgrade technologies. With the opening of the market in 1990, the competitive environment changed. New foreign assembly groups entered the market and intensified the competition. The incumbent firms reacted by rapidly upgrading their technologies and introducing new vehicles. Local supply firms began to feel the intense competition of foreign rivals entering the domestic industry along the entire value chain and from the increased technological demands of both, the new assembly groups, and the incumbent firms. As a result, many local indigenous supply firms defaulted, were bought up by foreign competitors, or had to downgrade to lower value-added products to stay competitive, as explored in the case study chapter.

With steady growth rates since the opening of the market in 1990, Brazil has been the second fastest growing production location in the global economy, underlining its importance in the global industry. Yet Brazil is one of only two of the largest production economies with no indigenous assembly firms with significant scale (the other being Mexico). Instead it has depended on foreign multinationals to take the lead and develop Brazil into the strong hub it is today (Ramalho and Francisco 2008; Shapiro 1994; Tewksbury 1930; Wolfe 2010).

Additionally, compared to its relative importance as a production hub in the world, Brazil has brought forth very few notable international firms in the industry. In 2014 only one Brazilian supply firm barely made it into the top 100 largest auto supply firms ranked by revenue (Automotive News 2013). This is surprising considering Brazil's vast production output and the time the indigenous firms had to develop the necessary firm specific advantages (mainly technologies) since the 1950s and the necessary international footprint since the opening of the market in the 1990s to become globally competitive.

The Chinese automotive industry

China has taken a different approach to the development of its automotive industry. Over the past two decades the Chinese automotive industry grew at a staggering speed. Domestic vehicle production has increased from a mere 481,970 vehicles produced in 1997 to a staggering 15,523,658 produced in 2012 (OICA 1998, 2013). The rapid growth in domestic production capacity was underpinned both by the investments of foreign multinationals from the advanced economies as well as the creation of indigenous Chinese car producers. The beginning of China's automotive industry goes back to the 1950s, when vehicles were produced locally for the first time by the indigenous manufacturer 'First Automobile Works' (FAW). FAW was founded with the aid of the Soviet Union, and it was incorporated in 1953 (Oliver, Holweg, and Luo 2009). In 1978 the automotive industry was chosen as one of the 'pillar' industries for development (Thun 2004, 2006). The aim of

China was to build up its own strong industry to catch up with developed countries, to create jobs, and to increase wealth and welfare for its citizens through owned 'national champion' firms (Sutherland 2001).

In the 1980s, the market opened to foreign investors, which were allowed to invest into joint-ventures with Chinese partner firms. At this time, the global automotive industry had been highly consolidated, while the Chinese industry was immensely fragmented. While the number of global assemblers was reduced through a number of M&A, the number of Chinese assemblers increased to over 100 during the same time (Liu and Zhao 2006; Ramasamy 2011). This left the majority of Chinese firms weak, as economies of scales through consolidation are crucial in the automotive industry.

In order to further integrate into the world economy, joining the WTO became necessary. Joining the WTO was supposed to bring a much needed competition into the Chinese market to enforce a long necessary restructuring process of the state-owned sector to develop a new breed of internationally competitive firms (Thun 2006). Investments from foreign firms rapidly increased and approximately US$ 12 billion was invested by 2003 (Thun 2006: 7). The foreign partners had better technologies, and the Chinese firms became dependent on their foreign partners. While it was hoped that the joint-ventures would lead to technology spillovers, some argue that the dominant foreign firms hinder the development of an indigenous automotive industry in China (Chang 2004).

By slowly opening its market, China rose to become the second largest economy in 2010 (World Bank 2010). For years it has attracted foreign direct investments (FDI) from developed economies and has become the second largest FDI recipient in the world, after the USA (UNCTAD 2011: 4). Lately, China even evolved to become one of the major sources of outward FDI. It appears that China has become a thriving hub for MNC global value chains. For efficiency reasons, and owing to state industrial policy, relationships between global assembly firms and local firms have been encouraged, and some local firms have been able to develop strong relationships with the foreign assemblers that design meticulously controlled global value chains (Anderson, Håkansson, and Johanson 1994; Johanson and Vahlne 2011; Nolan 2001b). The Chinese automotive market has become the most attractive and most important market for car sales in the world. In 2009, it overtook the USA as the largest market for passenger cars (Tian 2010) and has been steadily growing ever since. Moreover, in contrast to the traditional large markets of USA, Europe, and Japan, China is expected to grow further in the next decades. While the traditional markets are stagnant, China has the potential for further growth.

The dual strategy of opening the market to western firms and developing indigenous assemblers and suppliers appears to pay off, and many of China's most successful firms have been able to break into the global market and compete with western firms. For instance, SAIC has become one of the top ten assemblers by vehicle production, and Geely has been able to acquire Volvo and recently bought over 9% shares of Daimler. Additionally, some of China's largest suppliers were able to develop an international footprint and compete outside of China, such as Yanfeng, YAPP, and Fuyao (see case study chapter).

References

Abreu, A., L. Gitahy, J. R. Ramalho, and R. Ruas. 1999. *Industrial Restructuring and Inter-Firm Relations in the Auto-Parts Industry in Brazil*. London.

Amsden, Alice Hoffenberg. 1989. *Asia's Next Giant: South Korea and Late Industrialization*. Oxford: Oxford University Press.

Anderson, J., H. Håkansson, and J. Johanson. 1994. "Dyadic Business Relationships Within a Business Network Context." *Journal of Marketing* 58(4).

Automotive News. 2013. "Top 100 Global OEM Parts Suppliers." *Supplement to Automotive News*.

Baldwin, R. 2014. "Trade and Industrialization After Globalization's Second Unbundling: How Building and Joining a Supply Chain Are Different and Why It Matters." In *Globalization in an Age of Crisis: Multilateral Economic Cooperation in the Twenty-First Century*, edited by R. C. F. Feenstra and A. M. Taylor. Chicago: University of Chicago Press.

Bank, World. 2009. *World Development Report 2009: Reshaping Economic Geography*. Washington DC: World Bank. https://openknowledge.worldbank.org/handle/10986/5991

Bertrand, O. and M. Mol. 2013. "The Antecendents and Innovation Effects of Domestic and Offshore R&D Outsourcing: The Contingent Impact of Cognitive Distance and Absorptive Capacity." *Strategic Management Journal* 34(6): 751–60.

Cantwell, J. 2013. "Blurred Boundaries Between Firms, and New Boundaries Within (Large Multinational) Firms: The Impact of Decentralized Networks for Innovation." *Seoul Journal of Economics* 26(1): 1–32.

Cassis, Y. 1999. *Big Business: The European Experience in the Twentieth Century*. Oxford: Oxford University Press.

Chandler, A. D. 1977. *The Visible Hand: Managerial Revolution in American Business*. Cambridge, MA: Harvard University Press.

Chandler, A. D. 1994. *Scale and Scope: Dynamics of Industrial Capitalism*. Cambridge, MA: Harvard University Press.

Chang, HH-J.. 2004. *Globalization, Economic Development and the Role of the State*. London: Zed Books.

Coase, R. H. 1937. "The Nature of the Firm." *Economica*: 386–405.

Contractor, F., V. Kumar, S. Kundu, and T. Pedersen. 2010. "Reconceptualizing the Firm in a World of Outsourcing and Offshoring: The Organizational and Geographical Relocation of High-Value Company Functions." *Journal of Management Studies* 47(8): 1417–33.

Datamonitor. 2011. *Industry Profile: Global Automotive Manufacturing*. http://www.datamonitor.com/

Dembinski, P. H. 2008. *Enhancing the Role of SMEs in Global Value Chains*. Paris: OECD Publishing.

Dembinski, P. H. 2009. "Very Large Enterprises, Focal Firms and Global Value Chains." *Revista de Economia Mundial* 23: 107–30.

Dicken, P. 2011. *Global Shift: Mapping the Changing Contours of the World Economy*. 6th ed. New York: The Guildford Press.

Fisher, M. 2009. *Capitalist Realism: Is There No Alternative?* London: Zero Books.

Fujimoto, T. 2012. "The Evolution of Production Systems: Exploring the Sources of Toyota's Competitiveness." *Annals of Business Administrative Science* 11: 25–44.

Gereffi, G., J. Humphrey, and T. J. Sturgeon. 2005. "The Governance of Global Value Chains." *Review of International Political Economy* 12(1): 78–104.

Gereffi, G. and M. Korzeniewicz. 1994. *Commodity Chains and Global Capitalism*. London: Greenwood Press.
Ghemawat, P. 2001. "Distance Still Matters: The Hard Reality of Global Expansion." *Harvard Business Review* 79(8): 137–47.
Gibbon, P., J. Bair, and S. Ponte. 2008. "Governing Global Value Chains: An Introduction." *Economy and Society* 37(3): 315–38.
GTAI. 2013. *The Automotive Industry in Germany*. Berlin: GTAI.
Haspelslagh, P. C. and D. B. Jemison. 1991. *Managing Aquisitions: Creating Value Through Corporate Renewal*. New York: Free Press.
Hill, R. C. 1989. "Comparing Transnational Production Systems: The Automobile Industry in the USA and Japan." *International Journal of Urban and Regional Research* 13(3): 462–80.
Hymer, S. 1960. *The International Operations of National Firms: A Study of Direct Investment*. Cambridge, MA: MIT Press.
Johanson, J. and J. Vahlne. 2011. "Markets as Networks: Implications for Strategy-Making." *Journal of the Academy of Marketing Science* 39(4): 484–91.
Johnson, S. B. 2003. "Systems Integration and the Social Solution of Technical Problems in Complex Systems." In *The Business of Systems Integration*, pp. 35–55. Oxford: Oxford University Press.
Kaplinsky, R. 2004. "Spreading the Gains From Globalization: What Can Be Learned From Value-Chain Analysis?" *Problems of Economic Transition* 47(2): 74–115.
Kim, H. K. and S.-H. Lee. 1994. "Commodity Chains and the Korean Automobile Industry." In *Commodity Chains and Global Capitalism*, edited by G. Gereffi and M. Korzeniewicz, pp. 281–96. London: Greenwood Press.
Lee, N. and J. Cason. 1994. "Automobile Commodity Chains in the NICs: A Comparison of South Korea, Mexico, and Brazil." In *Commodity Chains and Global Capitalism*, edited by G. Gereffi and M. Korzeniewicz, pp. 223–43. London: Greenwood Press.
Liu, D. and Y. Zhao. 2006. "Ownership, Foreign Investment and Productivity: As Case Study of the Automotive Industry in China." Microeconomics Working Papers 21892, East Asian Bureau of Economic Research.
Lupa, M. 2008. *Volkswagen Chronicle: Becoming a Global Player*. Wolfsburg: Volkswagen AG.
Menz, M., S. Kunisch, and D. J. Collis. 2013. "What Do We Know About Corporate Headquarters? A Review, Integration, and Research Agenda" (August 19, 2013). Working Paper No. 14-016, Harvard Business School Strategy Unit.
Milberg, W. and D. Winkler. 2013. *Outsourcing Economics: Global Value Chains in Capitalist Development*. New York: Cambridge University Press.
Nolan, P. 2001a. *China and the Global Economy*. Hampshire: Palgrave Macmillan.
Nolan, P. 2001b. *China and the Global Business Revolution*. Basingstoke: Palgrave Macmillan.
Nolan, P. 2012. *Is China Buying the World?* Cambridge: Polity Press.
Nolan, P, J. Zhang, and C. Liu. 2007. *The Global Business Revolution and the Cascade Effect*. Basingstoke: Palgrave.
Nolan, P., J. Zhang, and C. Liu. 2007. "The Global Business Revolution, the Cascade Effect, and the Challenge for Firms From Developing Countries." *Cambridge Journal of Economics* 32(1): 29–47.
OECD. 2012. *Mapping Global Value Chains*. Paris.
OECD. 2013. *Interconnected Economies: Benefiting From Global Value Chains*. Paris: OECD Publishing.

OICA. 1998. *1997 Production Statistics*. http://www.oica.net/production-statistics/

OICA. 2013. *2012 Production Statistics*. http://www.oica.net/production-statistics/

OICA. 2016. *2015 Production Statistics*. http://www.oica.net/production-statistics/

Oliver, N., M. Holweg, and J. Luo. 2009. "The Past, Present and Future of China's Automotive Industry: A Value Chain Perspective." *International Journal of Technological Learning, Innovation and Development* 2(1–2): 76–118.

Pavitt, K. 2003. "Specialization and Systems Integration: Where Manufacture and Service Still Meet." In *The Business of Systems Integration*, pp. 78–91. Oxford: Oxford University Press.

Ramalho, J. R. and E. M. V. Francisco. 2008. "Labour Relations in the Modular System: Ten Years of the VW Experience at Resende, Brazil." In *Flexibility at Work: Critical Developments in the International Automobile Industry*, edited by V. Pulignano, P. Stewart, A. Danford, and M. Richardson, pp. 151–72. Hampshire: Palgrave Macmillan.

Ramasamy, B. 2011. "Trade Liberalization and International Production Networks: The Automotive Industry in China." In *Fighting Irrelevance: The Role of Regional Trade Agreements in International Production Networks in Asia*, pp. 77–99. New York: United Nations Publication.

Ruigrok, W. and R. van Tulder. 1995. *The Logic of International Restructuring*. London: Routledge.

Sapolsky, H. M. 2003. "Inventing Systems Integration." In *The Business of Systems Integration*, pp. 15–34. Oxford: Oxford University Press.

Shapiro, H. 1994. *Engines of Growth: The State and Transnational Auto Companies in Brazil*. Cambridge: Cambridge University Press.

Sturgeon, T. 2002. "Modular Production Networks: A New American Model of Industrial Organization." *Industrial and Corporate Change* 11(3): 451–96.

Sturgeon, T., J. Van Biesebroeck, and G. Gereffi. 2008. "Value Chains, Networks and Clusters: Reframing the Global Automotive Industry." *Journal of Economic Geography* 8(3): 297–321.

Sutherland, D. 2001. "Policies to Build National Champions: China's 'National Team' of Enterprise Groups." In *China and the Global Business Revolution*, pp. 67–140. Basingstoke: Palgrave Macmillan.

Sutherland, D. 2003. *China's Large Enterprises and the Challenge of Late Industrialisation*. London: RoutledgeCurzon.

Tell, F. 2003. "Integrating Electrical Power Systems: From Individual to Organizational Capabilities." In *The Business of Systems Integration*, pp. 56–77. Oxford: Oxford University Press.

Tewksbury, H. 1930. *The Automotive Market in Brazil*. Washington, DC: U.S. Government Printing Office.

Thun, E. 2004. "Industrial Policy, Chinese-Style: FDI, Regulation, and Dreams of National Champions in the Auto Sector." *Journal of East Asian Studies* 4: 453–89.

Thun, E. 2006. *Changing Lanes in China: Foreign Direct Investment, Local Governments, and Auto Sector Development*. Cambridge: Cambridge University Press.

Tian, Y. 2010. "China Ends U.S.'s Reign as Largest Auto Market (Update2)." *Bloomberg*, January 11.

UNCTAD. 2010. *World Investment Report 2010: Investing in a Low-Carbon Economy*. New York and Geneva: UNCTAD.

UNCTAD. 2011. *World Investment Report: Non-Equity Modes of International Production and Development*. Geneva: UNCTAD.

UNCTAD. 2013. *World Investment Report 2013: Global Value Chains: Investment and Trade for Development*. Geneva: UNCTAD.

Van Biesenbroeck, J. and T. Sturgeon. 2010. "Effects of the 2008–09 Crisis on the Automotive Industry in Developing Countries: A Global Value Chain Perspective." In *Global Value Chains in a Postcrisis World: A Development Perspective*, edited by O. Cattaneo, G. Gereffi, and C. Staritz. Washington, DC: The World Bank.

Wolfe, J. 2010. *Autos and Progress: The Brazilian Search for Modernity*. New York: Oxford University Press.

Womack, J. P., D. T. Jones, and D. Roos. 1990. *The Machine That Changed the World*. New York: Rawson Associates.

World Bank. 2010. *World Development Indicators*. Washington, DC: World Bank.

WTO. 2013. *Global Value Chains in a Changing World*, edited by D. K. Elms and P. Low. Geneva: WTO Publications.

2 Global value chains

The global value chain (GVC) framework has been developed as a response to the changing structure of global trade and investment, which is increasingly shaped through coordination of economic activity of the participating firms and geographic locations that are involved in the creation and production of a final product. Through the GVC framework one can look at the chain of separately successive value-adding activities to understand the entire value chain from extraction of raw material over R&D, production, manufacturing, and assembly to marketing, sales and after sales services for the final consumer, and recycling at the end of the product life-cycle. It has been a key tool for understanding the structure and dispersion of the activities performed in the world economy, as well as the performance and role of the participating nations and participating firms as actors in the value chain. This chapter sets out to introduce the GVC framework and explains the methods used for the GVC research in this book.

The firm in an era of business networks

In the past decades, the role of networks in which a firm operates has become increasingly important. Since the emergence of the resource based view of the firm in the 1950s and 1960s (Penrose 1959), the growth and success of firms has been mostly understood from its internal resources. Since the 1990s, the organization of economic activity has changed to systems that require more cooperative forms and lead to the creation of business networks with strong inter-firm ties that play a defining role for the growth and success of the individual firm. During the 1990s, the introduction of lean manufacturing principles brought along a need for greater inter-firm cooperation, to ensure 'just-in-time' and 'just-in-sequence' delivery (Womack, Jones, and Roos 1990). In the established networks of businesses, focal firms have established total quality management and continuous improvement processes not only within their own company but also embedded within their entire value chain (Kaplinsky and Morris 2000). Enabled by new communication technologies, focal firms have started to manage and control the up- and downstream activities in their respective networks.

Through a trend of refocusing on the core business, companies engaged in a wave of outsourcing and off-shoring that began in the late 1990s. Through the outsourcing and off-shoring, the economic activities in a value chain began to be dispersed among an ever increasing number of participating firms and across an increasing number of locations (Kaplinsky 2004; Ruigrok and van Tulder 1995). The outsourcing of activities went beyond the typical 'non-core' scope of outsourcing support functions and production capabilities to include core capabilities like R&D for particular components or modules (Bertrand and Mol 2013; Contractor et al. 2010). This has fundamentally changed the approach to R&D, as large turnkey suppliers are increasingly responsible for future innovations (Hatani 2005; McCann and Kim 2008; Mei 2008; Pavlinek and Zenka 2010). Moreover, by outsourcing some of the R&D activities, the need for close coordination in the value chains increased further, leading to close and very intense buyer-supplier relationships through extensive knowledge sharing and two-way interaction (Birkinshaw and Fey 2005; Frederick and Gereffi 2009; Gereffi, Humphrey, and Sturgeon 2005; Humphrey and Memedovic 2003).

As a consequence, the firm needs to be viewed as part of a collective network on which it depends, and its growth and success needs to be understood from a network perspective (Pyke and Sengenberger 1992). The GVC framework emphasizes that view and claims that firms increasingly focus on their networking capabilities, particularly their ability to manage the resources and capabilities that lie within the network and outside the legal boundaries of the firm. Fine goes so far as to describe the management of the value chains as the core competitive advantage of the firm: "there is no competency more critical than that of superior design of one's capability chain-from the final consumer all the way upstream to the sources of raw materials and new technological concepts" (Fine 1998: 71). Fine argues that the focal point of a firm's advantage can thereby be embedded in the external value chain rather than within the individual corporation. According to Fine, it is the ability to spot lucrative opportunities within one's value chain and to invest in these that differentiates top-performing firms from ordinary firms. Hence, 'superior competency portfolio management' is the most critical capability of top-performing firms and its competitive advantage (Fine 1998: 76). Similarly, Porter argues that much of the competitiveness of a firm can be determined through its external environment, including its the value chain, as this is "the arena in which competitive advantage is won or lost" (Porter 1987: 29).

Utilizing, maintaining and coordinating the capabilities of the outsourced activities within the firm's value chain requires conscious steering and controlling of the extended business network (Gereffi and Fernandez-Stark 2011; OECD 2013). Nurturing the parties that are involved and controlling resource allocation and capability building in one's value chains has become one of the most important tasks for the lead firms in the value chain. This factor becomes even more important as firms expand to become multinational and their value chains become spread across multiple nations.

Definition and analysis of GVCs

A global value chain is the descriptive chain of all the value-added activities required for the development, creation, sale, and distribution of a final product. In the early research the analysis focused on production networks that were defined as "a network of labor and production processes whose end result is a finished commodity" (Hopkins and Wallerstein 1986: 159). This concept was extended to include all process steps required for the final product, including conceptual product inception, research and development, multiple stages of material processing like production, manufacturing, and assembly processes, to logistics, marketing, distribution, sales, and aftersales services (Kaplinsky and Morris 2000). As an analytical framework, it thus entails the analysis of all the different value-adding stages in a chain of activities towards the final product (Coe, Dicken, and Hess 2008). Through fine-slicing of activities and restructuring of firms to focus on the 'core activities,' value chains today span over a multitude of firms that are involved in the activities (Chandler 1994; Kaplinsky 2004; Ruigrok and van Tulder 1995). Furthermore, after decades of internationalization efforts and offshoring activities, value chains, by their very nature, have become global, and they form complex networks of individual activities performed by different firms and across multiple participants (Gereffi 1999; Gereffi and Korzeniewicz 1994). Despite assumingly individual activities performed by legally or geographically isolated and independent participants, the activities within a GVC are found to be explicitly governed by lead firms in the value chain (Humphrey 1995; Humphrey and Schmitz 2001; Ponte et al. 2014). Lead firms are powerful, large, and mostly multinational corporations that can orchestrate the activities within a global value chain (Fold 2002; Sturgeon, Van Biesebroeck, and Gereffi 2008).

The literature on GVC developed from three different strands: research on global commodity chains (GCC), global value chains (GVC), and global production chains (Coe et al. 2008). The concept of global value chains emerged in the 1990s (most notably, Gereffi and Korzeniewicz 1994) and has increasingly caught attention as an alternative framework for understanding globalized industries (OECD 2013; UNCTAD 2013). However, value chains as such are not a new phenomenon. Indeed, one of the fathers of modern economics, Adam Smith, when describing the division of labor in his 1776 book *An Inquiry into the Nature and Causes of The Wealth of Nations*, describes in great detail the value chain of the apparel industry, more specifically of the production of a woolen coat (Smith 1776). More than two centuries later, value chain analysis has become more and more important, as the vertical disintegration and separation of tasks performed for the creation of a product has become global and spans multiple firms (Nolan 2012; Ruigrok and van Tulder 1995). This process has been further accelerated through revolutionary new production systems like lean manufacturing that enable the lead firms to effectively orchestrate outsourced value chains (Womack et al. 1990). Consequently, the separation of activities has been divided not only within the factory, as in the times of Adam Smith, nor just between firms, as described by Chandler (1977), but between countries in an ever more globalizing world.

Linkages, spatial spread, and governance structures

The GVC framework offers three dimensions of analysis: First, an 'input-output' structure that links together all the production and service activities in the value chain in a sequential manner of value-adding tasks – much as in Porter's understanding of value chains: "a firm's value chain is an interdependent system of network of activities, connected by linkages. Linkages occur when the way in which one activity is performed affects the cost or effectiveness of other activities" (Porter 1990: 41). Second, the 'territoriality' of the activities in the value chain and their special spread – this is particularly fruitful for macro-economic analysis at a national level, and research on competitiveness of nations, but it can also be used for international business research on questions like location choice or the configuration of international operations. The third dimension is the 'governance structure' of the value chain, in particular the inter-firm relations and dynamics at play (Gereffi and Korzeniewicz 1994). Analyzing governance structures allows to explain how some actors in the value chain can control and orchestrate the value chain beyond the limits of their own legal boundaries and can thereby allocate resources (e.g. financial, material, and human resources) to the different participating firms along the value chain (Gereffi 1994: 97). A core concept in GVC governance theory is that of asymmetrical relations between firms (Kaplinsky and Morris 2000; Li 2010; Schmitz and Humphrey 2000). It is assumed that a handful of powerful lead firms "reside at the top of the world production networks" (Li 2010: 14) and are able to determine the distribution of resources in the value chain thereby exerting power over the other firms involved in the value creating process. By analyzing the governance structures it is possible to understand how value chains are coordinated and controlled when power asymmetries occur, how resources are allocated along the value chain, and how individual firms and geographic locations (i.e. production hubs and ultimately the position of nations in the global value chain) develop and evolve over time (Gereffi and Fernandez-Stark 2011). For the purpose of this book, three areas of the GVC framework are further elaborated: First, the concept of governance in GVC; second, how GVCs link to development; and third, a unique methodological approach to explore the competitive dynamics in a particular value chain.

Governance in the GVC framework

Governance in the GVC framework is based on power asymmetries between firms involved in the value chain. The understanding of governance has developed over time, adapting the framework of analysis. Initially, Gereffi developed a dichotomous framework and distinguished between two different government structures; the 'producer-driven' and the 'buyer-driven' value chains (Gereffi and Korzeniewicz 1994: 7). Although this concept was later further developed into a typology of five different structures, it still offers a suitable starting point to understand the underlying principles of power asymmetries in the relationships in value chains.

Producer-driven value chains are mainly dominated and directed by large manufacturing firms at the core of the value chain, like IBM in the ICT industry or car assemblers in the automotive industry. Ruigrock and Van Tulder frame such value chains as "informal control hierarchies, where one core assembler is positioned as a monopolist at the apex of a hierarchical, closed network" (Ruigrok and van Tulder 1995: 78). In producer-driven value chains, the lead firm, which plays the central role at the core of the network, focuses on producing goods. It coordinates and controls backward and forward linkages in the network and exerts power over vast parts of the value chain, like sourcing of parts and raw materials as well as distribution of the final product. They are mostly the terminal firm in the value chain, i.e. directly selling to the final customer with well-developed brand names. The segments of the value chain in which the lead firms are positioned are often the most profitable and highly concentrated with high entry barriers for new entrants. Typical lead firms in such value chains are manufacturers of advanced products such as aircrafts, computers, or automobiles that require high investments and technological standards (Gereffi 1999).

Buyer-driven value chains, on the other hand, are controlled and coordinated by trading companies, brand-named merchandisers, or large retailers. The production process in these value chains is decentralized and distributed over several firms in exporting countries, often in peripheral countries with great distance to the final customer (Gereffi 1999; Gereffi and Korzeniewicz 1994). In buyer-driven value chains it is large retailers close to the consumer that dominate and direct the value chain through their purchasing power. An example of such a value chain is the apparel industry with large retailers such as Wal-Mart, Kmart, or Sears.

The three underlying principles for the determination of buyer- and producer-driven value chains are (1) the 'complexity of transactions,' that is the complexity of the information flow and knowledge transfer between the different actors in the value chain, (2) the 'codifiability of information,' which is the ability to codify and efficiently transmit information, and (3) the 'capability of suppliers' or level of competence (Frederick and Gereffi 2009; Gereffi et al. 2005). While complexity increases through new demands set by the lead firm, such as just-in-time supply or product differentiation, lead firms can also reduce complexity through product standardization or codification of the information (Gereffi et al. 2005).

Typology of GVC governance structures

The principles of the early product network research mentioned earlier eventually led to the development of five governance structures types, extending the dichotomy by adding three more elaborate intermediary concepts (Gereffi et al. 2005; Table 2.1). The typology of GVC governance distinguishes between five forms of governance, from 'market' structures determined by market forces at one side of the spectrum to hierarchy with fully vertically integrated firms at the other side of the spectrum. Between the two extremes are three types of hybrid forms of governance with semi-control. The structures are coined *modular*, *relational*, and *captive* structures, in which the lead firm takes increasing control over its non-equity business network. Such hybrid forms of governance do not require ownership of the firm. For instance, Japanese firms like Toyota have legally independent firms that in fact are dependent on and closely orchestrated by Toyota, led by former Toyota employees with loyalty to the Toyota group and considered part of Toyota's 'inner circle' (Cusumano 1985; Hill 1989; Womack et al. 1990).

Table 2.1 Types of global value chains

Governance type	*Market*	*Modular*	*Relational*	*Captive*	*Hierarchy*
Degree of explicit coordination	–	– to 0	**0**	**0 to +**	+
Factors determining governance setup					
Complexity of transaction	–	+	+	+	+
Codified interfaces	+	+	–	–/0/+	–
Capabilities in the supply-base	+	+	+	–	–

Three factors determine the governance type. While there are eight possible combinations of the factors, Gereffi et al. (2005), found only five governance types that are likely to occur.

Source: Author's own table, based on Gereffi et al. (2005).

Market governance structures consist of loose linkages where the cost of switching partners is low, much like in an ideal neoclassic market under perfect competition. Relationships are hands off and price competition is the determining factor for choosing a partner.

In *modular* value chains the lead firm controls the distribution channels and is the link between the finished product and the final customer. They know the customer and determine design requirements of the final product. However, many of the production competencies lie with the 'turn-key suppliers,' who produce key modules that require extensive knowledge and capabilities in R&D and manufacturing. Such 'turn-key suppliers' control their supply chain and take responsibility for the production processes, ensure quality standards are met, and make sure that suppliers have adequate technologies and competencies. The products are characterized as being differentiated and highly customized; yet suppliers use generic machinery to pool their capacities for their different customers and to limit transaction-specific investments. Hence, Sturgeon (2002) referred to modular governance structures that rely on turn-key suppliers as 'modular production networks' in which highly competent suppliers can be added to the global production system according to the demand (Sturgeon 2002).

Relational value chains are defined through the bilateral dependencies between suppliers and buyer, which is results from the complex interactions and information flows between the two firms. The relational supplier produces highly customized products that require high standards of technology and own product design capabilities, thereby being dependent on its buyer while the buyer is dependent on the supply firm's capabilities at the same time. Product specifications are set by the buyer, which thereby exert some degree of control over the supplier. Interactions between the two are frequent and the information exchange complex. The close linkages that are created can be managed through trust and reputation that has built over time or alternatively by ethnic or family ties (e.g. Menkhoff 1992). Relational suppliers often show a close spatial proximity to the buyer.

Captive value chains are characterized by buyers with considerable power over smaller suppliers. The suppliers are highly dependent on the buyer and have little R&D capabilities or intellectual property. However, as the complexity of the transaction is high, switching cost for suppliers is high. Therefore, the suppliers are closely monitored and controlled by the buyer.

Hierarchical value chains consist of highly vertically integrated firms. Parts production is owned by the lead firm, and the lead firm exerts managerial control over its subsidiaries and affiliates (Gereffi et al. 2005; Gereffi and Fernandez-Stark 2011: 9).

Power asymmetries in the GVC

While the types of governance structures mentioned earlier are mostly determined by the complexity of a transaction (i.e. information flow, codifiability, and capability of the supplier), additional crucial elements for governance are the power asymmetries between firms.

The ability of lead firms to exert control over parts of the value chain depends on their relative power over other firms. Power asymmetries between the firms involved in the value chain derive from the ability of a firm to gain control over crucial activities in the value chain, like control over large proportions of the market, either as buyer or seller. Through the ability to control a crucial link in the value chain power is distributed asymmetrically, with some firms dominating and dictating the activities along the up- or downstream value chain. Dembinski identified three sourced of advantages that vest a firm with power. First, the capacity to spread the economic activity globally; second, the ability or a price mark-up based on superior branding capabilities; and third, strong bargaining power towards the suppliers that allows the lead firm to reap the benefits of productivity advanced in the entire value chain (Dembinski 2009). In particular the bargaining power of one firm towards its supplier or buyer contribute to the firm's dominant position in the value chain (Porter 1979). A firm that controls a bottleneck in the value chain has control over supply or demand, which increases its bargaining power within the value chain. In that regard, the focal firm is the nexus of the GVC (Dembinski 2009).

Moreover, key innovations enabled the powerful firms to exert control over others. The ability to assume a powerful position in the value chain has been increased through the ongoing consolidation of lead firms that, when created, led to oligopsony structures in which few buyers can consolidate considerable power (Nolan, Zhang, and Liu 2007). In particular, technological advancements, contracting, and management capabilities enabled firms to control the extended value chain. Modern IT systems, for example, enable firms to transfer accurate information in real-time across the world and to share such information with other vendors at the effect of more control (Nolan 2001).

The most powerful firms in a GVC have been coined 'lead firms' in the literature (Fold 2002; Gereffi and Korzeniewicz 1994). Such lead firms have considerable power over their business network and are typically large firms that control significant areas of the value chain. The role of the lead firm has increased over time, as inter-firm interdependencies have intensified (Bair and Gereffi 2001; Coe et al. 2008; Schmitz and Navadi 1999). The influence of lead firms has increased to an extent that it can take the form of partial control over separate firms without the necessity of ownership. In its role as a coordinator, the lead firm in a value chain can be seen as a 'spider' in a web of businesses (Ruigrok and van Tulder 1995), controlling and establishing a network of connecting activities and production procedures. As a result of the vertical disintegration, exerting control beyond the firm's boundaries is a way to ensure and secure supplies of raw material and produced goods that meet all the requirements of the terminal firm. In behaving so, the nature of what can be seen as an individual 'firm' has greatly changed (Coase 1937).

Contemporary transaction cost theory assumes that firms need to take ownership to have some degree of control over other firms (Buckley and Casson 1976; Coase 1937; Williamson 2005). However, the GVC literature hints that such ownership may not be necessary. By strongly influencing or even partly controlling independent suppliers' operations, planning, and even strategies, the boundaries of the firms have become blurred. Yet such intertwined operations between individual entities do not resemble price-driven neoclassic arm's length relations as imagined in a perfect free market (Casson 1987; Williamson 1981). Inter-firm relations in a GVC do not fit the market-hierarchy spectrum, as they neither resemble Adam Smith's 'invisible hand' of free market transactions and intense competition between interchangeable firms, nor Alfred Chandler's 'visible hand' of internal planning and coordination within a firm (Li 2010). Nolan has coined the concept of the 'external firm,' in which the firm exerts influence outside its legal boundaries by planning and coordinating the activities within its value chain. The sphere of influence is not limited to its legal entity but expands to its value chain through conscious coordination and allocation of resources and tasks (Nolan et al. 2007). The GVC framework enables us to study the 'firm' in its extended form: as a network or group of cooperating firms, rather than as its legal entity. It is thus an elegant analytical tool to further our understanding of economic activity in a globalized world in the age of vertical disintegration.

Early conceptions of governance structures assumed unipolar GVCs, in which one lead firm dominates the entire value chain (Fold 2002). This concept of 'unipolar' value chains was recently extended to allow for 'bipolar' and 'multipolar' value chains (Fold 2002; Ponte 2014; Riisgaard and Hammer 2011; Sturgeon 2002). Although the 'lead' firm is often positioned close to the final customer, the powerful firms can sit at different positions along the value chain. For instance, large suppliers can orchestrate their upstream value chains without their customers being involved (Kaplinsky and Morris 2000). In multi-polar value chains multiple powerful firms can co-exist, each controlling a key stake in the value chain as well as exerting some degree of control over external up- or downstream activities. Even though power appears to be more equally distributed along such value chains, multipolar value chains differ from hands-off market structures, "because they are shaped by explicit strategic actions of powerful actors (both inside and outside the chain), even if they exhibit multiple foci of power and various kinds of linkages" (Ponte 2014: 359). Moreover, governance structures are not static but change over time as the determinants (i.e. complexity of the interactions between the firms involved) change. Changes can occur in the way they are managed and when new technologies influence the design and production system of the product (Gereffi et al. 2005).

Linking product architecture, knowledge-transfer, and degree of control

The extent to which the lead firm exerts power over the participating firms depends on the firm's power based on its dominant position for a crucial link or position in the value chain and the complexity of a transaction. The ability of a firm to capture a strong position for a crucial link in the value chain stems from the firm's competitive advantage, like superior product knowledge, systems integration capabilities, or access to the market. According to the resource-based view of the firm, the competitive advantage must be VRINE (valuable, rare, inimitable, non-substitutable, and exploitable) for the firm to utilize its advantage and gain power over other firms and to allow the lead firm to capture and control a quasi-oligopolistic position. While there may be powerful firms in all tiers along the value chain, most value chains involve a high number of far less powerful firms.

The complexity of the knowledge transfer in a transaction depends on the product characteristics, which are an important determinant for the governance structure. To get a deeper understanding of product characteristics it is possible to link the GVC framework to the literature about product architecture. In his product architecture typology, Fujimoto differentiates between integral or modular nature of a product and open and closed product architecture (Figure 2.1). Modular architecture products are such that allow a high degree of codification for the interfaces

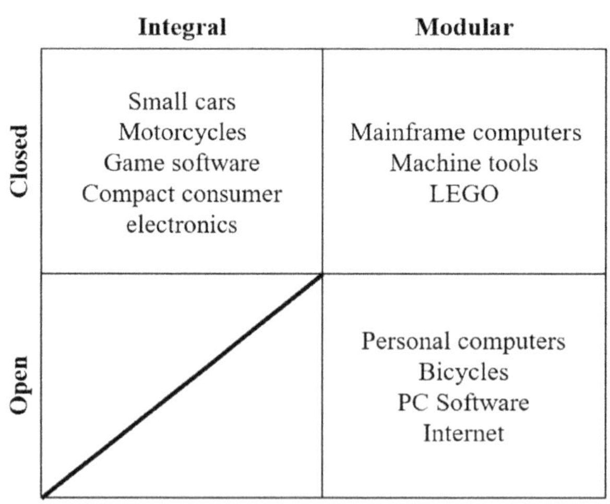

Figure 2.1 Basic types of product architecture

Source: Fujimoto (2007).

between components. Individual components can be matched through clearly defined interfaces to build a final product. Integral architecture, on the other hand, exists when interfaces are difficult to codify and are therefore difficult to standardize. Interdependencies of components are high, so changing one component has an impact on others. Detailed designs are only known to the firm and may be subcontracted to an outside firm, but the basic design of the tool system is contained within one company (Fujimoto 2007).

Open and closed differentiates between industry-wide standardization of interfaces and interface designs that are contained within the firm. Open architecture requires standardization at the industry level, while closed architecture occurs when it offers competitive advantage to the owner to define the interfaces at the product level. Since integral components cannot be standardized, this requires the architecture to be closed-integral; open-integral architecture is impossible.

The complexity of a transaction is to a large degree driven by the interfaces of components, i.e. the product architecture. Open-modular interfaces are standardized so that full information is codified and available outside the transaction. In closed-modular architecture knowledge about the interface designs is shared as part of the transaction. Even though the information is not publicly available, the information required to define the interface is fully codifiable. The most complex transactions involve closed-integral architectures. In such instances, the interfaces cannot be fully codified, for instance because the different components are interdependent. This means that any changes to one component requires adaptation of the other. At the time of the transaction the components and interfaces are not fully developed and defined, and they need further R&D before finalization. This requires the involved firms to co-develop the components, which entails a complex transfer of tacit knowledge. Individual components correspond with one another, and their performance is influenced by the performance of structurally separate components or modules (Fujimoto 2007; Ulrich 1995; Ulrich and Eppinger 2004). As Park and Ro write: "With integral product architecture, components are tightly coupled, creating the need for coordinated design and production processes to create optimal linkages between component to ensure optimum-product performance." (Park and Ro 2013). Transaction cost theory would suggest that for closed integral architecture, the firm would opt for a high degree of vertical integration. However this is not always the case. Increasingly, several firms are involved in the product development process, such as supply firms for highly specialized components, which they later supply to the production and assembly locations of the final firm (Hertenstein and Williamson 2018). Hence the co-development process for closed products requires systems integration at the firm level. Such co-development processes of close-integral products require extensive collaboration of the individual development centers of the involved companies and require extensive transfer of tacit knowledge between firms to ensure successful integration of components with no standardized interfaces. Moreover, the individual components of integral systems have a high degree of asset-specificity, i.e. can only be used for their predefined end-use. Suppliers and buyers in such transactions therefore have a high degree of dependency on one another. This has led to increased mixtures of semi-control by some firms over the external value chain, referred to by some as 'extended firm' (Fine 1998). The necessity for close interaction, the knowledge advantage of the systems-integrating firm, and the high levels of interdependency in integral architectures provides the lead firm with the potential to exert extensive power over the participating external firms both up- and downstream in the value chain.

Global value chains and development

The GVC linkages, spread of activities, and governance structure have an impeccable impact on the development of national economies. The localization of activities to an emerging market (spread of activities) and the integration of indigenous firms from the emerging markets into the GVC that are dominated by lead firms are two crucial aspects for development.

In today's globalized economy, the production of goods has been 'unbundled' from consumption (Baldwin 2014). Due to affordable international transportation and the reduction of trade barriers, activities can be located anywhere local advantages exist. Hence, the 'level of localization' of activities, which determines how many value-adding activities are localized to a specific location, is important to countries and can determine the strength of their local industries. As previous GVC research has shown, lead firms can allocate value-adding activities to different locations for both their own operations and operations of its extended value chain. Therefore their decisions play a crucial role in determining the level of depth for localization to a specific geographic area. Additionally, in globalized and highly consolidated industries dominated by a few large MNCs, such MNCs play a decisive role in the development of firms from the emerging markets, as the MNC often controls large proportions of the world market in its industry and has a high degree of power over the other participants in the industry, including such firms from the emerging markets.

GVC governance and firm-level upgrading

Upgrading refers to the process of achieving higher rents by outperforming the competition. In the value chain context, upgrading can be achieved through capability building that enables the firm to produce better products, increase its efficiency and productivity, or move into more skilled activities to create more value (Gereffi and Fernandez-Stark 2011; Humphrey and Schmitz 2001; Kaplinsky and Morris 2000). A commonly used typology of upgrading in the context of GVC differentiates between four ways of upgrading (Schmitz and Humphrey 2000).

The first way to upgrade is referred to as *process upgrading*, which can be achieved by an increase of productivity through process efficiency. This can involve processes within individual firms as well as inter-firm processes at the link between two firms in a value chain. Most commonly, process upgrading is achieved by reorganizing the production system, or by introducing superior processing technologies (Schmitz 1999). The second way to upgrade is *product upgrading*, which refers to the development of better or new products that achieve higher value-added. This can be achieved through product innovation or innovative product development processes and fast product updates, enabling the firm to move to more sophisticated and profitable segments (Gereffi 1999). *Functional upgrading* refers to changing the firm's function in the value chain by performing new activities. Examples are upgrading from manufacturing components to assembling systems or upgrading from manufacturing to designing products (Bair and Gereffi 2001). Finally, *chain or inter-sectorial upgrading* refers to upgrading across value chains by entering new value chains and applying the capabilities in the new, potentially more profitable sectors (Giuliani, Pietrobelli, and Rabellotti 2005; Humphrey and Schmitz 2002).

In early literature on upgrading, the ability to upgrade was derived from attributes within the firm (Hamel and Pralahad 1994; Teece and Pisano 1994). As Kaplinsky and Morris argue, these concepts fall short in capturing the systemic aspects of upgrading in value chains in which firms are linked together and where several firms can influence the potential for upgrading others (Kaplinsky and Morris 2000: 38). In particular lead firms play a decisive role for the prospects to upgrade other firms in the value chain. Multiple studies have documented the links between value chain governance and upgrading (Gereffi 1999; Giuliani et al. 2005; Schmitz and Humphrey 2000). Lead firm orchestration and coordination of global value chains include the allocation of activities within the value chain (i.e. selecting and allocating activities to capable supply firms), developing and enabling supply firms for technological upgrades (Giuliani et al. 2005), collaborative expansion to new (international) production hubs (i.e. location choice for FDI) (Hertenstein, Sutherland, and Anderson 2017), and restructuring and consolidating the supply chain (i.e. by encouraging mergers and acquisitions) (Nolan, Zhang, and Chunhang 2007). Consequently, the upgrading prospects of participating supply firms depends to a large extent on lead firms' orchestrating activities.

Scholars have studied the process of lead firm induced upgrading in the emerging markets, in which some of the supply firms otherwise lack in quality controls and production process standards to deliver the components to the requirements at a low price. Yet, the interactions and dynamics between the two firms involved are relatively unexplored. In oligopsony markets like the automotive industry, where a few buyers dominate the industry, multiple supply firms can fully depend on the lead firm. Moreover, with powerful lead firms being involved in assisting and nurturing the supply firms to upgrade their products, processes, or functions, supply firms from the emerging economies can be awkwardly dependent on the lead firm. Consequently, the challenge of upgrading has to be viewed within these wider perspectives of the business network or value chain in which a firm is embedded.

Methods for GVC research

In the quest to understand governance within the GVC, most studies relied on a single case study on the lead firm (Gereffi and Fernandez-Stark 2011: 12). However, as power asymmetries involve two or more firms, a more holistic approach to analyzing such asymmetries and its relational dynamics seems necessary. For this reason, the study presented in this book conducted a multiple vantage point approach, to include and analyze firms at multiple levels in the value chain. Through the multiple vantage point analysis it was possible to explore the inter-firm dynamics along several layers of the value chain, offering new insights into the competitive dynamics between firms and deepening our understanding of governance. The case study approach is especially useful for explorative studies (Yin 2003) and is, according to Gereffi et al. (2005), a particularly valuable approach for studies on the changing governance structures of global value chains. Through the case-study approach, a longitudinal view of the topic can be taken to document how certain decisions and changes in the strategy of the lead firm changes the economic environment of the supply firms and affects the indigenous firms' development over time. By using this approach this research exemplifies the value of in-depth case study research in the field of economics by highlighting findings of inter-firm process evolution that are difficult to capture with quantitative methods (Strauss 1987).

The case study was designed to include multiple vantage points of several firms from a single discreet value chain. This allows us to develop a holistic view of the firms' interactions and to triangulate the findings. The value chain is explored from four vantage points of firms at different positions in the value chain, to include the perspective of a lead firm, turn-key supply firms, component supply firms from the home country of the lead firm, as well as supply firms from the two emerging markets Brazil and China. Overall, the supply firms came from several different positions in the value chain. Selecting multiple cases of indigenous supply firms was important as multiple cases are more likely to yield generalizable and robust findings (Eisenhardt 1989; Yin 2003). Furthermore, the multiple vantage point approach enhances external validity (Gibbert, Ruigrok, and Wicki 2008).

Data collection and analysis

Several primary and secondary data sources were used for the multiple case study approach. For primary data collection the most common method was expert interviews in each case firm. Interviews were conducted with multiple individuals from the firms to gain different perspectives from employees (Eisenhardt and Graebner 2007). Interviewees came from different levels in the corporate hierarchy, from engineers to board members, from several different functions, typically from purchasing, sales, and R&D departments, and different geographic locations. Additional interviews were conducted with industry experts not related to the case firms, such as management consultants, top management of additional automotive firms, or policy makers, to supplement the primary case data (Gibbert et al. 2008). The best source of in-depth information proved to come from several weeklong observations of senior managers in their daily jobs, which enabled the asking of questions during daily routines. Several weeks in the purchasing, R&D, and production departments at some of the firms offered unique insights into their value chain orchestrating activities.

Most critical in all interview-based research is access to interviewees. Several approaches were used to gain initial access to the companies, the most successful being through personal contacts or connections through the university department. Additionally, establishing the initial contact at public events such as trade shows or industry conferences proved to be fruitful, even if the attending company representatives were often not from the desired department or function from within the firm. The least fruitful approach to gain access was through cold-calls of the official contact of a company. Yet even through this approach it was possible to gain access to some of the supply firms in the case study.

Once the initial contact was established the most effective strategy to get further access to the desired department, hierarchy level, and number of interview partners was through snow-balling, by utilizing the network of the contact who can refer to additional interview partners. This proved to work particularly well from top-down. I was in the fortunate position to have gained access to several C-level executives, all of which were extremely helpful to refer me to the right person. The other way around, however, proved fairly difficult. Managers seemed generally happy to recommend either peers or subordinates but were hesitant to refer me to superiors. All in all, I was able to conduct 104 interviews, the vast majority through snow-balling and follow-up interviews with colleagues of previous interviewees.

Additional secondary archival data was collected to support the primary data and to triangulate the data and so improve the accuracy of the picture emerging (Eisenhardt and Graebner 2007; Gibbert et al. 2008; Jick 1979). The documents used in this book came from internal company documents, annual reports, company web pages, magazines and newspapers, published interviews by company officials, and books.

Data analysis in the multiple vantage point approach

The multiple vantage point approach offers unique opportunities for within-case and cross-case analyses (Eisenhardt 1989; Miles and Hubermann 1994). As a first step, individual cases that triangulated all of the data, including observations, interviews, and documents, were written up (Jick 1979). This was followed by a cross-case analysis using replication logic across firms, treating each firm as a case. During the cross-case analysis alternative narratives can emerge depending on the interviewee's vantage point. This opened up insights for novel conceptual constructs and new theoretical relationships, as the different views complemented each other, sparking new questions for a deeper exploration of the topic.

Limitations of the multi vantage point approach

The multiple vantage point approach does not come without its limitations. First, as a case study approach, the findings are derived from a relatively small number of firms. Future research is required to test the proposed implications of such studies. Second, the multiple vantage point approach focuses on a single industry. While this provides deep insights into the dynamics of this industry, it limits the generalizability of the findings. Depending on size of industry, level of globalization, product characteristics, level of modularization, and codifiability, the interfirm relations and governance approaches may look very different in other industries, leading to different implications for development. Third, in this book, the study only includes Brazil and China. Both countries are relatively large, with strong industries and a high level of integration in the world economy. Yet their development is very different. This limits the generalizability in regards to implications for development as most emerging markets are smaller in size and face a different set of challenges.

References

Bair, J. and G. Gereffi. 2001. "Local Clusters in Global Chains: The Causes and Consequences of Export Dynamism in Torreon's Blue Jeans Industry'." *World Development* 28(11): 1885–903.

Baldwin, R. 2014. "Trade and Industrialization after Globalization's Second Unbundling: How Building and Joining a Supply Chain Are Different and Why It Matters." In *Globalization in an Age of Crisis: Multilateral Economic Cooperation in the Twenty-First Century*, edited by R. C. F. Feenstra and A. M. Taylor. Chicago: University of Chicago Press.

Bertrand, O. and M. Mol. 2013. "The Antecendents and Innovation Effects of Domestic and Offshore R&D Outsourcing: The Contingent Impact of Cognitive Distance and Absorptive Capacity." *Strategic Management Journal* 34(6): 751–60.

Birkinshaw, J. M. and C. Fey. 2005. "External Sources of Knowledge, Governance Mode, and R&D Performance." *Journal of Management* 34(4): 597–621.

Buckley, P. J. and M. C. Casson. 1976. *The Future of the Multinational Enterprise*. London: Macmillan.

Casson, M. 1987. *The Firm and the Market: Studies on Multinational Enterprise and the Scope of the Firm*. Cambridge, MA: MIT Press.

Chandler, A. D. 1977. *The Visible Hand: Managerial Revolution in American Business*. Cambridge, MA: Harvard University Press.

Chandler, D. D. 1994. *Scale and Scope: Dynamics of Industrial Capitalism*. Cambridge, MA: Harvard University Press.

Coase, R. H. 1937. "The Nature of the Firm." *Economica*: 386–405.

Coe, N., P. Dicken, and M. Hess. 2008. "Introduction: Global Production Networks – Debates and Challenges." *Journal of Economic Geography* 8: 267–9.

Contractor, F., V. Kumar, S. Kundu, and T. Pedersen. 2010. "Reconceptualizing the Firm in a World of Outsourcing and Offshoring: The Organizational and Geographical Relocation of High-Value Company Functions." *Journal of Management Studies* 47(8): 1417–33.

Cusumano, M. 1985. *Japanese Automobile Industry: Technology and Management at Nissan and Toyota (Harvard East Asian Monographs)*. Cambridge, MA: Harvard University Press.

Dembinski, P. H. 2009. "Very Large Enterprises, Focal Firms and Global Value Chains." *Revista de Economia Mundial* 23: 107–30.

Eisenhardt, K. M. 1989. "Building Theories From Case Study Research." *The Academy of Management Review* 14(4): 532–50.

Eisenhardt, K. M. and M. Graebner. 2007. "Theory Building From Cases: Opportunities and Challenges." *Academy of Management Review* 50: 25–32.
Fine, C. H. 1998. *Clockspeed: Winning Industry Control in the Age of Temporary Advantage*. London: Little, Brown and Company.
Fold, N. 2002. "Lead Firms and Competition in 'Bi-Polar' Commodity Chains: Grinders and Branders in the Global Cocoa-Chocolate Industry." *Journal of Agrarian Change* 2(2): 228–47.
Frederick, S. and G. Gereffi. 2009. *Value Chain Governance*. Briefing Paper, United States Agency for International Development.
Fujimoto, T. 2007. "Architecture-Based Comparative Advantage – A Design Information View of Manufacturing." *Evolutionary and Institutional Economics Review* 4(1): 55–112.
Gereffi, G. 1994. "The Organization of Buyer-Driven Global Commodity Chains: How U.S. Retailers Shape Overseas Production Networks." In *Commodity Chains and Global Capitalism*, edited by G. Gereffi and M. Korzeniewicz, pp. 95–122. London: Greenwood Press.
Gereffi, G. 1999. "A Commodity Chains Framework for Analyzing Global Industries." Working Paper, Duke University: Center on Globalization Governance and Competitiveness.
Gereffi, G, J. Humphrey, and T. J. Sturgeon. 2005. "The Governance of Global Value Chains." *Review of International Political Economy* 12(1): 78–104.
Gereffi, G. and K. Fernandez-Stark. 2011. "Global Value Chain Analysis: A Primer." Working Paper, Duke University: Center on Globalization Governance and Competitiveness.
Gereffi, G. and M. Korzeniewicz. 1994. *Commodity Chains and Global Capitalism*. London: Greenwood Press.
Gibbert, M., W. Ruigrok, and B. Wicki. 2008. "What Passes as a Rigorous Case Study?" *Strategic Management Journal* 29(13): 1465–74.
Giuliani, E., C. Pietrobelli, and R. Rabellotti. 2005. "Upgrading in Global Value Chains: Lessons From Latin American Clusters." *World Development* 33(4): 549–73.
Hamel, G. and C. K. Pralahad. 1994. *Competing for the Future*. Cambridge, MA: Harvard Business School Press.
Hatani, F. 2005. *Organisational Evolution of Global Supply Networks: Formation and Capabilities of the Toyota Group*. PhD dissertation, University of Cambridge.
Hertenstein, P., D. Sutherland, and J. Anderson. 2017. "Internationalization Within Networks: Exploring the Relationship Between Inward and Outward FDI in China's Auto Components Industry." *Asia Pacific Journal of Management* 34(1): 69–96.
Hertenstein, P. and P. J. Williamson. 2018. "The Role of Suppliers in Enabling Differing Innovation Strategies of Competing Multinationals From Emerging and Advanced Economies: German and Chinese Automotive Firms Compared." *Technovation* 70–71: 46–58.
Hill, R. C. 1989. "Comparing Transnational Production Systems: The Automobile Industry in the USA and Japan." *International Journal of Urban and Regional Research* 13(3): 462–80.
Hopkins, R. K. and I. Wallerstein. 1986. "Commodity Chains in the World-Economy Prior to 1800." *Review* 10(1): 157–70.
Humphrey, J. 1995. "Special Issue on Industrial Organization and Manufacturing Competitiveness in Developing Countries." *World Development* 23(1).
Humphrey, J. and O. Memedovic. 2003. "The Global Automotive Industry Value Chain: What Prospects for Upgrading by Developing Countries." UNIDO Sectorial Studies Series Working Paper, Vienna: UNIDO.

Humphrey, J. and H. Schmitz. 2001. "Governance in Global Value Chains." *IDS Bulletin* 32(3).
Humphrey, J. and H. Schmitz. 2002. *Developing Country Firms in the World Economy: Governance and Upgrading in Global Value Chains*. INEF Report, Duisburg.
Jick, T. D. 1979. "Mixing Qualitative and Quantitative Methods: Triangulation in Action." *Administrative Science Quaterly* 24(4): 602–11.
Kaplinsky, R. 2004. "Spreading the Gains From Globalization: What Can Be Learned From Value-Chain Analysis?" *Problems of Economic Transition* 47(2): 74–115.
Kaplinsky, R. and M. Morris. 2000. "A Handbook for Value Chain Research." Working Paper, IDRC.
Li, L. 2010. *Convergence and Transformation of Telecommunication Industry: The Cases of Telecommunication Service Provider and Equipment Manufacturer*. Cambridge: University of Cambridge.
McCann, P. and H. Y. Kim. 2008. "Supply Chains and Locational Adjustment in the Global Automotive Industry." *Policy Studies* 29(3): 255–66.
Mei, L. M. L. 2008. *Study on the Automotive Industrial Upgrading in China Based on Global Value Chain*. 2008 4th International Conference on Wireless Communications, Networking and Mobile Computing.
Menkhoff, T.. 1992. "Xinyongor How to Trust Trust? Chinese Non-Contractual Business Relations and Social Structure: The Singapore Case." *Internationales Asien Forum* 23: 26–288.
Miles, M. B. and A. M. Hubermann. 1994. *Qualitative Data Analysis: A Sourcebook of New Methods*. 2nd ed. Beverly Hills, CA: Sage.
Nolan, P. 2001. *China and the Global Economy*. Hampshire: Palgrave Macmillan.
Nolan, P. 2012. *Is China Buying the World?* Cambridge: Polity Press.
Nolan, P., J. Zhang, and C. Liu. 2007. *The Global Business Revolution and the Cascade Effect*. Basingstoke: Palgrave.
Nolan, P., J. Zhang, and C. Liu. 2007. "The Global Business Revolution, the Cascade Effect, and the Challenge for Firms From Developing Countries." *Cambridge Journal of Economics* 32(1): 29–47.
OECD. 2013. *Interconnected Economies: Benefiting From Global Value Chains*. Paris: OECD Publishing.
Park, J.-K. and Y. K. Ro. 2013. "Product Architectures and Sourcing Decisions: Their Impact on Performance." *Journal of Management* 39(3): 814–46.
Pavlinek, P. and J. Zenka. 2010. "Upgrading in the Automotive Industry: Firm-Level Evidence From Central Europe." *Journal of Economic Geography* 11(3): 559–86.
Penrose, E. T. 1959. *The Theory of the Growth of the Firm*. New York: Wiley.
Ponte, S. 2014. "The Evolutionary Dynamics of Biofuel Value Chains: From Unipolar and Government-Driven to Multipolar Governance." *Environment and Planning* 46(2): 353–72.
Ponte, S., I. Kelling, K. S. Jaspersen, and F. Kruijssen. 2014. "The Blue Revolution in Asia: Upgrading and Governance in Aquaculture Value Chains." *World Development* 64(12): 52–64.
Porter, M. E. 1979. "How Competitive Forces Shape Strategy." *Harvard Business Review* 57(2): 137–45.
Porter, M. E. 1987. "Changing Patterns of International Competition." In *The Competitive Challenge: Strategies for Industrial Innovation and Renewal*, edited by D. J. Teece, pp. 27–57. Cambridge, MA: Ballinger.
Porter, M. E. 1990. *The Competitive Advantage of Nations*. New York: Free Press.

Pyke, F. and W. Sengenberger. 1992. *Industrial Districts and Local Economic Regeneration.* Geneva: International Institute for Labour Studies.

Riisgaard, L. and N. Hammer. 2011. "Prospects for Labour in Global Value Chains: Labour Standards in the Cut Flower and Banana Industries." *British Journal of Industrial Relations* 49(1): 168–90.

Ruigrok, W. and R. van Tulder. 1995. *The Logic of International Restructuring.* London: Routledge.

Schmitz, H. 1999. "Global Competition and Local Cooperation: Siccess and Failure in the Sinos Valley, Brazil." *World Development* 27(9): 1627–50.

Schmitz, H. and J. Humphrey. 2000. "Governance and Upgrading: Linking Industrial Cluster and Global Value Chain Research." Working Paper 120, IDS.

Schmitz, H. and K. Navadi. 1999. "Clustering and Internationalization: Introduction." *World Development* 27(9): 1503–14.

Smith, A. 1776. *An Inquiry Into the Nature and Causes of the Wealth of Nations.* London: W. Strahan and T. Cadell.

Strauss, A. 1987. *Qualitative Analysis for Social Scientists.* New York: Cambridge University Press.

Sturgeon, T. 2002. "Modular Production Networks: A New American Model of Industrial Organization." *Industrial and Corporate Change* 11(3): 451–96.

Sturgeon, T., J. Van Biesebroeck, and G. Gereffi. 2008. "Value Chains, Networks and Clusters: Reframing the Global Automotive Industry." *Journal of Economic Geography* 8(3): 297–321.

Teece, D. and G. Pisano. 1994. "The Dynamic Capabilities of Firms: An Introduction." *Industrial and Corporate Change* 3(3): 537–56.

Ulrich, K. T. 1995. "The Role of Product Architecture in the Manufacturing Firm." *Research Policy* 24: 419–40.

Ulrich, K. T. and S. D. Eppinger. 2004. *Product Design and Development.* 3rd ed. New York: McGraw-Hill.

UNCTAD. 2013. *World Investment Report 2013: Global Value Chains: Investment and Trade for Development.* Geneva: UNCTAD.

Williamson, O. E. 1981. "The Economics of Organization: The Transaction Cost Approach." *The American Journal of Sociology* 87(3): 548–77.

Williamson, O. E. 2005. "The Economics of Governance." *American Economic Review* 95(2): 1–18.

Womack, J. P., D. T. Jones, and D. Roos. 1990. *The Machine That Changed the World.* New York: Rawson Associates.

Yin, R. 2003. *Case Study Research: Design and Methods.* London: SAGE Publications Ltd.

3 Volkswagen – lead firm and orchestrator

The Volkswagen AG is a German manufacturer of passenger cars and commercial vehicles headquartered in Wolfsburg. With over 10.3 million vehicles sold in 2016, Volkswagen has become the largest automotive producer in the world, for the first time overtaking its Japanese rival Toyota. Even though Volkswagen was founded in 1937, it was not until December 1945 that Volkswagen began producing passenger cars in serious volumes, as the company was assigned to manufacture armaments and war machinery between 1939 and 1945. Volkswagen is a relative latecomer in the automotive industry compared to the likes of Daimler or Ford, which built the first automobiles in 1886 and 1896 respectively. Nevertheless, it is of little surprise that Volkswagen would one day become one of the largest automotive manufacturers of the world. Large volume production is at the very heart of Volkswagen, which translates into 'people's car' and was founded under the German Nazi regime to produce an affordable car for the masses. The ambition and objective to become a serious volume producer began right after the Second World War, with the production of the 'Volkswagen Type 1,' more commonly known as the 'Volkswagen Beetle' or 'Bug' as it is called in the US. In 1971, annual production of the Volkswagen Beetle peaked at 1.3 million units. On 17 February 1972, a total of 15,007,034 Beetles had been produced, surpassing the first truly mass-produced vehicle and previous record holder, the Fold Model T, which was produced from 1908 to 1927. By the end of production in 2003, a total of over 21 million Volkswagen Beetles were produced, still holding the record for the most produced passenger car in the world. Other successful models followed, like the iconic Transporter series and later models like the Passat or Golf, which helped Volkswagen to grow organically.

Despite the success of some of Volkswagen's own vehicles the firm did not base its strategy on organic growth alone. Over the years, VW has become one of the most aggressive acquirers in the automotive industry. Mergers and acquisitions have a long tradition in the Volkswagen group, with the first acquisition taking place on 1 January 1965, when Volkswagen bought the Auto-Union GmbH, which would later be known as AUDI. With the acceleration of globalization in the 1980s the automotive industry began a global consolidation through a wave of M&A. Volkswagen was one of the most active players and acquired a number of European manufacturers: in 1985, Volkswagen first bought 51% and later in the same year

75% shares of the Spanish producer SEAT. In 1991, after the dissolving of the USSR, Volkswagen acquired the traditional Czech manufacturer Skoda. In 1998 Volkswagen acquired Bugatti and Bentley, two luxurious super car manufacturers, to widen the segment and integrate superior technology into the company. Later the same year, the Volkswagen daughter AUDI acquired the Italian super sports car manufacturer Lamborghini. Through these acquisitions, Volkswagen was able to offer a wide spectrum of passenger cars in its portfolio, and the focus for acquisitions shifted to commercial vehicles.

In 2006, the attention shifted from passenger cars to commercial vehicles, and Volkswagen acquired MAN, a manufacturer of heavy commercial vehicles. The MAN acquisition supplemented the portfolio of light commercial vehicles produced under the Volkswagen brand. This was followed by the purchase of first 38% and then 67% of the voting rights of the Scandinavian Scania, a producer of heavy commercial vehicles and an increase of the stake in MAN to 55% and later 75%. Through the acquisitions of MAN and Scania, Volkswagen was able to add the full range of commercial vehicles to its product portfolio.

Somewhat out of line is the acquisition of Porsche. After a long takeover battle between the two companies and leading families behind them (Porsche and Piech), Volkswagen was finally able to acquire Porsche in 2009 after accumulating a 49.9% stake. After the takeover battle was won, Porsche was fully integrated into the Volkswagen group and became one of the key developing brands besides AUDI and Volkswagen.

In 2012, AUDI's subsidiary Lamborghini acquired the Italian based producer of motor bikes, Ducati. This marks the last grand acquisition of Volkswagen, after which the company extended to product portfolio beyond automobiles. As of 2017, Volkswagen owns 12 brands, most of which have been acquired (Volkswagen, Volkswagen commercial vehicles, AUDI, Porsche, SEAT, Skoda, Bugatti, Bentley, Lamborghini, Ducati, MAN, and Scania). Of its eight passenger cars brands, five are considered mass producers (VW, SEAT, AUDI, Skoda, and Porsche) and three are luxury or sports vehicle manufacturers (Bugatti, Bentley, and Lamborghini). Through its subsidiaries, Volkswagen offers a broad product portfolio from a wide range of passenger cars, including small vehicles like the Volkswagen Up!, to sports utility vehicles (SUV – like the Touareg), sports vehicles (Porsche), luxury vehicles (Bentley), and super cars (Bugatti and Lamborghini), and the full range of commercial vehicles from small (VW Transporter) to heave trucks (MAN) and busses (Scania), to motorbikes (Ducati).

The internationalization of Volkswagen

Volkswagen was an early adapter to the pressures of globalization, and it began internationalization soon after production of passenger cars started in December 1945. In October 1947, just 22 months after the start of production, Volkswagen exported its first vehicles to the Netherlands. Five years later, in September 1952, Volkswagen established its first foreign representation office and import company, the Volkswagen Canada Ltd., in Toronto. This was the beginning of an aggressive internationalization strategy, first via exports and later international production. In October 1953, just one year after its first international office, Volkswagen had opened 82 international representative offices and exports totaled at 68,754 vehicles, accounting for 44% of the vehicle production in Germany.

In 1953, Volkswagen began to internationalize its operations through localization of production. The company laid the foundation of its first international production plant in Brazil (Volkswagen do Brasil Ltda.). What started as a complete knock-down plant to assemble fully produced kits, soon became a full localized production plant for the Volkswagen transporter in 1957 and for the VW Beetle in 1959. What followed were investments to open production plants in South Africa in 1956, Mexico in 1964, Belgium in 1971, Brazil in 1976, Argentina in 1980 and finally China, to form a joint-venture with SAIC in 1984 and a second joint-venture with FAW in 1991. After the opening of the seven international production sites through greenfield investments, Volkswagen refocused on the European market through its M&A activities, through which Volkswagen acquired operations in Spain, Czech Republic, the UK, and Italy. The market entry in China in 1984 marked the last transcontinental greenfield investment for over a decade until Skoda entered the Indian market in 1999. The early market entry to China also proved to become the single most important factor for the impressive growth that made Volkswagen one of the top three largest automotive producers in the world. Through the early investment in 1984, Volkswagen was one of the first international automotive manufacturers to enter the Chinese market and enjoyed first mover advantages that set Volkswagen up to achieve high market shares. After China's succession to the World Trade Organization in 2001, almost all international greenfield investments from Volkswagen focused on China. Since 2001, Volkswagen opened 16 production plants in China alone and only four new plants in other countries of the world (one in each Russia, India, the USA, and Mexico). Because of its early investments in China, Volkswagen has been able to establish itself as the leading automotive assembler in the growing market. In 2016 Volkswagen sold 3.873 million vehicles with its joint ventures in China, which accounts for 37% of its global sales.

Volkswagen's global operations

In 2016, over 200 different vehicle models rolled off Volkswagen's production lines, totaling over 10.3 million produced units per annum, an average of over 28.000 vehicles produced per day. To achieve such impressive numbers, Volkswagen operates over 119 production plants around the world. Of the 119 plants, 70 are assembly plants for finished vehicles and 49 are component manufacturing sites (Figure 3.1). The component manufacturing sites produce engines, transmissions, turbo chargers, compressors, axles, and seats. The production plants are located in 31 countries across four continents. Volkswagen developed a standardized assembly line for vehicle plants. When fully build, each plant can have an annual capacity of approximately 300,000 vehicles. With very significant sales and production overseas, Volkswagen's global operations are a complex network of

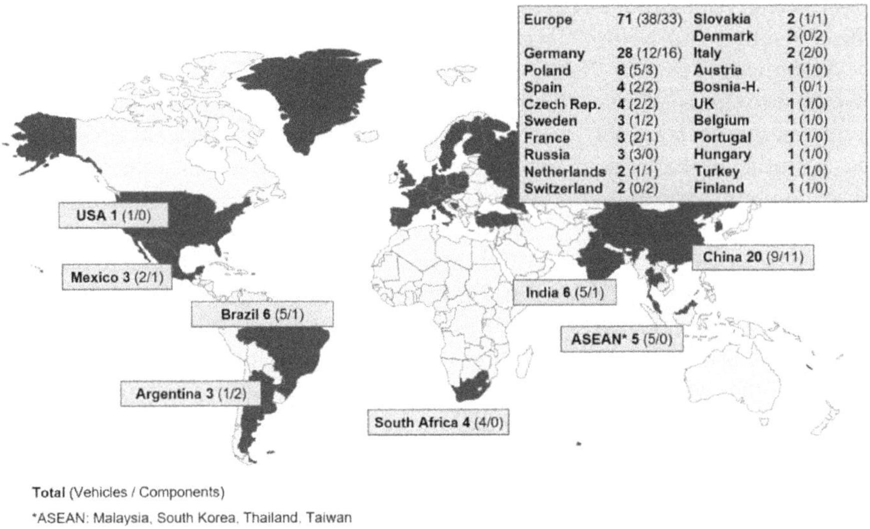

Figure 3.1 Volkswagen's global production footprint in 2016

Source: Author's summary from company information (Volkswagen Navigator 2016 and website).

tightly controlled plants. As shown in the next chapter, economies of scale and the new product architecture require a close cooperation between the international plants and tight control from the headquarters in Wolfsburg to run global operations smoothly.

Supply firms play a key role for production to run smoothly. To ensure smooth upstream supply chain operations, Volkswagen collocates key suppliers to the majority of its production lines. Each assembly plant focuses on the production of a small number of particular vehicles. Most assembly lines can produce several vehicles that are based on the same platform. The tooling change for metal stamping takes less than 30 minutes so that two different vehicles can roll off the assembly line in a single day. When Volkswagen develops a new vehicle its assembly line is selected based on capacity and proximity to the final target market.

The evolution of Volkswagen's product architecture

At the center of the passenger car as a product is its platform, which norms and standardizes the mounting points for all the components and systems that are assembled for the final product. A key event in the evolution of vehicle platforms is Volkswagen's introduction of its new platforms logic, the MQB, MLB, MSB, and MNB, which are used globally and replace the old PQ platforms, drastically reducing the number of platforms from over ten to just four across several brands within the Volkswagen group (including AUDI, Porsche, SEAT, and Skoda). MQB stands for Modularer Querbaukasten,' where MB translates loosely to 'Modular

Kit' and Q, L, S, and N stand for the engine mounting: Q for 'quer' (transverse), L for 'laengs' (longitudinal), S for 'standard' (which is only used for sport vehicles like Porsche), and N for 'Nutzfahrzeuge' (commercial vehicles – currently in development). The P in PL/PQ stands for 'passenger car' and Q or L for 'quer' (German for transverse) or 'longitudinal' engine mounting.

In the past decades, VW went through several platform updates that showcase the evolution of the product architecture. In the 1950s the earliest vehicles did not share common parts or platforms but were each developed from the ground up. As early as the 1970s Volkswagen realized it could create synergies and achieve economies of scale by using common parts in several vehicles. The first shared platform was the PQ1/A01, introduced in 1974 for the Volkswagen Polo, Volkswagen Derby, and AUDI 50. This was followed by many different platforms, most of which were used by only two to three different vehicles of similar size. The first platforms that were shared by more than three vehicles were developed after the rise of the Japanese automotive industry, the success of the lean manufacturing principles, and the success Japanese assemblers had by reducing the number of platforms. The PQ34/A4 was Volkswagen's first platform following the Japanese example and was used for nine vehicles. Shortly after, Volkswagen developed the PQ35/A5 platform, which was used for 19 vehicles. The two platforms were developed in 1997 and 2003 respectively to catch-up with the Japanese platform and lean manufacturing strategy. In 2012 VW introduced its latest platform logic, the MQB, MLB, MSB, and MNB, which replaced the old PQ platforms for a further drastic reduction of platforms from over ten to just four. The new platforms are rolled out globally, which means local platforms, a necessity during the previous platform setup, have been eliminated. While in the past both Brazil and the joint-ventures in China had their own platforms to develop vehicles for the local markets, these vehicles will now be based on the new global platforms, which are developed at the headquarters in Wolfsburg.

The objective of these new platforms was to further increase the use of common parts, enabling the firm to use the same standardized component in several vehicles rather than developing or customizing the components for specific vehicles. A high rate of common parts allows the firms to utilize the economies of scale for such components. The target standardization rate for the new MQB platform is 70% of the value of parts in the vehicle, decreasing the material costs by approximately 20% (Interview, Volkswagen case).

> The new platform works like a shelf, in which we can put all the developed components. If we develop a new vehicle, we can simply take the existing components and fit them together for the new car. A bit like LEGO.
>
> (Interview, Volkswagen case)

The increased use of common parts has an important implication for the structure of the supply base and the integration of supply firms from the emerging markets. Therefore the product architecture directly influences the prospects for participants in Volkswagen's value chain. In particular during the R&D phase, the impact the product architecture has on the inter-firm relations has become apparent.

Volkswagen's product development process

The development of passenger cars is separated into three distinct sections, each of which is developed independently from the other. The most important section is the vehicle platform, which lays out the basic structure of the vehicle, defining the mounting points for all other components and systems. To allow the use of interchangeable off-the-shelf components, the components are modularized with standardized mounting points. The second most important section is the powertrain, which includes the engine, gearbox, exhaust system, and control systems, and it requires a high degree of coordination between components (including chassis components) for superior performance. It is therefore developed as a whole system. The third section is the vehicle body, which is the most distinctive characteristic for the customer and includes the exterior design and body parts (e.g. stamped metal parts, windows, or lighting systems) and interior design and parts like seats, dashboard, door panels, entertainment systems, safety equipment like belts and airbags, or air conditioning systems.

The core development of the three distinct sections is separated, although each section influences the design and performance of the other. The reason for a separate development of the sections is that each section has a different life cycle. The platform has the longest life cycle and is rarely updated, as any update makes all the readily developed components for that platform obsolete. Once developed, the platform is relatively static. For this reason, the new MQB platform was already developed in a way to allow large battery cells to be installed, years before VW launched its first hybrid vehicle to make use of this functionality. Because of its central and structure giving nature, a platform launch must coincide with the launch of a new vehicle and potentially requires a new engine design. Hence it is the most complex system to be updated. Similarly, the powertrain has a relatively long life cycle, with an engine family often in use for 12 or more years with only relatively minor version updates. The body has the shortest life span, with approximately seven years (at VW, other assembly firms reduced the lifetime to just 3–4 years) with little facelifts between the intervals for a new generation. The reason for the frequent updates of the body is that the body is the defining part of a vehicle to the customer, as it is what is ultimately recognized as the vehicle. Unlike the body, the vehicle platform and power-train can be used across multiple generations of distinctive vehicles. Consequently the vehicle platform is rarely updated and not constantly being re-developed. The body and the power-train, on the other hand, are constantly being updated through new projects. Both are developed independent from one another but use a similar, standardized product development process.

The standardized development process for new vehicles takes approximately 48 months and is divided into four separate segments: concept phase, development phase, serial development phase, and production phase or roll-out. The concept phase lasts 12 months and consists of four milestones: concept initiation, product premise development, product definition, and product feasibility. The concept initiation kicks off the development process for the predefined range of specifications for the vehicle that have been defined during a strategic decision phase to refine the product portfolio prior to development during which design studies, market research, and technology scouting all contribute to detailing and validating the concept. The product premises refine the predefined range. The design concept follows the premises, defines the exterior and interior design of the vehicle, and finishes on month 43 with the milestone product definition. At this point, full scale design studies have been produced and approved by the board of management, including external and internal design. What follows are feasibility checks, which include technological feasibility, manufacturing capabilities and capacities, business case, and market response. With the milestone 'concept decision,' the project enters the development phase, and the lead is handed over from the design team to the developing engineers.

The development phase is the most critical, as all of the approximately 15,000 components are developed during this phase, including intensive functional testing for the components. Because of the integral nature of an automobile the phase requires a high degree of communication between the engineers to reconcile the different components. The special dimensions and boundaries for each component are defined in a vehicle cutting plan to avoid overlapping (for instance, the open position of the ashtray once overlapped with a specific gear stick position). At milestone 'design decision' all components are defined and alternatives reduced to the final range of components that will be used in the vehicle. At this stage, Volkswagen has completely finished and fully working vehicles for test driving. What follows is extensive testing and refining of the components to eradicate any errors until the design freeze milestone. This is the most important milestone, as it finalizes the design and development stage. After this milestone, 24 months prior to production, computer-aided design (CAD) files should not be changed anymore. Up until the design freeze all prototypes have been produced using tools and machines for prototyping. After the design freeze the final tools for mass production are produced at very high investment costs. The project now enters the serial development phase, with extensive durability testing. The lead shifts from the developing engineers to production engineers, who define the production logistics, production line layout, and facilities for the first production, and produce and prepare all the required tools and machinery, including a transition phase for a quick transition of the product line, which is still producing previous models. This phase ends in the launch approved milestone, after which the roll-out is implemented, followed by a pre-serial approval production trial series, the pilot series, and finally the start of production at full scale.

Volkswagen's international R&D configuration

Not all R&D efforts occur centralized at a single R&D central. Instead, Volkswagen has three principal developing firms among its eight passenger car brands: Volkswagen, AUDI, and Porsche. Each of the three developing brands is

Table 3.1 Number of engineers and roles of Volkswagen's R&D centers

	Germany	*USA*	*Brazil*	*VW China*	*FAW-VW*	*S-VW*
	P, T, S, R, M	T	A	T, A, S	T, A, S	T, A, S
Number of employees	>10,000	>1000	>500	>400	1,220	>1,400

Development functions:
P (product design, core development for products)
A (adaptation and application of products for a specific market)Research:
T (technology scouting, competitor analysis through reverse engineering,)
S (specific market knowledge)
R (research: advanced engineering, material science, collaborations with universities)
M (processing and production methods)

Source: Author's own table, based on fieldwork and company information.

responsible for one of the different global vehicle platforms (MQB, MLB, and MSB, respectively) and the platform specific engine groups.

Despite the international dispersed production network, core functions such as R&D remain relatively central at the headquarters in Wolfsburg (for VW branded R&D). For the MQB platform based vehicles, Volkswagen operates seven development centers in five different countries (Table 3.1). The most important R&D center is located at the VW headquarters in Wolfsburg, Germany. Here, Volkswagen employs the most R&D engineers and develops all platforms, components, and powertrains within the scope of Volkswagen's R&D. Furthermore, all Volkswagen branded vehicles are designed and developed in Wolfsburg. Prior to the new global vehicle platforms, selected vehicles were developed outside of Wolfsburg. E.g. Brazil had its own local platform, the BX-platform. The VW Gol was developed in Brazil but based on the old Golf platform, and the VW Bora and VW Lavida (based on the old Jetta platform) were developed in the two Chinese joint-ventures, FAW-VW and Shanghai-VW, respectively. Even before the introduction of the new global vehicle platforms, the vehicles developed locally in Brazil and China were derivative of previous VW vehicles that were developed in Wolfsburg. Since the introduction of the new global platforms the VW Gol has been discontinued and newer versions of the China specific vehicles are being developed in Wolfsburg. While the core development of all new vehicles is based in Wolfsburg, adaptations are developed locally. These include such adaptations as exterior and interior design to accommodate for specific consumer tastes of the Chinese market.

Five of Volkswagen's international R&D centers are located in their biggest and most important markets: the USA, Brazil, and China. The only country with more than one R&D center is China, where Volkswagen established three R&D centers, one for each of the two joint-ventures with Chinese partners and one wholly owned center for centralized coordination and as a link back to Germany.

The domestic and overseas R&D centers have different functions and roles in VW's R&D process. The main role of the domestic R&D center is platform development and core product development. The overseas R&D centers have two principal roles. First, to adapt centrally developed vehicles and apply them to each market. Such adaptations include technical specification adaptations to meet government regulations (e.g. emission standards or quality and safety regulations), as well as adaptations to meet the specific consumer tastes (e.g. entertainment systems, adaptations to language and interface, interior design, chrome and color choice, gear shift preferences, engine size preferences, chassis suspension preferences, seating preferences, etc.). The knowledge necessary for these specific adaptations is best created in the local environment through an embedded R&D center close to the customer and regulating body.

The second role of the local R&D centers is to scout for technologies that are specifically developed in these locations. Such scouting activities involved re-engineering newly launched vehicles from competitors, collaborations with universities or other institutions in knowledge clusters, and market research to understand consumer tastes and trends in the market.

Before the roll-out of the new platforms, Volkswagen had planned to expand its R&D activities in China, to delegate more responsibility and core development to one of its joint-ventures for the development of a 'budget car' under a new brand that would allow Volkswagen to compete in low price segments in the emerging economies. In autumn 2014, however, all efforts to localize the project in China were rolled back, and the team was relocated to Wolfsburg in Germany, which goes to show that Volkswagen centralized core R&D to Germany. Senior managers in the R&D department said R&D was centralized for three reasons: first, to consolidate R&D efforts after the wave of M&A, second to gain more control at headquarters through the centralized approach to prevent knowledge flows to joint-venture partners in China, and third because of the product architecture of the new Volkswagen group platform design, the MQB, which allows for centralized R&D.

The role of suppliers in innovation and development in Volkswagen

Volkswagen proudly presents itself as the world's most innovative and technologically advanced automotive assembler with the deepest knowledge and understanding on a breadth of technologies in the automotive industry, like powertrains, chassis development, powertrain integration, driver comfort, safety, and driving experience. With over 20,000 engineers working in research and development worldwide, and more than 5 billion Euro annual budget for R&D, Volkswagen is one of the giants in the industry. None the less, suppliers play a key role in Volkswagen's vehicle development process and add know-how, technology and innovations, along the entire value chain. For instance, VW's internally developed and manufactured engine models require the technology and knowhow of the leading injection system suppliers BOSCH, Continental, Delphi, or Denso. With increasingly strict regulations on emission standards worldwide, engines need to continuously improve to become more efficient, a process in which key suppliers play a key role and are deeply involved. The expertise of technology service providers such as Ricardo, a combustion engine and powertrain expert in the industry, are also sought after for ambitious niche products such as the Bugatti Veyron 16-cylinder engine, which boasts more than 1,000 horsepower. Key suppliers are also deeply involved in non-powertrain technologies, such as control systems, entertainment systems, gear shift systems, and steering systems with the aim of enabling VW to develop and build its vehicles to perfection through simultaneous engineering from the most capable engineers along the value chain.

Most components are not readily available on the market but have to be customized for the specific vehicle. Due to the integral nature of the vehicles, supply firms are deeply involved in the overall vehicle development process. This is because any adaptations to one component can influence the performance and functionality of another. The more performance oriented the vehicle, the higher the interdependencies between components. Because of such interdependencies, engineers from Volkswagen and the supply firms of integral components and systems need to be in constant exchange throughout the vehicle development process. Due to the outsourcing of non-core activities and the increased R&D capabilities in the supply base, key suppliers are involved in the development process from the very early stages on. Some firms are involved even before the vehicle development process, during the strategic decision process of what vehicles to develop. Especially suppliers with own strong R&D competencies and innovative products are involved early on in the process. How early a specific supply firm is involved in the process depends on the nature of the specific component developed in the supply firm. The nature and product architecture of the component defines the role of the supply firm and its development capabilities. For highly integral components that are predominantly developed by the supplier, supply firms are involved in the vehicle development process from the first day. Components with fewer interdependencies require less knowledge exchange. Supply firms of such components are involved at later stages of the process.

Volkswagen differentiates between four types of relationships with suppliers: *innovating*, *developing*, '*produce per blueprint*,' and *commodity* suppliers. *Innovating suppliers* independently develop own innovations, ideas and technologies and pitch them to Volkswagen, 'push' their innovative capabilities, and are involved in the vehicle development process before concept design phase (Table 3.2). Examples of such innovations are anti-brake locking systems (ABS), which was first developed by a supply firm before it eventually became industry standard. Such innovating suppliers are of strategic importance to Volkswagen because they can add new innovative technologies to the vehicles that help differentiate from the competition. Such innovations can occur in a wide variety of components, from interior or exterior design like lightning technologies for LED solutions important for the body to important powertrain technologies like injection systems to increase the engine efficiency, reduce fuel consumption, and lower CO2 exhaustion. Supply firms that 'push' their innovative ideas and technologies to the assemblers are ahead of the assembly firm in terms of innovation for their respective component. Maintaining a good relationship and offering opportunities to add superior new technology to premium vehicles (Porsche and Audi),

Table 3.2 Involvement of supply firms in the vehicle development process

Supplier type	*Involvement in vehicle development process, from Concept Phase (CP), over Design Phase (CP), Serial Development (SD), to Pre-serial Stage (PS).*				*Contract duration*
	CP	*DP*	*SD*	*PS*	
Innovating suppliers	X	X	X	X	Entire production life-cycle
Developing suppliers		X	X	X	Entire production life-cycle
'Produce per blueprint' suppliers			X	X	Interchangeable/no long-term contracts
Commodity suppliers				X	Ad-hoc orders on free market

Innovating suppliers have innovation capabilities, like product designs and superior market information. The suppliers propose new ideas and designs to the assembly firm at the conceptual stage.

Developing suppliers have own R&D capabilities. The supplier develops components based on the particular specifications of the assembly firm.

'Produce per blueprint' suppliers have no significant R&D capabilities. They produce simple, mostly mechanical products based on the blueprints provided by the assembly firm.

Commodity suppliers have no significant R&D capabilities. They produce standardized commodities.

Source: Author's own table, based on fieldwork.

combined with the potential to expand the use of the technology to volume brands of Volkswagen, Skoda, and SEAT, are key factors for VW to be one of the most attractive first buyers for such technologies. However, it is the supply firm that can choose its first customer to introduce new technology to the market.

Developing suppliers have superior component or system knowledge and develop their components or systems independently from the assembler. All technical drawings are made at the supply firm, and Volkswagen is dependent on their development capability. Volkswagen orders the supply firm to develop a specific component and 'pulls' the product development capabilities from such supply firms to use their expertise to co-engineer the newest components with the combined expertise of the assembly firm and the supply firm. In this case the assembler lays out the features and specific requirements and requests the supplier to develop components for the next generation of vehicles. The developing supply firms are involved in the development process after the concept decision milestone (Table 3.2). Supply firms with own strong R&D capabilities but no innovation capabilities are also of strategic relevance, not as a source for differentiating technology but as a key partner in the R&D process. Such supply firms are more difficult to be substituted by competing supply firms, because they customized their components to the particular needs of Volkswagen and own the intellectual property rights and drawings for the components. As these firms have large upfront investment costs they also receive long term contracts for the full duration of the production life cycle of a particular vehicle.

'*Produce per blueprint' suppliers* have no development capabilities. Technical drawings and designs are made and provided by Volkswagen, and the supply firm only manufactures the components. Suppliers of relatively simple, mostly mechanical, products receive blueprints from Volkswagen as sub-contractors to manufacture the components as per the blueprint that has been developed from Volkswagen engineers. The supply firm has little to no design and development capabilities and focuses solely on the manufacturing of the component. These firms are only involved in the later stages of the vehicle development process, when first prototypes are built and tooling is prepared for the mass production and first mass produced prototypes and attempts have to be performed, around 24 months prior to start of production (Table 3.2). 'Produce per blueprint,' suppliers are of little strategic relevance, as they can be easily interchanged. The highest investment for this group is the tooling, which is owned by Volkswagen and not the supply firm. Hence these firms mostly receive shorter contracts and are governed by an arm's length price driven mechanic. The barriers of entry are low, and the firms are relatively easy to substitute. With no firm specific advantage, such supply firms have no bargaining power. As a result, firms in the 'produce per blueprint' category are governed via hands-off price mechanisms.

Finally, *commodity suppliers* for products such as chemicals or steel, which supply standardized materials, are involved only 12–24 months prior to start of production, to ensure availability of the material (Table 3.2). However, as the properties for the materials are known, and no customization or adaptation has to be applied at the supply firm, such suppliers are not involved in the vehicle development process unless new components require the use of novel material like carbon fibers or particular resins with special specifications. In such cases, the supply firm can be involved in the early stages of the component development. Finally, commodity suppliers fall into two different distinct categories. Some commodity suppliers, in particular such that offer internationally standardized commoditized components such as nuts and bolts, are small and often local companies in close proximity of manufacturing hubs. Such supply firms are governed the same way as the 'produce per blueprint' category supply firms, even though no drawings are required from Volkswagen. Hence even less knowledge transfer between the firms is required. Commodity suppliers of mass materials like steel or chemicals, on the other hand, are governed differently. These supply firms are multinational firms like ThyssenKrupp or BASF with large scale manufacturing capabilities to produce sheet steel or car paints with specialized chemicals. Specialized metal alloys or plastic resins with particular characteristics require IPR and can therefore often be produced by only a handful of firms. However, unlike multinational automotive supply firms, the commodity suppliers are more diverse, supplying multiple industries and being less dependent on a single automotive assembler. Assemblers such as Volkswagen make up only a small percentage of their sales. Therefore, automotive assemblers have less bargaining power over such firms compared to auto component suppliers. Prices are mostly determined by global market prices rather than dictated by the assembler. And since very little knowledge transfer is required for such commodities, the inter-firm ties are loose and resemble hands-off market driven relations.

Since the majority of R&D activities have been centralized within Volkswagen, supply firms involved in the R&D process, with regular meetings for knowledge exchange and regular testing of prototypes in Wolfsburg, need to be in close geographic proximity to Volkswagen. For highly integral components or systems the engineers of the supplier meet with Volkswagen's engineers as often as once a week. This requires the suppliers' R&D center to be in close geographic proximity to Volkswagen, for an efficient simultaneous engineering process.

By mapping its supply firms according to strategic relevance, Volkswagen can select the most capable supply firms to take on new activities and extend their role in the value chain. For instance, the most capable supplier of the most complex door component is selected for the assembly of the door. In addition to developing and manufacturing its component, this supplier then orchestrates the upstream value chain, including other door components, and takes on the role of a module supplier. Similarly, key supply firms are selected to expand their production and serve Volkswagen in additional countries or regions.

Volkswagen's approach to value chain orchestration

The purchasing strategy is closely linked to the product architecture and has been adapted since the introduction of the new platforms. The use of common parts, the rate of standardization and modularization of components and the global use of components are made possible by the product architecture and change the requirements for supply firms. As the number of platforms has been reduced to just four, and the use of standardized platforms has been globalized, so has the procurement strategy. Instead of purchasing different components for each vehicle and the different markets, the exact same component can be used globally. Consequently, the Volkswagen group has gradually centralized its procurement processes since the late 1990s in conjunction with its product architecture evolution and introduction of global vehicle platforms. Volkswagen harmonized its global purchasing strategy to meet the requirements of the new platform strategy, avoid parallel development of the same component in the markets, and further enjoy the benefits of economies of scale. What has been a gradually evolving strategy now peaks in a global unified purchasing strategy. With global platforms in place, common parts can be sourced worldwide. To achieve maximum economies of scale, few global supply firms are selected to supply the common parts to all of Volkswagen's production sites worldwide. In particular for highly customized components and systems, this approach enables the company to reduce development expenses.

From regional to global purchasing

Before the introduction of lean manufacturing techniques in the 1990s, every manufacturing plant was responsible for its own sourcing of parts and components. Very few vehicles shared their platform with others, which meant the number of carry-over components was small and each production line could only produce one specific vehicle. Components were sourced from local supply firms depending on the demand of the individual production plant. There was no central coordination or alignment of the supply base across multiple production plants unless they were in close geographic proximity to one another. With the introduction of the PQ platforms several vehicles were based on the same shared platform and several production plants needed to purchase the same components for the first time. Consequently, sourcing changed from plant-based to regional responsibilities. Wolfsburg purchased the components for all of Volkswagen's production plants in Europe, Ingolstadt the components for AUDI branded vehicles in Europe, Sao Bernardo do Campo the components for Latin America, ChangChun the components for the joint-venture with the Chinese assembler First Automotive Works (FAW), and so on. This was already a major step to increase the benefits of economies of scale in the supply base and to start building a common supply base for the large production regions.

With the introduction of the global platforms MQB, MLB, and MSB, the purchasing strategy was further centralized to a single global purchasing center in 2012. All the important decisions for the markets are made at headquarters, and all suppliers are nominated by the central committee at Wolfsburg, undergoing a standardized system of requirement checks, firm visits, quality improvement processes, and alignment of supply chain systems before approval. While much of the daily routine work and supplier relations work can be decentered, key decisions are made centrally. All the important negotiations with the supply firms for any location in the world now occur at the headquarters of the Volkswagen Group in Wolfsburg, Germany. Through the centralized approach Volkswagen further increased its bargaining power over supply firms, as they now negotiate for larger batch purchases that often span across multiple continents.

Cornerstones of Volkswagen's global purchasing strategy

Four principles were introduced with the global purchasing strategy. First, the introduction of a new central sourcing committee across the 12 brands of the Volkswagen group and involving representatives from several departments. Second, the reduction of supply firms for any particular component by developing global suppliers that are present at all production hubs. Third, and somewhat in contrast to the first, a multiple supplier strategy in order to remain independent from the suppliers and to maintain the competition between suppliers. And fourth, a local-to-local strategy to increase the localization of parts production. In order to reduce risks from supply chain delays and to hedge against currency fluctuations, parts should be produced in close geographic proximity to Volkswagen's assembly lines.

In the globalized purchasing strategy, VW installed a central sourcing committee at headquarters in Wolfsburg through which all supplier nominations and supply contracts go, allowing the firms to compare and contrast the quality, price, capabilities, and long standing relationships of all the firms that supply components to the VW group. Through the new strategy, VW centralized all important decisions regarding its supply chain and moved the decision power to Wolfsburg. The new strategy extends beyond the Volkswagen brand and includes all 12 currently active brands. The central sourcing committee enables Volkswagen to truly globalize purchasing. It includes senior managers from several departments, such as purchasing, research and development, production, quality, finance, and representatives from the brands, to synthesize supplier databases, cost comparison across brands and regions, and previous experiences with supply firms to create a single point of purchasing. "We want one face to the supplier, so that all negotiation are done with the same people who have all information and full transparence before the purchasing decisions. Through the committee, we can finally compare prices and negotiation practices across all brands" (Interview, Volkswagen case). "Everyone important sits in those meetings. It is torture for our suppliers, if someone is not happy." (Interview, Volkswagen case). The committee is responsible for all the important decisions for all the brands and all markets.

The second principle of the new purchasing strategy is the reduction of supply firms. The purpose of the reduction of supply firms is to further increase the economies of scale and increase Volkswagen's bargaining position. Through the introduction of globally standardized components, Volkswagen can source components for all its over 100 production plants from a single supplier. This has several additional advantages for Volkswagen. It reduces the complexity of knowledge transfers necessary during the simultaneous engineering process of new vehicles. The complexities involved in orchestrating and controlling its global supply chain and supply firms are also reduced. Furthermore, Volkswagen can ensure that quality standards and functionality are met for all components. Moreover, it increases Volkswagen's bargaining power with the increased volumes per purchase for individual suppliers. "We can now negotiate prices for orders to all our plants worldwide, which increases the magnitude of a single order and puts us in a strong position" (Interview, Volkswagen case).

Reducing the number of supply firms is achieved in two ways: first, by reducing the number of individual components to be used for the assembly of vehicles. This is achieved through the higher number of carry-over components and by combining individual components to modules. Volkswagen allocates additional activities such as sub-assembly to the most competent supply firms, to move from components supply to modules that are then shipped to the assembly plant. Second, rather than nominating different supply firms to supply the same component in the different regions, Volkswagen can nominate one firm to supply to all of its over 100 production plants worldwide. Internal documents at Volkswagen showed that the company was able to reduce the average number of suppliers for any particular component from above ten in the early 2000s to as few as two to three worldwide in 2014.

In contrast to the reduction of direct suppliers, Volkswagen also introduced a multiple supplier strategy, which means that they want to have at least two or three supply firms for every component. The multiple supplier strategy reduces risks in the supply chain, as it makes Volkswagen less dependent on a single supply firm in case production is disrupted because of natural disasters or bankruptcies of supply firms. For a lean production system with close to zero stock and just-in-time delivery, such failures in the supply chain can quickly have critical consequences. Mitigating such risks has become a major concern for large manufacturing firms. While this seems to counter the strategy mentioned earlier to reduce the total number of supply firms, it has become an important cornerstone and necessity after the experience of the tsunamis that hit Japan in 2011. The tsunami eradicated key supply firms in the value chain that proved very difficult to substitute. Moreover, the multiple supplier strategy allows Volkswagen to strengthen its bargaining position and compare prices with multiple active supply firms. Through the combination of the two strategies, the reduction of globally active supply firms together with the multiple supplier strategy, Volkswagen creates a global competition of globally active supply firms in its supply base rather than the previously regional orientation.

To achieve the global harmonization of its supply base Volkswagen follows a strict local-to-local strategy through which Volkswagen localizes as much value-added activities in the value chain as possible. The local-to-local strategy enforces that the production of components is in close geographic proximity to the Volkswagen assembly plant. This allows smooth transportation, which is important for just-in-time and just-in-sequence delivery of a lean production system. Moreover, large local content ratios make Volkswagen less dependent on exchange rate fluctuations and the global macroeconomic environment. It is also important in countries with high import duties. The local-to-local strategy requires the supply firms to operate internationally and to develop a footprint in all the regions Volkswagen produces (on all continents). The strategy is enforced in two ways: first, one of the selection criteria for supply firms is to have a location in close proximity (less than 300 km) to the supplied manufacturing plant, which in the case of carry-over components requires the supply firm to maintain the capabilities in close geographic proximity to most manufacturing plants of Volkswagen globally. Second, Volkswagen actively incentivizes existing supply firms to localize production in close proximity to their global manufacturing sites by offering long-term supply contracts in the new locations. Volkswagen may not renew contracts with firms that are not able to comply.

Supplier selection criteria and strategic role for Volkswagen

Supply firms are selected on a project basis to supply parts and components for the production life cycle of a vehicle. When a new vehicle is rolled out into production an assembly plant is selected for the pilot roll-out, followed by additional assembly plants, including international plants, to ramp up production to the expected volume. The supply firms are selected by the central sourcing committee for the particular project prior to start of production (SOP):

> Our purchasing is oriented by individual projects. A project can be for a platform, when the engineers develop a component that is used across all vehicles of the platform. Or, it can be for a vehicle, if components are developed for a specific vehicle, like body parts. Where the new vehicle is rolled out does not matter, because all the lead developers are in Wolfsburg [Volkswagen's headquarters].
>
> (Interview, Volkswagen case)

Most supply firms are selected for the entire production life cycle, especially if they are innovating or developing firms. 'Produce per blueprint' and commodity suppliers may be swapped during production. Once running, the mass production of vehicles runs relatively smoothly and requires only few and small updates and efficiency programs. Therefore key supply chain decisions and integration of the supply firms occurs during the previous product development phase.

Due to the dynamics in the R&D process the developing engineers have a significant impact on the final decision of supply firms of innovating and developing suppliers. Because of the close interaction during the vehicle development process, the role the development engineers at Volkswagen plays in the supplier nomination process for the group of developing suppliers is decisive. Well-functioning engineering teams with good relationships are important. To ensure well-functioning teams, the engineers working on a project can effectively select the involved supply firms. Furthermore, the Volkswagen engineers get deep insights into the specific capabilities of the supply firm – with a strong impact on the choice of supply for the next project. If the Volkswagen development department had a good experience with a particular developing supplier it will want to resume working with the supply firm. This way the supply firm can develop strong ties with the assembler and win follow-up projects that are out of the scope of its contracts, significantly strengthening the ties between the two firms. The developing engineers of Volkswagen and the supply firm work closely together during the development phase of the project. Relationships are developed through weekly meetings.

Once the project is over the engineers' team will immediately be allocated to new projects. With over 200 vehicles, Volkswagen has a full pipeline of future development projects, which start immediately after one project phases out (i.e. after start of production). The engineers that were involved in previous projects now take on new projects and take with them their relationships to the core supply firms and their experience, influencing which firms to nominate for the new projects. The longer the supply firm is involved during the simultaneous development process the stronger the relationships that are established. New supply firms may be proposed by procurement departments, but it is the engineers that have the final say, and new firms have very little chance of winning a development project.

The influence of the developing engineers erects barriers of entry for new entrants to the supply industry. New entrants need to gain the trust by the engineers and develop good working relationships in order to become part of the 'inner circle' and be recognized as value experts and partners during the simultaneous engineering project. However, first entry is often prohibited by the selection of incumbent supply firms. Especially supply firms from the emerging markets such as Brazil or China that tend to lack a good reputation, who are rarely considered as potential suppliers from the developing engineers.

Supply firms that are not involved in the vehicle development, i.e. 'produce per blueprint' suppliers, commodity suppliers, or even developing suppliers of components that require little knowledge exchange between engineers due to the few interdependencies to other components, do not enjoy such advantages. For such supply firms the engineers have much less say during the selection process so that the procurement and quality departments can make the final decision. Such suppliers are selected based on price and are governed by a price mechanism. Therefore it is easier for new entrants to enter the value chain in this group but difficult to develop ties with the assembler to win follow-up projects.

Apart from the relationships between R&D departments, the purchasing department developed a systemic supplier matrix to distinguish between strategic relevant and less relevant suppliers and to document the capabilities and competencies of each supplier (Table 3.3). Strategic relevant supply firms are all firms with innovation and development capabilities, as these firms have capabilities that Volkswagen depends on during its vehicle development process. Such firms are highly integrated in the R&D process, have regular exchange with Volkswagen, and are difficult to substitute or change. Volkswagen therefore develops an intimate

Table 3.3 Supplier categories and relevance to Volkswagen

Supplier category	*Exemplary component*	*Exemplary supply firm*	*Supplier characteristics*	*Involvement in R&D*	*Strategic relevance*
Innovating suppliers	New innovative products: ABS, driver assistance systems, lighting solutions	BOSCH, Marquardt	Often large multinational enterprises; some niche manufacturers	48–60 months prior to start of production (SOP)	Highly relevant
Developing suppliers	Technologically demanding parts & systems: interior parts	Fuyao, Yanfeng, Witzenmann	Mostly large multinational enterprises	36–48 months prior to SOP	Relevant
'Produce per blueprint'	Mechanical components: white body parts, engine mounts	ASIMCO, CIE Automotive	Mostly local enterprises, some multinationals	12–24 months prior to SOP	Little relevance
Commodity suppliers	Steel, chemicals, nuts and bolts	BASF, ThyssenKrupp	Often large multinational enterprises; some local enterprises	12 months prior to SOP	Little relevance

Source: Author's own table, based on fieldwork.

relationship with such supply firms to ensure their services for the future. Long-term supply contracts are the norm for such suppliers. 'Produce per blueprint' suppliers and commodity suppliers are easier to substitute or change and therefore often have short-term contracts.

Volkswagen's supplier development program

Volkswagen has established a supplier development program, through which it can support its supply firms to become more efficient, adapt to new technologies, upgrade its processes, or take on new activities within the value chain. Through annual audits and firm visits, Volkswagen is well aware of the capabilities and challenges of its supply firms. The data on supply firms is further enhanced by open book relations to most of its smaller supply firms. Volkswagen can identify development gaps in its supply base. By mapping all supply firms according to strategic relevance and capabilities, Volkswagen can identify the most relevant cases for further development or identify possible candidates to take on new responsibilities and tasks in the value chain, for instance when components are combined to be supplied as a module in the future.

The supplier development program works like a consulting service from the assembler to the supply firms. Volkswagen sends expert teams to the supply firms, for instance to establish shop floor management tools or upgrade the processes of the supply firm. Rather than charging the supply firm for the services, Volkswagen offers them free of charge. The supply firm agrees to share the gains made from the increased efficiency. Supply firms that receive the services are able to upgrade their processes or products, or even value chain activities, if chosen to perform new tasks.

Through its supplier development program, Volkswagen can increase efficiency in the supply base and secure a better grip on actively coordinating the activities within the global value chain by allocating specific activities to the most capable supply firms.

Collocating supply firms to new markets

When entering a new country with manufacturing capabilities, Volkswagen aims to build up a local supply base. Localization of Volkswagen's production capabilities is a gradual process. It starts with CKD (complete know-down) plants, to which fully finished vehicle kits are shipped for final assembly. This is followed by a gradual localization of components and parts production. As a mass producer, VW's strategy is a strategy of economies of scale. Localizing production is only feasible if large volumes can be expected. For new Greenfield investments in assembly plants, Volkswagen has developed a standardized blueprint for production facilities that follows a ramp-up in two steps. The final manufacturing plant consists of two identical, mirrored production sites. At first, only one half of the production site is gradually built, until it reaches its capacity limits. If further production increase is expected the second half is built. The final facility has a production capacity of approximately 300,000 vehicles annually under full load.

Throughout the gradual ramp-up of assembly capacities, Volkswagen starts the localization of parts and component manufacture. In the past, localizing the production of components has been mostly driven by national policies that incentivized a high ration of value-added activities in the target country. For instance, Brazil gradually increased the local content requirements to incentivize the local production of components. With the introduction of the global purchasing strategy, Volkswagen shows its own interest in building a local supply base.

Establishing a local supply base can be done in two ways: either the assembler nurtures existing local supply firms so as to enable them to meet its technological and quality requirements, or the assembler incentivizes its existing supply firms from abroad to collocate to its new manufacturing location. As purchasing managers explained, the second option is favored:

> We try to bring our own supply firms wherever we go. . . . When we bring our own suppliers, they already know exactly what we need. . . . We have made a good experience with them. We know they can meet our requirements. [Brining our own supply firms] is faster and easier for us, than establishing or helping local supply firms.
>
> (Interview, Volkswagen case)

Collocating existing supply firms to new production hubs has several advantages for Volkswagen. It is much faster than nurturing new supply firms. Developing a new supply firm to become an audited and qualified supplier takes years, according to Volkswagen interviewees. It also requires less development effort by Volkswagen, as the supply firm already has all the capabilities required for the production. If existing supply firms are collocated they are responsible for establishing the required knowledge, skills, and capabilities. If Volkswagen nurtures new supply firms, then Volkswagen has to localize such capabilities. Moreover, collocating existing supply firms requires less knowledge transfer and coordination of supply firms and supports Volkswagen's strategy to reduce the number of global supply firms.

4 Participants from the advanced markets

BOSCH

The BOSCH GmbH is a German firm producing white goods, industrial equipment, and automotive components. The company was founded in 1886 by Robert Bosch and is one of the oldest automotive suppliers in the world. The automotive division of BOSCH is the largest automotive component supplier in the world, with a revenue of US$ 51.4 billion (43.9 billion EUR) in 2016. As the largest supplier, BOSCH's revenue surpasses some of the well-known assembly firms such as Kia (approx. US$ 47 billion) or Suzuki (approx. US$ 26 billion).

BOSCH's automotive division produces key components such as gasoline systems, diesel systems, chassis control systems, brake control systems, sensors, airbag control systems, driver assistance systems based on radar and video sensors, starter motors, entertainment and multimedia systems, electronics, and steering systems. With new business units in automated driving, connected vehicles, electronic powertrain, and automated manufacturing techniques through Internet of Things technology, BOSCH is developing new products to adapt to the ongoing technological revolution in the automotive industry.

Turn-key suppliers like BOSCH have developed a global footprint that is on par with the largest assembly groups and have taken on the role of a lead firm for their upstream value chain, with power over supply firms in the same way as large assemblers. In 2016, 80% of BOSCH's revenues were made outside of Germany, with 20.8% made in the Asia Pacific region, 18.6% in the rest of Europe, 12.3% in North America, and 1.4% in South America. The company has around 440 subsidiaries in 60 countries, highlighting how global the company is. Its automotive division is active in all important production hubs in the world, with production plants that are in close geographic proximity to the major assembly lines. The interviewees have highlighted the importance of the global footprint as a competitive advantage to be selected by assemblers as a global supplier.

BOSCH adapting its R&D process to sync with Volkswagen

BOSCH is a developing and innovating supplier. With US$ 8.137 billion (6.959 billion EUR) spending in R&D, BOSCH is one of the most R&D intensive companies in the world and a key innovator and developer in the automotive industry.

As a developer and producer of key automotive modules and components of highly integral nature, like anti-lock braking systems (ABS), or engine injection systems, BOSCH has a very close working relationship with assemblers such as Volkswagen. When one of the most important customers, Volkswagen, changed its purchasing strategy, demand shifted from regional adapted components to globally standardized. Reacting to these changes, BOSCH adapted its global R&D and production configuration. R&D of core platform development was centralized and production plants reconfigured, so that BOSCH is able to comply to the local-to-local policy of its customer.

The market for BOSCH's products is very different from that of finished vehicles. Vehicles are first developed and finalized and then produced and sold to individuals with predefined performance, functionality, and features. System components, on the other hand, do not have predefined performance specifications before being sold to the customer but need to be extensively customized to the client's needs (i.e. the vehicle in which they are to be used). The adaptation and customization of the component is decoupled from its core principal development. The timeline for customization needs to be aligned with its customers, as BOSCH needs to be able to meet deadlines and start production on the vehicle. The overall customization requires high investments and intensive knowledge exchange between BOSCH and the potential buyer during the customization and development process. Because of the high upfront investment, the supply contract for the component extends over the entire production cycle of the vehicle.

Because of the different nature of the market for components compared to vehicles, the R&D process of BOSCH differs from that of Volkswagen. While the R&D process of Volkswagen is linear, in the sense that first the vehicle is in development, and then put on the market, the process for firms of highly customized products is split into two different processes: first, core product development independent of the client and vehicle requirements, and second, product customization and development in close interaction with the client.

The new product development encompasses the capability, knowledge, intellectual property (including patents), and core products (hardware and software) needed for the development. For instance, the driver assistance systems were developed independently from the assemblers in the core product development process. Other innovations included control systems like ABS, flex fuel systems that allow use of ethanol as a substitute for gasoline, or innovations in the injection systems like high pressure diesel injection systems with high frequency controlled injections for optimal performance. Once developed the new product can be pitched to assembly firms and BOSCH can choose which client to first approach with the new product.

Since some products have an impact on customer perception of the final vehicle, assemblers tout for such innovative components to be selected first and bring new innovations in their vehicles to the market. This is in particular the case for premium vehicles that differentiate via innovative features. However, as a supply firm BOSCH chooses the first customer wisely to generate attention and attract additional future revenue for new products.

But before the product can be sold to the assembler it requires intensive customization for each specific vehicle. Since almost all components of BOSCH are highly integral in nature, a high level of customization is required to successfully integrate the component or system into the overall vehicle. This is when the second development process begins, that of customization and adaptation to the specific vehicle requirements. This process needs to be synchronized with the vehicle development process of the assembler. Because of the integral nature of the components adaptation and vehicle specific developments begin approximately three–four years prior to the start of production. In Volkswagen's vehicle development process this is during the concept and development phase, at the very beginning of the process. Most of BOSCH's systems and components (e.g. injection systems, control systems) have two-way interdependencies to other components. This means that other components in the vehicle that are not necessarily developed by BOSCH influence the performance of BOSCH's product, and vice-versa. For instance, driver assistance systems require configuration with other components such as sensors and other assistance systems, control systems like engine control or brake control, chassis architecture, bumpers, engine, or differentials. All these different parts and systems influence each other's performance. But they are developed by a number of different companies that come together for the development of the final vehicle. The interdependencies require BOSCH's engineers to be in regular exchange with both, engineers from the assembler as overall systems integrator, and the engineers of other suppliers of core systems. Furthermore, BOSCH needs to be in contact with its own suppliers throughout the development process in case internal components have interdependencies with other components within the product of BOSCH or even with the systems and components of other supply firms. For the development of its own products and systems, BOSCH takes on the role of systems integrator, thereby linking the upstream development activities with those of Volkswagen's overall systems integration (see Figure 4.1).

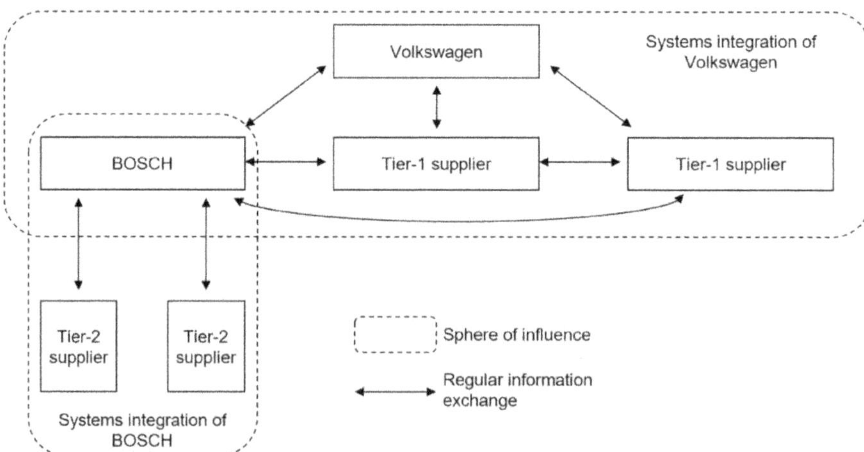

Figure 4.1 Interaction during the vehicle development process

Source: Author's own figure, based on fieldwork.

Through the ongoing modularization of the vehicle architecture, the task of systems integration has been pushed down the value chain to the tier-1 suppliers. Supply firms of modules are increasingly responsible for entire systems rather than individual components. Hence, supply firms such as BOSCH increasingly take on more systems integration activities.

> We now handle more suppliers during development phases, compared to the past. . . . We supply systems instead of components. Steering systems, not hydraulic parts for steering support. Gasoline systems, not nozzles and pumps. . . . Because of this, we now have to develop in the same way [as assemblers], and work together with multiple component and material suppliers.
>
> (Interview, BOSCH case)

Configuring the international R&D activities

Bosch has a very international R&D structure, with 13 R&D locations in total, of which five are in its home country Germany and eight in foreign locations in China, India, Japan, Russia, Singapore, and the USA. As the world's largest automotive supplier, BOSCH serves global assembly firms around the world. The international R&D centers are primarily responsible for product adaptation for the specific market as well as some technology scouting and market research activities through local collaborations, research labs, and local universities. To facilitate efficient interactions with their suppliers, assemblers have established a 'simultaneous engineering' process in which all involved parties simultaneously develop the components and systems for the new vehicle which is centrally coordinated, assembled, and tested (as a holistic system) by the assembler. During this simultaneous engineering process, BOSCH's engineers meet with an assembler's engineers and managers as often as once per week to closely coordinate the development process. To enable this close interaction it is important that the R&D activities of BOSCH are located in close geographic proximity to the customer and that engineers can communicate with the assembler to efficiently co-develop their components for the project. BOSCH's close proximity of R&D to large assemblers provides the company with an advantage over less internationalized companies.

While collocating of the adaptation and customization process is essential, core product development is independent from the vehicle development process of the customer. Consequently, the majority of BOSCH's core R&D activities are still located in the company's home market in Germany, where advanced engineering, research (including material science and production process advances), and core product development takes place across the five German R&D centers. In addition to the German core development center, BOSCH established a R&D center in Palo Alto that has the unique role to develop new products incorporating IT-enabled future technologies such as future entertainment systems and connected, IT-assisted, and automated driving technologies.

Adapting the purchasing strategy

In alignment with the adapted R&D processes, and the demand for global components, BOSCH changed its purchasing strategy. BOSCH's new purchasing strategy, which was introduced in 2012, closely resembles that of Volkswagen and consists of the same cornerstones: the centralization of procurement, the reduction of direct supply firms, a local-to-local policy, and a multiple supplier strategy. The overall aim was to strengthen the bargaining power and centralize the supplier knowledge. However, because of BOSCH's vast international footprint and because of the scattered and diverse nature of BOSCH"s supply base, BOSCH has not been able to centralize its global purchasing to the extent of Volkswagen. The majority of BOSCH's suppliers are medium-sized privately owned companies that do not necessarily have the resources to rapidly internationalize in support of BOSCH's centralized purchasing demand.

BOSCH introduced a central sourcing committee. Compared to Volkswagen, BOSCH's central committee has a stronger regional focus split in four regions in Europe, North America, Asia, and Latin America. Rather than making all decisions central, regional sub-offices can coordinate locally sourced parts and materials. BOSCH actively internationalizes its supply base to move to a more global purchasing strategy:

> We do incentivize our supply firms to go abroad and collocate to our important production hubs. But only slowly. Our supply firms are often quite small and not as international as tier-1 firms like us. Therefore we can only gradually globalize our purchasing, as our supply base becomes more international.
>
> (Interview, BOSCH case)

Furthermore, each region is responsible for the global purchasing of the components that are developed in these regions. 'Produce per blueprint' components and materials that require no development at the supply firm are purchased globally where possible and economically feasible. However, since most of the supply firms have only a regional footprint, BOSCH often purchases such components on a regional basis. Moreover, BOSCH has fewer innovating and developing supply firms in its upstream value chain. Instead, the company relies more on 'produce per blueprint' and raw material suppliers with hands-off relations.

Similar to Volkswagen, BOSCH has introduced strategies to reduce the number of direct supply firms.

> The fewer supply firms the better. Why? For three reasons: First, fewer supply firms means larger firms, with more capital to be invested into research. This becomes increasingly important, because we see that components that were relatively simple in the past become more and more high-tech. Second, larger supply firms have power to be more resilient to economic downturns. And third, they are able to develop an international footprint which we will need from our suppliers in the future.
>
> (Interview, BOSCH case)

To reduce the number of supply firms, BOSCH incentivizes the regional supply firms to develop a global footprint. BOSCH encourages M&A between the supply firms to accelerate the consolidation and to build a global and capable supply base: "[We] sometimes encourage mergers [between suppliers] to develop stronger suppliers. . . . If we know that a company is for sale, we can find suitable buyers" (Interview, BOSCH case). But M&A are not the only way to strengthen the supply base. BOSCH also modularizes component suppliers where possible.

> The extent to which we modularize our suppliers is very limited. We buy materials and some mechanical parts, but not large modules like [the assemblers]. . . . What we do, is encourage our suppliers to expand their product portfolio. Rather than buying injection molded parts from several suppliers, and metal components from others, we want to move to batch orders of different components from a single supplier.
>
> (Interview, BOSCH case)

Despite the efforts to reduce the number of supply firms, BOSCH also introduced a multiple supplier strategy.

> Ideally, we aim for three to four suppliers per component. At the moment, we often have more – but regional. For instance, we may have two supply firms in Europe, three in China, and four in Americas. In the future, we would like to have three global firms.
>
> (Interview, BOSCH case)

Similar to Volkswagen, BOSCH has established a supplier development program through which it provides consulting services to its supply firms for continuous process and quality improvements and to increase efficiencies. The profits gained by the increased efficiency are shared by the two companies by lowering component prices. This requires an open book relationship, which BOSCH can enforce upon its supply firms when they are dependent on BOSCH as a client.

As seen throughout the case, BOSCH adapted its own sales, R&D, and product configuration in support of Volkswagen's global product architecture and purchasing strategy. Moreover, BOSCH subsequently adapted its own purchasing strategy, mimicking Volkswagen to some extent, to reconfigure its own supply base in the same fashion.

Schaeffler

The Schaeffler Group (Schaeffler AG) is a German supplier of anti-friction bearings, engine components, chassis components, transmissions, dampers and clutch, and transmission systems. With annual revenue of 13.2 billion EUR, Schaeffler is one of the top 20 global automotive supply firms by revenue. The company was founded in 1946 as INA (Industrie GmbH) by the two brothers Dr Wilhelm Schaeffler and Dr Georg Schaeffler and had early success after the invention of needle roller bearing cage in 1949 by Georg Schaeffler. In 1965, the two brothers went on to found LuK (Lamellen und Kupplungsbau GmbH), which quickly became the world's largest clutch manufacturer and drive train specialist and was merged into the Schaeffler Group in 1999. Through the additional acquisition of FAG (Fischers Aktiengesellschaft), a leading firm and innovator of the ball mill that enables mass production of ball bearings, Schaeffler became the global leader for precision bearings. In 2003, FAG, LuK, and INA formed the Schaeffler Group as it is known today. As a manufacturer of components and systems, Schaeffler suppliers to assemblers directly, as well as to other tier-1 supply firms. The company claims that it supplies "all major automotive manufacturers worldwide" (Schaeffler 2015).

Over the years, Schaeffler has established a strong international operations footprint. Schaeffler started to seriously globalize its operations and adapt to the growing need for global supply firms. The Group's earliest foreign direct investments were made as early as 1956 in Hagenau, France. Further early expansion followed, with investments to Llanelli in the United Kingdom in 1957, Sao Paulo, Brazil, in 1958, the opening of a production plant in Puebla, Mexico, in 1975, a production plant in Skalica, Slowakia, in 1991, and production plants in Ansan in South Korea and Taicang, China, in 1992 and 1995 respectively. However, the largest and most aggressive internationalizing began after forming the Schaeffler Group in 2003. In 2007, Schaeffler opened new production plants in India, China, and Hungary, as well as a research and development center in China, and in 2014 they opened a production plant in Ulyanovsk, Russia. In 2015, a second production plant was opened in Puebla, India, which focuses on torque converters for US and Japanese automobile manufacturers for the US market. Between 2007 and 2016, Schaeffler established an additional five production plants in China alone to operate a total of seven production plants at four locations in China, as well as one localized R&D center. Even though Schaeffler was not a producer of integral components at the time, these investments to China were strongly encouraged by assembly firms, especially Volkswagen, with strong growth trajectories and a need for deep localization. "Take Taicang, for instance. When we opened that plant, it was purely because Volkswagen told us to do it. At that point, Schaeffler had no vision to enter the Chinese market, but we had to follow our biggest customer" (Interview, Schaeffler case).

As of 2015, the Schaeffler Group operates 74 plants worldwide, with approximately 60,000 employees. Each of the production plants is in close proximity to an automotive cluster led by a major assembly firm. As a traditional German company with strong roots in Europe, 48 of the 74 plants are based in Europe, 14 in the Americas region (including 2 plants in Brazil), five in the Asia Pacific region and seven in China, of which the Taicang plant is now the largest production plant of Schaeffler's worldwide. The production plants are designed to allow for just-in-time and just-in-sequence delivery for customized system solutions, as well as common mass production for standardized components. The global production network is established, so that Schaeffler can maintain cost efficiency and reliability of supply through cross-network supplying from different plants as demand shifts. Efficiency gains have recently been achieved from increased interconnected plants and machinery within the network through modern "Industry 4.0" machines.

Upgrading in the value chain

Schaeffler started out as a typical tier-2 supplier, albeit for high precision and high value-added components. Precision bearings are mechanical components that are modular rather than integral so that little exchange of tacit knowledge is required during the development process. As a producer of bearings, Schaeffler was a typical producer of what are called modular components in the product architecture literature: components that have standardized interfaces with other components and are therefore easily interchangeable. As a consequence of its product architecture, Schaeffler had no close ties to the assemblers. At the turn of the century, the Schaeffler Group realized it had to upgrade to maintain its position as a high value-added supply firm in the industry. Three trends in the automotive industry required rapid adaptation and rethinking of the business model: first, the accelerated globalization of the industry, and growing demand for supply firms to develop an international footprint in which assemblers often support the supply firms it had close ties to; second, the ongoing product architecture evolution that changed the role of top tier supply firms from component manufacturer to sub-assembler of whole systems; and third, the increasing role of digitalization for the industry in both production systems as well as changing nature of key components on the vehicles through the emergence of alternative power-train systems and connectivity of components.

A central strategy has been to upgrade the capabilities and value chain position from a component supplier of modular components to a systems integrator of highly integral products that require close interaction with the assembler. Schaeffler has made an effort to move up the value chain through two distinct strategies: first, through internal incremental innovation and development, and second, through M&A of supply firms of integral products or system integrators in the automotive supply industry. This requires a new thinking in systems rather than individual and isolated components:

> In an increasingly networked world, it is no longer expedient to optimize individual components or production processes in isolation. Only those who understand and integrate the entire system will be able to offer maximum possible efficiency and customer benefit. . . . To be able to develop innovative drive solutions for energy-efficient hybrid and electric vehicles, Schaeffler needs to understand the entire drivetrain including the driving behavior of the car.
>
> (Schaeffler 2015)

To adapt its product portfolio, provide more modules and system solutions, and become a systems integrator, Schaeffler undertook a series of M&A. In 2000, Schaeffler acquired REGE Motorenteile GmbH in 2000, a system provider in the area of mechanical processing and assembly of complex components such as cylinder heads, piston rods, engine blocks, and gear systems. However, the aspired transfer of systems integration knowledge to Schaeffler's core components did not materialize because of the very different nature of REGE's components compared to Schaeffler's, which require different approach to building systems. Consequently, REGE was sold off in 2008. Instead, Schaeffer made an attempt to upgrade into systems in the same year by taking over the larger Continental AG. However, the timing shortly before the financial crisis was unlucky and the takeover attempt ultimately failed as the credit market froze. In 2011 the Schaeffler Group had to reduce its stake from 75.1% to 60.3% (for 1.8 billion EUR) to maintain liquidity. The Schaeffler Group subsequently further reduced its shares and as of 2016 owns 46% of Continental's shares.

Adjusting R&D processes

As a producer of non-integral components, Schaeffler's core R&D process was somewhat independent from the vehicle development process of the assemblers. The 6,650 R&D staff at Schaeffler worldwide registered a total of 2,643 patents in 2015, making Schaeffler one of the most innovative companies in the world. The deep level of technological knowledge can be exemplified with what seems to be a rather simple product: bearings. Schaeffler operates an 'Acoustics Network' that offers improvements and investigation into any kind of noise or vibration and is therefore a leader in the field of electronic motors. The Schaeffler Group developed a very methodically innovation system. At its core is the annual 'Technology Dialog' that sets the fundamental direction of future R&D efforts for a time period of five to ten years. It incorporates different aspects, such as consumer demand, mega trends, current product portfolio, firm capabilities, and the firm strategy. This Technology Dialogue helped Schaeffler to identify future demand for new components and modules, enabling the company to gradually upgrade towards modules and systems. Through incremental development Schaeffler started to move from components to developing modules, such as the dry double clutch system developed by the Schaeffler daughter LuK in 2007, a fully-variable hydraulic valve control system in 2009, a sensor bottom bracket for e-bikes in 2011, and an electric axle system for electric powertrains in 2013. Through these efforts, Schaeffler has successfully upgraded from a component producer of modular parts to a systems integrator for integral products.

Adjustments for close collaboration with assemblers

In order to upgrade and develop a deeper understanding of the finished vehicle, close collaboration with the assemblers are inevitable. Schaeffler has been able to develop closer ties to the assembler by focusing on products that play a key role in reducing the fuel consumption and CO2 emission of vehicles. This has been achieved by developing deep knowledge of the components, as well as becoming a leader in high-tech processing methods for production. For its deep knowledge in key technologies, Schaeffler has been rewarded by becoming a strategic supplier for Volkswagen and is consequently now deeply involved in the development process of new engines and vehicles. To upgrade from a modular component producer to an integral systems supplier, Schaeffler had to adjust its R&D system towards a close simultaneous development process with the assemblers.

One requirement for close collaboration with the assembler is to collocate the R&D activities with that of the customer. As of 2015, Schaeffler operates a total of 17 R&D centers and additional market research centers in 19 countries. The international R&D centers' primary role is product customization and adaptation to specific vehicles in the simultaneous engineering process during the vehicle development phase. The R&D centers are distributed to be in close geographic proximity to R&D clusters of the major assemblers: e.g. five in the Americas region and one R&D center in China.

The limits of Schaeffler's orchestration activities in the value chain

As one of the top 20 large suppliers in the global automotive industry by revenue, and at the brink of becoming a top systems integrator through the acquisition of Continental, the Schaeffler group clearly aspires to be one of the largest and most influential supply firms in the industry. Similar to firms like BOSCH, Schaeffler aspired to position itself as a lead firm in the automotive value chain. However, several setbacks and failures in the past decades show the limits of Schaeffler's influence in its own upstream value chain and indicate that the firm is not at the level of the likes of BOSCH. The group of top systems integrators with similar orchestrating roles as the assembly firm appears to be very small. The following three examples highlight the differences between the top turn-key suppliers such as BOSCH and Continental, to the large but much less influential firms such as Schaeffler. First, the ability to globally centralize its purchasing falls beyond that of Volkswagen and BOSCH. Second, the supplier development program, while existing, is not as impactful as that of BOSCH or Volkswagen, as Schaeffler struggles to implement open book relations to its suppliers, most of which are not dependent on Schaeffler as a client. And third, the ability to establish production hubs is limited at best.

Unlike Volkswagen and BOSCH, the purchasing of Schaeffler is structured much more regional. Purchasing is divided into four regions: Europe, Americas, Greater China, and the Asia Pacific region. These regional purchasing offices are responsible for all production plants in the region. However, no cross-regional purchasing is made as of 2015 for further volume bundling, the way Volkswagen or BOSCH introduced in their purchasing systems. One reason Schaeffler seems to lack behind in terms of globalized purchasing may stem from the failed Continental takeover efforts, as both companies have started combining their procurement to achieve higher volumes but could not fully integrate and consolidate due to the subsequent divestment.

Schaeffler's supplier development program is a second indication that Schaeffler has little power over its supply firms. Through its development program Schaeffler tries to improve the quality provided by the suppliers by "coordinating extensively" (Schaeffler 2015). The program includes process optimization and logistics optimization. However, as Schaeffler is typically only one of many buyers to its suppliers, and most supply firms are not dependent on Schaeffler as a customer, the willingness to develop an open book relationship and let Schaeffler see and optimize internal processes are limited. Moreover, many of Schaeffler's supply firms are family enterprises too small to justify expensive optimization programs.

Schaeffler follows similar strategic purchasing goals and wants to consolidate its purchasing through supplier reduction and supply base internationalization, as currently Schaeffler has approximately 33,000 supply firms from 80 countries. Despite its attempts, efforts to internationalize the supply base have shown relatively little results. Schaeffler's purchasing volume for a single production location does not justify collocating production for most of the supply firms. Especially, because most of the supply firms are relatively small German family owned businesses. Only in locations where Schaeffler's production plant is itself part of a larger production cluster is it able to attract supply firms to collocate.

The example that underlines Schaeffler's limited ability to orchestrate and restructure the value chain the most is that of a failed attempt to establish its own production hub by collocating several of its supply firms. In 1991, Schaeffler made a deal with the local authorities in Skalica, Slowakia, to establish a thriving production cluster around Schaeffler. The idea was simple: Schaeffler would invest in a greenfield production plant and invite its supply firms to collocate in close proximity. More and more supply firms were supposed to follow until the cluster gained momentum and further production industries would collocate to benefit from the infrastructure and knowledge in the cluster. What sounded good on paper turned out to become a costly mistake for Schaeffler. While Schaeffler committed to the idea and opened one of its largest production plants at that time, not a single supply firm would follow. Schaeffler was unable to create the critical mass to attract their suppliers to collocate:

> We have tried to collocate our suppliers with us, but with limited success. Whenever we followed [an assembly firm like] Volkswagen in China, it was easy to convince our suppliers to follow us as well. However, our production plant in Slovakia is a disaster. We invested there, because we thought we could pull other firms with us and build a cluster around us, but that never materialized. We are just not big enough to build an industrial cluster around us, like Volkswagen is.
>
> (Interview, Schaeffler case)

To date, Schaeffler is the only operating firm in this location, an isolated production plant detached from the large production hubs in Europe's automotive industry, resulting in hefty transportation and logistics costs to run operations.

Brose

Brose was founded as an automotive trading company in 1908 by 24-year-old Max Brose, a son of a coachwork manufacturer who watched as the motorization of automobiles changed the industry. The trading company quickly grew and expanded its product portfolio to include all important automotive parts at that time such as tools, wind screens, lights, horns, mirrors, speedometers, jerry cans, shock absorber, ignition plugs, and even automobile clothing such as jackets, helmets, and glasses. In 1919, Brose pivoted his business model and entered a new phase, as he moved the company from trading with automotive components to developing and producing his own components. The first patent for a "Schlingfederbremse" (a spring breaking system) was filed in 1919. This innovative component allows the window lifter to stop and hold the window in place in any position. This simple idea marks the beginning of a great automotive company. For almost 50 years this product becomes the key product of the Brose Company, with further break through inventions around the same component.

In the 1960s, Brose developed the first electronic window lifter. The first assembly firm to implement this technology were the two German assembly firms BMW and Mercedes. Additionally, Brose began to upgrade. The company used its acquired knowledge and capabilities to develop further key technologies and products. For instance, its electronic drive system was used for other components, such as electronic seat positioning systems, which became important as the automotive industry started to focus on comfort.

In the late 1980s Brose performed a functional upgrade and became a systems supplier for modularized doors. As the supplier of electronic window mechanics, Brose had capabilities in the most complex technology of doors and was therefore the ideal firm to add assembly activities of additional door components. This fell into the era of a new production system: The lean manufacturing system. The modularized door was first used in 1987 in the AUDI 80 (a Volkswagen daughter). From then on, Brose was not only responsible for the development of key components of the door but took on new responsibilities for the development, production, and assembly of the entire system, including logistics and quality controls for the upstream value chain. Additionally, the in-house production system was revolutionized, and Brose opened a new production plant in Germany in 1997 that produced "in the tact of the automobile assembly firm": just-in-sequence, and for just-in-time delivery. This became the model plant for all new production plants of Brose worldwide – which were collocated to the target assembly firm. The blueprint production plant marked the beginning of a new phase of internationalization and collocation in the auto industry.

The upgrading to a systems integrator and successful supplier of modules further opened doors for product upgrading, as Brose acquired key capabilities and knowledge for systems integration. Brose added complementary key components for the door system into its product portfolio, such as locking systems (acquired from BOSCH in 2002). Additional key developments were made in weight reduction to overall vehicle weight in order to reduce fuel consumption and CO2 emissions. Brose thereby enabled assemblers to comply with the tightening emissions regulations. Further product upgrading outside the key door system was achieved through acquisitions such as the acquisition of the Siemens-VDO Electric Motor Drives division or the Continental Cooling and Fan division in 2007. By 2016, Brose's additional divisions included a powertrain division, which develops and produces braking systems (including ABS and electronic parking brakes), and an electronic steering and transmissions division. Through its leading position in the automotive industry, Brose claims that at least every third vehicle on the road has one or more Brose components installed.

As shown throughout its history, Brose is not only a firm with development capabilities but also innovation capabilities that constantly innovates new features for automobiles. As such, Brose is at the forefront of innovation, ahead of the assembly firms, and in a good position to bargain with its customers. This makes Brose strategically one of the most important supply firms in the industry and enables Brose to develop very close ties to its customers. In fact, the close relations lead to numerous opportunities to expand its role in the global automotive value chain in the past and enabled Brose to perform one of the most aggressive and impressive internationalization strategies.

Global operations and reaction to VW's changes

Parallel to the introduction of lean manufacturing, modularization, and the inherited upgrade and increased responsibility of Brose began the age of globalization. In 1988, Brose opened its first international production plants in the United Kingdom and Spain. What followed was a rapid internationalization of the company. In 1993, Brose opened its first North American production plant in Mexico. One year later, three development and sales offices were opened in Detroit (USA), Tokyo (Japan), and Paris (France). From 1997 on, Brose expanded its new just-in-sequence production plants, and all international offices follow the same appearance. This included Brose's joint-venture in China, which was opened in 1999, and a rapid internationalization of sales offices. By 2008, Brose had over 50 sales representation offices in international locations. What followed was a rapid internationalization of production capabilities to collocate to the production plants of the assembly firms.

In 2009, Brose opened its second joint-venture in China together with Shanghai STEC Transportation Electric Company Ltd. It produced electronic window lifter, seating systems, and door systems. Its customers were SAIC-Volkswagen, Changan Ford Motor Company, and SAIC-General Motors. The rapid growth of the Chinese market led to further investments. In 2011, Brose localized a research and development center in Shanghai and invested into a new production plant in Chongqing. By then Brose operated five locations in China. In 2012, Brose opened its new production plant in Beijing, the second plant for door systems in China and the seventh location. Further Asian production plants opened in Thailand (a joint-venture with Delloyd Electronics) in 2009, and in South Korea in

2011 through the Mando-Brose Corporation, and a joint-venture with Mando for the production of electronic motors for Mando steering and braking systems. An additional production plant opened in Pune, India, in 2011. In 2014, Brose opened a production plant in South Africa for seating and door systems. As Brose said on their homepage: "Manufacturers are increasingly managing the juggling act between globalization, localization and customization with global platforms and modular systems. Brose has successfully faced up to this challenge and produces identical seat systems on three different continents." The purpose of this internationalization was to follow the western assembly firms, which incentivized Brose to open production plants in the growing markets. As an interviewee said: "We don't have a good experience with customers in China. They cannot develop, only copy. They are good in producing, but not as partners to develop products" (Interview, Brose case).

In parallel to its impressive globalization, Brose established a global purchasing strategy similar to Volkswagen. Through its 'global sourcing network,' Brose involves its supply firms in its R&D and production, demands constant product-optimization, invites supply firms to collocate, enforces open book relationships, and ensures quality requirements. In exchange, Brose offers long-term contracts and stable supplier relations:

> We involve our suppliers in our development, production and business processes at an early stage. This generates a close, intensive exchange of know-how, ideas and expertise – and ensures optimum product realization. In return, we offer our suppliers excellent opportunities for development, attractive conditions and long-term partnerships.
>
> (company webpage)

As an interviewee said: "We bring German supply firms with us to China, if we have a good relationship with them" (Interview, Brose case).

Mahle-Behr

The Mahle Behr GmbH & Co. GK is a German automotive supplier that resulted from the merger of two traditional German automotive suppliers, Behr and Mahle, in 2013. The group specialized in air conditioning and engine cooling systems. Before the 2013 merger, both Mahle and Behr were in the top 50 of the global automotive suppliers list of 2012 (Automotive News 2013). Through the merger, the Mahle Group was able to enter into the top 20 of the global suppliers by revenue, with an approximate revenue of over US$ 12 billion in 2014 (Automotive News 2015).

In 1905, Julius Friedrich Behr joined a local car cooling workshop and overtook the small company in 1907. By 1910 he managed to move from repairs to manufacturing and opened a small production plant near Stuttgart, Germany. Its engine cooling was used in iconic models, such as the Ford Model A, the Mercedes 'Silberpfeil,' and the VW Beetle. Key inventions were the wind channel for cooler testing and the oil cooling system developed in cooperation with Porsche. However, the Second World War disrupted operations. In 1957, Behr upgraded its product portfolio and added air conditions for passenger cars. Until the merger, these two products were the core business of Behr.

Mahle was founded in 1920 as a combustion engines testing company. However, it was the piston unit that made the company profitable, as Mahle was the first company to build pistons from lightweight metals such as aluminum (patented in 1927). Mahle continuously upgraded its product portfolio via further products in the engine group, such as aluminum cylinders in 1951, aluminum motor blocks in 1976, camshafts in 1988, new cooling concept for diesel engines in 2001, or the full plastics oil filter in 2003. By 2015, the Mahle Group was a leading automotive component manufacturer with four core business units: engine systems and components, filtration and engine peripherals, thermal management, and mechatronics. Its engine systems and components division includes piston systems, cylinder components, piston rings, pins, connecting rods, bearing brushings, and cylinder liners. The filtration and engine peripherals division includes air intake modules through to the combustion chambers and exhaust gas recirculation. The thermal management unit is of crucial importance to combustion engines and increasingly for new electronic driver trains as well. It includes cooling water pumps, water flows, and oil cooling systems.

The wide spectrum of products was achieved through a number of portfolio optimization M&As in recent years. In 2005, Mahle developed its first whole engine, which was used in a university student lead formula race. In the same year, Mahle acquired Cosworth Technology Ltd., with production in the USA and the United Kingdom, which laid the basis for Mahle Powertrain, as well as Brockhaus Soehne GmbH, a German steel and measurement instruments company. In 2009, Mahle followed up with the acquisition of KTM Kuehler GmbH, a cooling system producer. In 2013, Mahle acquired Behr to strengthen its thermal management unit. Further upgrading was achieved through the acquisition of the InnoWa Membrane GmbH in 2012 for the filtration business unit, the acquisition of the Slovenian based electric motor manufacturer Letrika, including its manufacturing plants in Slovenia, Bosnia-Herzegovina, Belarus, China, and Brazil, and it complemented this with a follow up acquisition of the Japanese company Kokusan Denki in 2015, a specialist in ABS and ESC units, dynamic driving control, and steering assistance. An additional acquisition followed in 2015, when Mahle carved-out the thermal business unit from Delphi, making Mahle the second largest automotive supplier for thermal management.

Through such acquisitions Mahle was able to constantly upgrade its products and develop into a systems integrator within the global automotive value chain. However, the basis for innovation and development capabilities has already been established throughout its long history – which enabled the company to integrate the acquired knowledge effectively and bundle the competencies in a way to develop new ones. The prerequisites were previous development capabilities and strong absorptive capacity by the engineering teams.

Global operations and reaction to VW's changes

The Mahle Group operates production plants in over 170 locations around the world, the majority of which has been established in close proximity to the customers. China has been the main focus on Mahle's recent organic growth. Mahle entered China late – the first operations were established in 1999. Since then Mahle has drastically increased its presence in the growing market, opening more than one new location per year. In 2015, Mahle operates 22 locations with approximately 7,000 employees.

Interestingly, the core clients in China are the global assembly firms, rather than indigenous Chinese firms. The driver attracting leading western supply firms to the Chinese market have been the western assemblers such as Volkswagen:

> On the one hand, MAHLE's customers in China come from the who's who of the global automotive industry. This means that they expect the same specifications and standards as in Germany, the USA, or Japan, which requires identical production conditions and above all, employees with the same level of qualifications.
>
> (company homepage)

The Chinese assemblers, on the other hand, handle projects rather differently: "They are accustomed to working without long schedules and in-depth processes" (Interview, Mahle case). If circumstances change, like expected sales of a vehicle, "the business partner is expected to respond to this change of heart – both quickly and flexibly. Any difficulties that may arise also need to be solved instantly" (Interview, Mahle case).

Adjusting to changing R&D processes for global platforms

Mahle set up a widespread network of R&D centers to accommodate to its global clients. Mahle employs approximately 6,000 engineers in research and development. These work in 15 major R&D centers, which are distributed to ensure collocation in all major automotive hubs: Stuttgart, Northampton, Detroid, Tokyo, Shanghai, Pune, and Sao Paulo (Germany, Great Britain, the USA, Brazil, China, India, and Japan respective). Such a network of collocated R&D centers is necessary for Mahle, due to the nature of its products. Mahle produces highly integral systems and has a unique systems knowledge in engine thermal management and engine peripherals. Such systems require extensive information exchange with the other developing firms like engine manufacturers or assemblers. Mahle is deeply involved in the engine development process of Volkswagen. Since emission standards are different in regions (e.g. EU, NAFTA, China), engines are adapted to meet different regulations. This requires Mahle to have R&D centers in close proximity to where the engines are adapted to local requirements. "Mahle has established itself as a leading global development partner to the automotive and engine industry" (Mahle 2015). "Vehicles on the whole are becoming increasingly complex, since more and more components and systems are networked and interact with each other" (Mahle 2015).

Components such as engine cooling systems are highly integral. Mahle-Behr is therefore closely cooperating with the assemblers and is an integral part of the vehicle development process. Thermal management of engines is crucial for combustion engines to achieve maximum efficiency and research emission standards. Mahle's expertise in thermal management is highly valued by the assemblers and engineers developing the new generations of engines. Furthermore, thermal management is also important for future electronic drive train systems (especially for battery cooling).

Global purchasing

Mahle-Behr purchases mostly raw materials such as aluminum, steel, copper, and resins. Such supply firms are in itself large global suppliers like ThyssenKrupp, BASF, or DuPont, which are not receptive for open book relations. Therefore, Mahle has limited power over its supply base. Still, Mahle has a centralized global purchasing approach. Recently acquired firms have been integrated into the purchasing system of the Mahle Group, since the acquired companies had common suppliers. Even for the year 2015, the integration of the purchasing departments enabled the company to leverage purchasing synergies, which goes to show how similar their supply base was. Only the compressors units have autonomous purchasing departments. All other business units are unified in a global purchasing department for volume bundling and supply firm reduction. And like most large firms, Mahle carries out supply visits and reviews and supplier development for smaller suppliers, such as component manufacturers and sub-contractors.

Marquardt

The Marquardt Group is a producer of what would traditionally be seen as a relatively simple product: switches. However, Marquardt is now a producer of R&D intensive high-tech systems and therefore an ideal case study to explore how technology advances change the value proposition and role of supply firms below what used to be called the first tier of supply firms. As technology advanced, switches, sensors, and controls have evolved to become high-tech components. Like the previous supply firms, Marquardt moved from a manufacturer of simple components, to take on design and R&D for entire systems, and has thereby established itself as the leader for 'drive authorization systems,' 'operating components,' and 'switches and applications.'

The Marquardt Group was founded in 1925 as a producer of switches for household appliances. During the Nazi Regime, and in the aftermath of the Second World War, the company lost most of its employees and machinery to the French occupants. However, a severe shortage of surface mount light switches in Germany kept the company from going out of business. Beginning its own R&D, Marquardt developed complete switching keyboards for appliances in the 1960s. Customer demand rapidly evolved in regard to the design of the switches, and smaller, slimmer switches were developed for high volume production. This allowed the company to enter the automotive market in 1978 as a supplier of small standard switches, such as snap-action and control switches. It was not until the 1990s that Marquardt moved to high value-added products and became a leading technology driven company, as the microprocessor changed the function of switches. As an early adopter of the new technology, Marquardt introduced the first microprocessor based power-controlled units for electro power tools at the appliance expo in 1991. Marquardt was able to introduce the same technology to the automotive industry. Through the adaption of micro processed switches, Marquardt became an innovating supply firm in the industry and played a key role in future innovations. The use of microprocessors in switches marked a milestone in the product evolution towards high-tech switching and control systems. One year later, Marquardt established itself as a leading automotive switch producer by introduction the smallest dust and water protected volume production snap-action switch that enabled inventions such as central controlled electronic seat positioning. With two consecutive innovations, Marquardt became a strategically important supplier to the assembly firms. Marquardt proved the ability to upgrade and innovate and used the momentum for a further functional upgrade in the value chain. In the next five years, Marquardt moved from component to system supplier, and in 1997 introduced its first driver authorization system with electronic key and ignition switches to set new standards in theft protection. Through the incremental innovation and development, Marquardt developed an originally simple component into a high-tech security system of high value.

Since the introduction of the first driver authorization system in 1997, Marquardt moved up the value chain and focused on the development of entire systems rather than components. Marquardt moved on to develop multifunctional control panels and console systems for vehicle cockpits. In 2003, the first keyless system was developed by Marquardt, again setting new trends for the industry. Material research enabled the company to introduce high-gloss control panels that add luxury and quality perception to the vehicle and set a new standard for premium cars in 2004. It also enabled the company to rapidly expand its product portfolio of interior design, interior trimming, and user interface components of the vehicle. In 2007, Marquardt developed a groundbreaking electronic gear selection switch for a completely new product: the 'shift by wire' gear switch, where the gearbox is shifted through electronic controls rather than mechanically. This requires complex systems integration of the control unit, switching unit, gearbox, and engine control units by the assembler, in which Marquardt is highly integrated in the long-term strategic development plan of the assemblers and has become a key partner and innovator in the value chain. Marquardt plays a key role and is now deeply imbedded in the long-term strategic development plans of the assemblers.

Other key innovations include the electronic steering column lock for key-less systems (2010), the 'BlueID Drive' system to lock, open, and start vehicles using identification on smartphones (2011), a touchpad for use in vehicle cockpits (2012), a move into other industry segments such as e-bikes or boats (2013), technology for even smaller robust switches (2014), and a battery management system for electronic vehicles (2014). Such innovations are based on in-house research and development efforts that go well beyond the expected innovation by the assemblers and makes Marquardt a strategic supplier that pushes innovation and technology down the value stream. This was rewarded by VW, which nominated Marquardt as an 'A-Supplier' in 2014.

The ascent to a strategically important system supplier further helped the company to quickly establish an international footprint. Marquardt was initially a late adopter to the internationalization trend. The first foreign subsidiary, headquartered in Cazenovia, New York, USA, was founded in 1981 as an export supporting office and expanded to a production plant in 1985. But it was not until the 1990s that Marquardt begun to seriously and rapidly expand its international operations.

In 1991, Marquardt acquired the tool switch manufacturer Russenberger, including its subsidiaries in France, Spain, and Tunisia. Five years later, Marquardt entered the Chinese market by opening the Marquardt Switches Shanghai production plant. In the same year, Marquardt also opened a joint-venture with the Indian switch manufacturer RG Keswani in India. In 1999, Marquardt opened a new production in Switzerland. By 2000, Marquardt further expanded its global footprint, entering the Indian and the US markets through the acquisition of the Indian R. G. Keswani company and a new green field investment in the US. In 2006, a new subsidiary was opened in Romania. 2012 saw a year of several milestones in terms of building a global footprint. A new administrative and R&D center was opened in Shanghai, China. In the same year, a new production line opened in Romania and the production of a new plant in Tunisia and Mexico. Further subsidiaries were founded in Macedonia in 2014 and Pune, India, in 2015.

This very rapid internationalization to establish a global footprint was necessary due to the requirement shift of the global assembly firms, to which Marquardt had suddenly become a key supply firm, and which increasingly required their top suppliers to establish a global footprint since the introduction of lean manufacturing in the 1990s. The process was rapidly accelerated at the turn of the century, when Volkswagen introduced a new purchasing strategy and accelerated even more after the new introduction of the MQB platform and the fully globalization of purchasing by Volkswagen in 2012. The majority of Marquardt's production locations were selected at the invite of the assembly firms to collocate with their production.

But the support from the assembler was not limited to help the company to internationalize. Marquardt also received support to upgrade its manufacturing processing from the assemblers. In 2003, the company redesigned its production lines to meet current just-in-time and just-in-sequence production standards. The new plant in Rietheim-Weilheim, Germany, became the new standard layout for future production lines worldwide. This was designed with the support and expertise of Volkswagen.

Witzenmann

The Witzenmann GmbH is a relatively small German producer of flexible metal elements. With annual revenue of just over 500 million EUR and around 4,000 employees worldwide, Witzenmann can still be considered a typical German 'Mittelstand' company. Witzenmann's products are used for industrial purposes, in the construction industry, in the aerospace industry, and in the automotive industry. Products include components that are close to the engine or used in the exhaust system, such as flexible metal hoses, tubes and pipes, pipe supports, special connection fittings, and compression fittings. Through the flexibility of the metal pipes, the pipes can absorb heat induced material extension, vibrations, and noise from the engine and are thereby used to decouple the engine from the vehicle chassis. Furthermore, Witzenmann has developed an expertise in exhaust systems, including thermodynamics to simulate exhaust flows for optimal re-circulation and a knowledge that positions Witzenmann close to the engine developers of the assembly firm. With over 40% of the revenue, the automotive industry is the most important industry for Witzenmann.

The company was founded in Pforzheim, Germany, in 1854 as a producer of jewelry. In 1877, the company expanded to Paris, where the founder Heinrich Witzenmann met Eugene Levavasseur. Together, the duo developed the first metal tube, which laid the groundwork of the company today. Through a number of early developments and patents, the company quickly became the market leader in flexible tubing. After reviving the company in postwar Germany, Volkswagen became the most important customer of Witzenmann and would remain its most important customer and co-developer. At the same time, the product portfolio was expanded with complementary products via the acquisition of the Fleitmann GmbH in 1960 (a German producer of shower hoses) and the Metallslangfabriken Huddinge AB in 1969 (a Swedish producer of metal tubes).

Today, Witzenmann operates in 24 locations in 19 countries across Europe, the Americas. and Asia, and it has established itself as the market leader for flexible metal tubing solutions. As the industries leader, Witzenmann supplies all major assemblers in the world, including increasingly new entrants from China, such as BAIC, SAIC, or FAW.

Apart from the early acquisition of the Swedish Metallslangfabriken company in 1969, the internationalization of Witzenmann began in 1979 with the founding of a subsidiary in France. 1985, Witzenmann licensed a Czech company to produce Witzenmann tubes for East Europe. The rapid internationalization began with the introduction of lean manufacturing and the increasing need for a global footprint of supply firms in the 1990s. 1989, Witzenmann established a subsidiary in Spain. The year 1993 marked the first foreign direct investment into East Europe, as Witzenmann opened a subsidiary in Slovakia and acquired the license in the Czech Republic. Further subsidiaries were established in France, Italy, and Belgium. In 1996, Witzenmann invested outside of Europe for the first time and established a subsidiary in the USA.

The internationalization was further accelerated around the turn of the century and the increased modularization of vehicle platforms and the demand for standardized components worldwide. Between 1999 and 2003, Witzenmann entered key markets in the automotive industry, especially in emerging markets, and it opened subsidiaries in Brazil, China, India, Korea, and Russia. This was followed by additional investments into India in 2008, a new production line in Russia in 2011, as well as the market entry into Japan, a new production plant in Poland, and a new production line in the US in 2012. In 2015, Witzenmann opened a production plant in Mexico to solidify its position in the North American market. As the interviewee said, the company always collocated with assemblers by invitation of the assemblers.

While the production of the component remains relatively low-tech, the science behind its development has become high-tech and very demanding. The optimal design of the tubes require knowledge in exhaust flow dynamics, thermal management, thermal expansion, and noise and vibration reduction. The assemblers constantly develop new exhaust systems for combustion engines, in which exhaust gases are recycled to reduce nitrous gases as required by increasingly strict emissions standards. The flexible tubes from Witzenmann play a crucial role in the exhaust system development and an integral part of engine development. The key value-added for the automotive industry is the flexible metal tube that enables to assembler to decouple to engine from the vehicle chassis, which in turn drastically reduces noise and vibrations in the vehicle and increases driving comfort.

Global purchasing

As a relatively small company compared to the likes of Volkswagen, BOSCH, Continental, or Schaeffler, Witzenmann has a much smaller impact on its supply base through purchasing strategy changes. Unlike the industry's giants, Witzenmann is not able to attract smaller supply firms to collocate with them if they decide to open a production plant in a new location. Furthermore, as a traditional tier-2 or at times even tier-3 company, Witzenmann is further up in the value chain. Its supply firms are therefore either very small supply firms, or for most parts, raw material suppliers, mainly metals, some resin, and industrial gases for processing and testing. These firms in turn are often giant multinationals, which themselves have a global footprint, and to which a company like Witzenmann is a small customer.

References

Automotive News. 2013. "Top 100 Global OEM Parts Suppliers." *Supplement to Automotive News.*

Automotive News. 2015. "Top 100 Global OEM Parts Suppliers." *Supplement to Automotive News.*

Mahle. 2015. *Annual Report*. https://www.mahle.com/

Schaeffler. 2015. *Annual Report*. https://www.schaeffler.de/

5 Participants from Brazil and China

Metal Leve/Mahle

Metal Leve is a Brazilian piston maker that was established in 1950. Today, it has become the leading supplier of forged and sintered automotive components in Latin America, producing pistons, rings, bearings, filters, valve trains, lingers, and ring inserts. Metal Leve has seven subsidiaries across Brazil and one in Argentina. In 2012, Metal Leve generated approximately 70% of its revenue from supplying automotive assembly groups, 37% domestically in Brazil and 33% from abroad. With production facilities in Argentina, and significant revenue from exports, Metal Leve is one of Brazil's most internationalized automotive component producers, with a solid position in the automotive value chain.

As a producer of forged and sintered engine components, Metal Leve is a typical 'produce per blueprint' manufacturer that receives the drawings and tools for the components from its clients. This means the components are developed by its clients and not Metal Leve. Its clients are both tier-1 suppliers as well as assembly firms. But as a 'produce per blueprint' supplier, Metal Leve has a relatively shallow relationship to its clients and is not involved in the R&D processes. What Metal Leve offers is manufacturing capacity and process expertise but no superior knowledge of the components and the systems in which they are used.

With the introduction of the first international vehicle platforms in the 1990s, the assemblers increased the use of common parts, often by importing components from foreign suppliers. This increased the competition with foreign suppliers, and Metal Leve had to upgrade its capabilities and products to stay competitive. This required new capital and external knowledge. In order to rapidly upgrade its technology, Metal Leve, like many other suppliers from Brazil, had to establish relationships with overseas competitors. Being unable to upgrade on its own, Metal Leve entered a number of partnerships with foreign competitors that could transfer knowledge and technology to Brazil.

To this end, Metal Leve entered an agreement with the German supplier Mahle in 1996, which were offered a share in the company for the transfer of technology. The assembly firms played a key role in establishing the partnership with Mahle.

> The merger with Mahle was strongly advised by the assemblers. It was either that, or the German company would come to Brazil with its own production, and we would lose the contract with our customer. This would not benefit either of us.
>
> (Interview, MML case)

Mahle increased its share in Metal Leve in its effort to internationalize and injected further capital to sustain Metal Leve's position in the Latin American market. By 2016, Mahle has become the largest shareholder, owning 60.81% of Metal Leve, followed by Mahle Industriebeteiligungen GmbH with 9.29% and Credit Suisse Hedging-griffo Asset Management with 5.32%, giving Mahle a controlling stake of 71%. After the de-facto takeover, the company was renamed Mahle Metal Leve. The injected capital from Mahle enabled Metal Leve to strengthen its domestic position by consolidating the industry through a number of acquisitions, like the acquisition of Metallurgy Mogi in 1998.

The consolidating of the Latin American market was important to maintain the position in the rapidly harmonized global market. In the early 2000s, competition with foreign competitors increased as the assembly firms decreased the country-specific components through the steady roll-out of vehicles based on the new platform with increasingly standardized carry-over components. At the same time, the pressure to internationalize increased for the supply firms, and Metal Leve slowly began internationalizing its Latin American operations with the help of Mahle. In 2007, Metal Leve acquired Dana Indústria, a local manufacturer of bearings. In the same year, the company began its international expansion with the acquisition of Evidal, an Argentinian based valve producer that was subsequently renamed Mahle Argentina. The shift in purchasing strategy of Volkswagen in the early 2010s, one of Mahle Metal Leve's most important customers, accelerated Mahle's efforts to further restructure its Latin American business. Metal Leve was used as the legal entity that was to become the spearhead for Mahle in Latin America. Other operational units in Latin America were subsequently restructured to become part of Mahle Metal Leve, including businesses for additional products and in other Latin American countries. In 2010, Mahle decided to merge its Brazilian based piston rings business into the company. In 2013, after Mahle increased its shareholding in the Behr Group from 36.8% to 51%, Mahle Metal Leve incorporated Behr's Brazilian operations, which was renamed Mahle Behr Gerenciamento Térmico Brasil Ltda. The integration of Behr's Brazilians operations further expanded the technological capabilities and product portfolio of Mahle Metal Leve, strengthening its position in the lead firms' value chain.

The rapid succession of technology upgrading mergers and acquisitions took place as an effort of Mahle to restructure its Latin American business, at the

Table 5.1 Global market share in pistons market

Company	*Global market share*
Federal Mogul	60–70%
Mahle	10–20%
Reihnmetall Automotive	>5%

Source: Author's own table, based on report from the European Commission (Commission).

decision of the headquarter in Germany and in close alignment with the changing requirements of the assembly firm. Metal Leve was integrated into the value chain by being bought out by a foreign competitor and is now controlled from a headquarters in a foreign country. Other examples of Brazilian high tech supply firms that were acquired by overseas companies in the time period are Plascar, PST Electronica, and Sabo.

Metal Leve's position in the global automotive value chain

Metal Leve has been fully absorbed by the Mahle Group, as it has become the major branch for pistons in Latin America for Mahle. The piston rings business has been highly consolidated in the global automotive industry for quite a while, with Federal Mogul from the USA as the largest manufacturer in the world with an estimated market share of > 60% of the global automotive market (see Table 5.1). As the second largest piston rings manufacturer, Mahle sought opportunities to expand and catch up to Federal Mogul in the past decades before revising its strategy to prepare for the electrification of the powertrain in the 2010s. In its efforts to increase its global footprint and market penetration, Metal Leve played an important role in Mahle's expansion to the Latin American market.

Similar to Metal Leve, multiple automotive suppliers were acquired by foreign firms in the wave of global consolidation that followed the new product architecture and the globalization of standardized components. As some interviewees expressed, the automotive component industry has been sold out to foreign investors.

Autometal/CIE automotive

Autometal was a Brazilian auto supplier of stamped metal components such as white body and chassis parts. Founded in 1965, the company enjoyed early success and was quickly established in the local Brazilian automotive industry to become a major supplier of metallurgy and later plastic injection components. Stamped metal components are typical 'produce per blueprint' components that require little exchange of tacit knowledge between buyer and supplier. And because of the heavy weight of metal parts and high transportation cost associated with them, such parts are often sourced locally. Therefore, the market of stamped metal components has stayed fragmented while other parts of the industry consolidated on a global level. Assemblers put little pressure on the supply base for stamped parts to consolidate because transactions to 'produce per blueprint' producers are easy to manage. Moreover such products have few competitive advantages from large scale production vis-à-vis localized manufacturing.

As a manufacturer of such components, Autometal survived the first wave of foreign competition entering the Brazilian market when the market opened in 1990. However, with the increased use of global platforms, and the overall consolidation of the global supply base steered by large assemblers like Volkswagen, Autometal fell victim to an emerging group of global supply firms in the 2000s when it was acquired by the French company CIE Automotive.

CIE Automotive is a global supplier for forging, casting, machining, metal stamping, tube forming, aluminum, and plastic components. The company was created from the merger between the Egaña group (founded 1996) and Aforasa group in 2002. CIE Automotive is a young automotive supplier in the industry. Its strategy has been to inorganically grow via (international) M&A, to develop a global footprint in the metal processing and machining sector of the auto supply industry. Since the foundation of the original company Egaña in 1996, the group has been involved in almost 70 M&A transactions to develop into a global supply firm. The Brazilian company Autometal was one of the earliest targets and was acquired in 2000 by Egaña as a major acquisition in the Latin American region to strengthen the footprint in this region and to date plays a key role for CIE in the region.

CIE Automotive offers a variety of manufacturing services as a subcontractor to produce a wide range of components: crankshaft, CV-joints, axle shaft, axle beam, gearbox housing, clutch housing, ladder frame, steering housing, camshaft cover, turbo housing, differential housing, brake drum, body in white, steering columns, brake booster, seat structure, emblems, ash trays, trim parts, roof system products, or diesel, and gasoline injection rails. The company has a diversified customer base from assembly firms to tier-1 suppliers. Its largest customers are Renault and Chrysler, each of which amount to 7% of CIE's revenues, followed by Daimler and Ford (with each 6%) and Volkswagen and General Motors (with each 5%). The remaining customers are below the 5% revenue mark, and almost 30% of CIE's revenue comes from customers that contribute less than 1% to its revenue.

CIE Automotive is a classical 'produce per blueprint' supplier that receives the drawings from its customers and provides manufacturing services to its clients. As such, CIE has very little product ownership advantages. Instead, its advantage lies in its processing and manufacturing expertise. Combined with the diversified customer base, CIE has no significant market leader position for any of its key components.

Industrias Arteb

Established in 1934, as Artur Eberhardt Group, Arteb initially manufactured head lights, taillights, and side lights for the automotive aftersales market in Brazil (which is now sold under the brand Lynx Vision). Since 1959, Arteb supplied lights directly to the four major assembly groups, Fiat, Ford, General Motors, and Volkswagen.

When the Brazilian market opened in 1990, new assembly groups rushed into the market with new modules, and the big four assemblers had to rapidly introduce new passenger car models with the newest technology. As the market opened to new assembly groups, Arteb successfully expanded its customer base, supplying lights to brands such as AUDI, Fiat, Ford, GM, Hyundai, Mercedes, Mitsubishi, Renault, Toyota, Troller, and Volkswagen. With four production facilities in Brazil, Arteb had a production capacity of over 800,000 lighting units per month and gained a 27% market share in lighting products for assembly groups in Brazil.

However, the new competition at the assembly level also accelerated the introduction of global platforms in Brazil, in which lighting systems used new technologies and are increasingly sourced from global suppliers. At this crossroads, Volkswagen decided to phase out its new vehicle, based on its then-common PQ platform logic. Consequently, Arteb began to struggle for its position in the market. The big four assemblers tried to rapidly upgrade their local supply base in order to compete with the new entrants at assembly level. A popular method was to encourage the local supply firms to sign Technical Assistance Agreements with foreign competitors that owned superior technological capabilities. Volkswagen was no exception to that and advised Arteb to upgrade its Technical Assistance Agreements with foreign partners.

In the rapidly changing market, Arteb had to quickly expand its capabilities to accommodate for the new designs, technologies, and lightning systems of its existing customers. For this reason, Arteb expanded its license agreement with the German automotive lights producer Hella, an internationally renowned and large automotive supplier at that time that was already capable of producing the newest lights for almost all vehicles on the market. The contact with Hella existed through a previously established technical assistance agreement between the two companies and was further facilitated through the lead firm's pressure. Additional technical assistance agreements were signed in 1994 with Japan's Koito, Italy's Carello, and Austria's ZKW.

Equipped with the leading-edge technology, Arteb tried to solidify its position in the Latin American market by expanding its production capacities. To this end, Arteb established a new production plant in Gravataí in 1998, within General Motor's industrial complex, and in Camaçari in 2001, in close proximity to the Ford Company. Expanding its production required fresh capital, which Arteb received from Hella and IFC (part of the World Bank Group) in 1998. Still, the holding family behind Arteb was able to maintain their majority stake in the company. When it became evident that the family was not willing to sell Arteb, Hella divested its equity stake in 2003 and terminated its licensing agreement. Arteb maintained its Brazilian ownership. However, without its key licensing agreement with Hella, Arteb was in a situation where it had to develop its own lightning systems.

To this end, Arteb set up its own R&D facility, Centro Tecnológico Arteb, for US$ 100 million. The R&D center is a critical component of Arteb's strategy. Its purpose is to enable Arteb to develop new high value-added front-end lightning modules independently to maintain their product portfolio. However, the timing coincided with rapid technological changes in the lighting systems industry and new vehicle development processes. At that time, the assemblers shifted towards more simultaneous engineering and co-designing of components for the upgraded product architecture that require new development processes. Accordingly, the focus of the R&D center was to develop new capabilities for lightning products and upgrade the development process to install simultaneous engineering techniques and routines. "We had to enhance our design capabilities, to accommodate the [assemblers] requirements. We now have a team of designers that is involved in new vehicle designs from day one." (Interview, Arteb case).

Whether or not Arteb will be able to maintain its position in the market is questionable for two reasons. First, the divestment from Hella came at a critical time when the introduction of new technologies changed the market for lightning systems. Second, the industry is under massive pressure to globalize and expand its production capabilities internationally. So far, Arteb has been avoiding the pressure to globalize. The company's goal is to become the largest automotive lighting supplier in Latin America. The company is looking to leverage its leading position in Brazil, to supply other automotive markets in the region, especially Argentina. "For foreign markets, we focus on Argentina. We try to win projects in North America and Mexico, but the Brazilian Real was too strong" (Interview, Arteb case).

Arteb's position in the global automotive industry

With the decision to stay independent of Hella, Industrias Arteb made the decision to remain a relatively small and local supply firm in the Latin American region. This is a risky move in an industry that is currently consolidating on a global level, with five very large lighting system suppliers with a global market share of over 10% and a number of additional relevant companies which each have a global market share of over 3% (see Table 5.2). As a relatively small supplier, Industrias

Table 5.2 Global market share in automotive lightning systems

Company	*Global market share*
KOITO MANUFACTURING CO.,LTD.	16%
Valeo	15%
Magneti Marelli	14%
Hella	11%
Stanley	10%
Visteon	6%
Samlip	4%
Ichoko	4%
Magna	3%
ACH	3%
Other	14%

Source: Author's own summary, based on company information.

Arteb is endangered to lose relevance for the assembly firms. With no global footprint, and no relevant market share in the global market, Industrias Arteb will find it difficult to maintain its market position even in the Latin American region.

Furthermore, the lighting industry is currently undergoing massive technological changes that are coming both from within the industry and from converging trends in the automotive industry. Future technologies that are coming from within the lighting industry include the move to LED and laser supported lighting systems for enhanced visibility fields through stronger and more focused light beams that do not distract other participants in the traffic. Furthermore, headlights are increasingly developed as adaptive headlights that turn the beam around the curve for a better view. Such adapting headlights need to be connected to the steering system for correct adaptation of the light beam. Converging trends from formerly unrelated aspects in the automotive industry that have an impact on the lighting system include, for instance, automated driving. In support of automated driving, future lighting systems have to support sensors and camera systems that are part of the automated driving system. Such sensors need enhanced visibility without distracting external participants in the traffic through visible and invisible lighting to ensure proper functioning. This is achieved by integrating the lighting system into the overall automated driving system through additional feedback and data exchange and constant adaptation of lighting in dependence on weather and light conditions.

Large companies such as Koito, Valea, Magneti Marelli, Hella, or Stanley are better positioned to upgrade their products and serve future demands in the fast technologically changing environment. First of all, these companies have larger budgets for the required R&D, have easier access to financing M&A deals to buy additional technologies such as laser technologies, or build the capabilities in-house from the scratch. More importantly, however, is their integration into the value chain of the globally leading automotive assembly firms that helps them co-engineer headlights together with the assembly firms and suppliers of automated driving systems. Through the close interaction, the lightning systems suppliers stay on top of the leading-edge technology through constant exchange of information and a close relationship to the customer. Future demands and trends are discussed years before they are implemented, providing the supply firms with the necessary time to adapt to the changes.

Iochpe-Maxion

Iochpe-Maxion, founded in 1918 as a wood processor, is Brazil's largest automotive supplier and the only Brazilian supplier that made it into the top 100 list of global automotive suppliers by revenue. The groups' main products are wheels, chassis components, and frame and stamped components.

As of 2014, Iochpe-Maxion supplies all major assembly groups, such as Daimler, Ford, Fiat, GM, VW, Renault, Toyoa, Volvo, PSA, as well as Tata from India. With 30 production plants in 14 countries, Iochpe-Maxion is not just the largest but also the most internationalized Brazilian automotive supplier, generating a significant portion of its revenue outside South America (which accounts for 40.8% of its revenue): 23.9% in North America, 28.0% in Europe, and 7.3% in Asia. Iochpe-Maxion followed a very focused strategy that included a complete overhaul from its original product portfolio to achieve such impressive growth. The process started in the 1990s when the company started focusing on the automotive and railroad industries, divesting from unrelated businesses such was wood processing. In 2000, as purchasing shifted to regional structures and the pressure to internationalize increased, Iochpe-Maxion sold 50% of its railway equipment business to Amsted Industries to focus on maintaining and expanding its position in the automotive industry. The automobile business, originally one of the smallest business units, contributed 93% of the company's revenue in 2014 with the remaining 7% coming from related railroads industry.

With the shift to a global purchasing of lead firms in the 2000s, Iochpe-Maxion rapidly internationalized through a number of cross-border mergers and acquisitions. In 2009, the company entered the North American market by acquiring the wheel business of America's Meritor, which was subsequently re-named Fumagalli Automotive Wheels. In late 2010, Iochpe-Maxion acquired the wheels production plant in Mexico from the Nugar S.A.P.I. de C.V. company to further solidify its position in the NAFTA region. The Mexican operations were expanded with the acquisition of the Galaz Group in 2012. In the same year, Iochpe-Maxion acquired Hayes Leymeny, a US based manufacturer of steel and aluminum automotive wheels. To increase its firepower for the bolt-on acquisitions, Maxion continuously divested from other products, such as high value-added structural chassis components, brake systems, interior trimming, and lock systems. The company realized that it had to develop a global footprint for one component in order to stay competitive in the globalizing market environment. Refocusing the business helped Maxion to achieve this goal. However, in the process, Maxion divested from high value-added components that offer high profit margins. Maxion decided to divest from such high profit components because these components experience high levels of international competition, strong pressure for consolidation, and are effectively dominated by a handful of large incumbent supply firms from the triad region of North America, Europa, and Japan. In this environment, Iochpe-Maxion was losing in the market for high value-added components due to its limited R&D and design capabilities as well as lacking research in material sciences and process technologies.

The divestment from the high-value-added products enabled Maxion-Iochpe to aggressively internationalize through acquisitions and establish itself as one of the globally leading manufacturers in the less crowded and consolidated market environment of steel wheels, which are a relatively simple and low technological driven products. As of 2014, the wheel business makes approximately 80% of the groups automotive business, and Maxion-Iochpe has successfully established itself as a global market leader in this segment.

While the acquisitions in the wheel sector enabled the company to upgrade its wheel products, the total product portfolio of Iochpe-Maxion was downgraded through the focus on what is the simplest and lowest value-adding product of its prior portfolio. Maxion-Iochpe has established itself as a global player in a little value-added position in the global value chains of the foreign assembly groups. The downgrading process proved to be necessary to catch-up in a segment where the global competition had no advantage through advanced technologies that could not be quickly developed by the Brazilian company.

Maxion's position in the global automotive value chain

The internationalization and expansion of Iochpe-Maxion is one of the most impressive trajectories of any Brazilian company and one of the few success stories of firms from the emerging markets in this case study. Maxion is the only Brazilian automotive supplier that ever made it into the list of top 100 automotive suppliers in terms of revenue (2013, 2014). Through its focus on wheels, Maxion has been able to establish itself as the leading automotive wheel manufacturer in the industry, with a global market share of 10% (see Table 5.3). This is an impressive result for a Brazilian company during a time in which most Brazilian automotive suppliers lost out to international competition and were bought by foreign multinational firms. It has been made possible by focusing on a product that requires very little interaction with the assembly firms, as it has no interaction to other components in the vehicle. Hence, supply firms that originated from the same countries as the largest assembly firms had no advantage from close proximity of R&D activities to its clients. Instead, cost advantages and an effective use of funds made available from divesting from other business units enabled Maxion to rapidly expand to other regions and establish a global footprint required to become a leading firm in the wheels industry.

However, its shining success has been somewhat tarnished in recent years. Maxion dropped of the top 100 automotive suppliers list of 2015 and 2016. Maxion has little chances to make it back onto the list with its focused approach on a relatively low value-added component that shows little opportunity for above normal growth. The company has an extremely focused product portfolio compared to most other

Table 5.3 Global market share in automotive wheels

Company	*Global market share*
Maxion Wheels	10.1%
Central Motor Wheel Co., Ltd.	5.1%
Dicastal	3.8%
Enkei	2.9%
Topy	2.9%
Wanfeng	2.7%
Ronal	2.7%
Mefro	2.6%
Borbet	2.6%
Magnetto	2.2%

Source: Author's own summary, based on company information.

top 100 automotive suppliers. With such a focused industry specialization and little requirement for close interaction with the assembly firms, Maxion is not in a prime position to receive support from its clients to perform value chain upgrading. Since the component requires relatively little knowledge transfer between supplier and buyer and is not affected much by the current technological developments in the industry, Maxion cannot expect to expand beyond its current business through in-house capability development.

Even within the relatively simple wheel industry, Iochpe-Maxion has a strong focus on the low value-added steel wheels, rather than on high value-added aluminum wheels. Steel wheels require relatively little technological know-how or R&D capabilities. To escape its low value-added position and stimulate future growth, Maxion Wheels would have to upgrade via M&A to acquire additional technologies for higher value-added components such as aluminum or carbon fiber wheels, or diversify its product portfolio again.

Yanfeng

Yanfeng is a producer of automotive interior systems and China's most successful auto supplier. As one of two of the Chinese case studies, the company belongs to the Huayu Automotive Systems Co., Ltd. (in the following HASCO). HASCO is the component manufacturer subsidiary of the SAIC Motor Corporation Ltd., China's largest state-owned automotive producer that has joint ventures with Volkswagen and General Motors since 1984 and 1998 respectively. HASCO is the largest automotive component supplier in China. As a holding company, the HASCO conglomerate consists of 28 business branches that are active in a wide range of components. The 28 business branches range from wholly-owned subsidiaries to joint ventures with foreign partners. As part of the SAIC group, the pre-existing network ties that SAIC had developed to foreign companies proved to be instrumental in Yanfeng's later success. As a subsidiary of HASCO, Yanfeng had strong relationships with assembly groups since its inception: "At the moment we make 60 % of our revenues from SAIC [including their two joint-ventures with VW and GM] and 40 % from external OEMs, but we provide parts and services to all OEMs in China" [interviewee, Yanfeng case]. Most of the senior management of Yanfeng and its parent company HASCO previously worked in the assembly joint-ventures, where they were able to establish personal relationships with the foreign assemblers. This included the chairman Hu Maoyuan (previously a managing director of Shanghai GM) and the vice president Xun Yizhong (former deputy manager of the cylinder shop and assistant to the plant manager of Shanghai VW). Through its network ties, Yanfeng was able to rapidly internationalize and develop into a large multinational supplier. Yanfeng's foreign investment projects have been linked closely with its relationships to foreign firms. Yanfeng utilized its business networks at two different levels. First, it exploited the vertical networks with General Motors, which it previously established in China. Second, it drew from its horizontal network ties with its international joint-venture partners.

Yanfeng originated as a joint-venture between HASCO and Visteon, a US based leading supplier of electronic components. "We are expanding into the global markets using the joint-ventures. . . . We are expanding into the US, into Germany, into developing and developed markets" [interviewee, Yanfeng case]. The horizontal relationships also provided learning opportunities to increase its international competence: "Through the joint-ventures, Chinese managers get international experience, because they have to travel overseas to the joint-venture partner" [interviewee, Yanfeng case].

Initially, all technological capabilities originated from its joint-venture partner Visteon, which had a centralized R&D center in Michigan, USA. Over time, Yanfeng was able to take over some core activities from its joint-venture partners, and thereby upgrade its position in the global automotive value chain through process, product, and functional upgrading. Opportunity arose when Yanfeng's joint-venture partner Visteon had to file for bankruptcy in the US in May 2009. HASCO (Yanfeng's parent firm) was able to inject capital into Yanfeng-Visteon. Through the capital injection, Yanfeng-Visteon was able to build much needed production facilities in Harrison Township, Ohio, close to GM (operational in 2011). The bankruptcy of Visteon in 2009 was the first opportunity to become technologically independent from the foreign competitor. Yanfeng was able to acquire the electronics business from Visteon and buy out Visteon from the joint-venture, including all of the Visteon operations in the US (Hertenstein, Sutherland, and Anderson 2017). The takeover enabled Yanfeng to rebrand the former joint-venture, and establish a strong independent brand name "Yanfeng" rather than 'Yanfeng-Visteon.' This was partly because the Visteon brand was "not strong enough" and had a tarnished reputation [interviewee, HASCO case], but mostly to expand the presence of its own brand internationally, in order to strengthen its own network position within GM's global value chain. The acquisition also marks Yanfeng's first large international investment and is a significant commitment to its network ties with General Motors. The operations that Yanfeng acquired from its joint-venture partner Visteon supplied General Motors in the US. The injected capital from HASCO and the integrated operations from Visteon enabled Yanfeng to further rapidly develop an international footprint within General Motors business network. New production facilities were built in Kalol, India (in 2011).

In August 2013, four years after the initial investment, Visteon agreed to sell its remaining shares in the joint-venture to HASCO for US$ 1.2 billion. At that time, Yanfeng-Visteon had already established three locations outside of China, two in the US and one in India. These now became fully integrated into Yanfeng and performed under the Yanfeng brand. Through its investments, HASCO committed to the business network of General Motors and has become a global supplier of interior trimming and seating to General Motors, eliminating the relationship with its former joint-venture partner Visteon. It has fully established its position in General Motors' business network, with the necessary scale and global presence to fulfil this role without further horizontal network partners.

International R&D configuration of Yanfeng's electronics business

Due to the historic trajectory, the USA still plays a central role in the R&D activities of Yanfeng's electronics business and enables the company to closely interact with its US customers during the vehicle development process. Because of its strong market presence in China, and the growing localization of R&D activities of large assembly firms in China, Yanfeng established an R&D location in Shanghai, China. Many testing facilities have been relocated to China to build the capabilities in the company's home market. Nevertheless, the R&D center in the USA still plays the central role for Yanfeng's core product development and as source of core technologies and the new product development capabilities. The Chinese R&D location is mainly involved in product adaptation and customization. Capabilities for core product development for indigenous Chinese assemblers in China is only gradually being developed as the Chinese assemblers build up their development capabilities.

Break-through and making of a global giant

Yanfeng's break-through came through its ties to a second joint-venture partner. In 2015, after Yanfeng-Visteon had turned from joint-venture to wholly-owned subsidiary of HASCO, Yanfeng founded a new joint-venture, the Yanfeng Automotive Trim Systems Co. Ltd, together with Johnson Controls. The joint-venture was created when Johnson Controls divested from the majority of its interior business. As the interior business suffered for many years from low profit margins, Johnson Controls pivoted its business model to focus on its core businesses: heating and cooling equipment, controls for buildings, and batteries for cars (the company carved out its automotive seating business a year later, which created Adient – the world's leading automotive seating business). In the new joint-venture, Yanfeng owned 70% of the shares, while Johnson Controls retained the remaining 30%. The joint-venture immediately became the world's largest supplier of automotive interior systems, as it continued all of the former operations from Johnson Controls interior business. It produced cockpit systems, central consoles, door panels, and roof systems.

As the majority holder, Yanfeng's brand name was used for the new joint-venture. Overnight, the Yanfeng brand became a recognizable and serious brand in the automotive supply business. Since all of Johnson Controls' former interior operations were integrated into the joint-venture, Yanfeng Interior Trim had a global footprint with more than 90 manufacturing sites in over 17 countries and global customer base from inception. Yanfeng relocated headquarter of the joint-venture to Shanghai, while all remaining operations remained untouched. This means the core product development is still located in the US, as is the majority of the business activity. Nevertheless, an additional R&D center was created in China to strengthen the capabilities for the increasingly important market.

Through the Yanfeng Interior Trim joint-venture, Yanfeng joined the ranks of one of the largest automotive suppliers in the world – and China's most recognizable brands in the automotive industry. In the 2015 top 100 supplier list by revenue, Yanfeng ranks 18th, the highest rank of any supply firm from the emerging markets ever reached (Automotive News 2015).

Yanfeng's position in the global automotive value chain

Yanfeng is the most successful automotive supply firm from emerging markets and has recently established itself as a leading company for interior parts in the highly competitive automotive market. The company focuses on door panels, instrument panels, and consoles for the assembly firms. In order to achieve such growth, Yanfeng, as a subsidiary of HASCO, skillfully utilized its close ties to SAIC and its two joint-ventures with Volkswagen and General Motors to grow on the back of the rapidly growing Chinese market for mass produced vehicles. In order to gain access to leading edge technologies, Yanfeng initially relied relatively little on cross-border M&A but instead established alliances through technology assistance agreements and in particular joint-ventures with leading automotive suppliers such as Visteon or Johnson Controls. When opportune, Yanfeng used the crisis of its partners to acquire additional shares and gain more control over its joint-ventures or entirely take over the operations, as in the asset-swap with Visteon. Through such moves, Yanfeng has been able to establish the 70–30 joint-venture Yanfeng Automotive Interior Systems Co., Ltd. together with Johnson Control, which immediately became the largest automotive interior supplier in the world. With an approximate market share of 24%, Yanfeng overtook the likes of Faurecia or Grupo Antolin and the captive suppliers Hyundai Mobis and Toyota Boshoku (Table 5.4).

Yanfeng's market share for interior systems in general is not equally reflected in all business units. For instance, in the automotive seating business, Yanfeng does not yet play a key role in the global market, despite its joint-venture with the market leader Adient. The two giants Adient and Lear are far out of reach for Yanfeng, and even the followers Toyota Boshoku, Magna, and Faurecia each have significantly larger market shares (Table 5.5).

Table 5.4 Global market share in automotive interior business

Company	*Global market share*
Yanfeng	24%
In-house	20%
Faurecia	14%
Grupo Antolin	7%
Hyundai Mobis	7%
Toyota Boshoku	6%

Source: Author's own summary, based on company annual reports.

Table 5.5 Global market share of automotive seating companies

Company	*Global market share*
Adient	34%
Lear	16%
Toyota Boshoku	7%
Magna	6%
Faurecia	6%
TS Tech	2%
Other	28%

Source: Johnson Control Investor Relations information.

Nevertheless, Yanfeng in undeniable one of the most successful cases of automotive supply firms from the emerging markets and has established itself as a core tier-1 supplier to assembly firms.

YAPP

YAPP is a global supply firm of plastic fuel tanks for passenger cars and commercial vehicles. The company was founded in 1988 and is part of the HASCO group. With 24 production locations and operations in Germany, India, USA, and Russia, YAPP has become one of the largest automotive plastic fuel tank suppliers in the world. Compared with Yanfeng, YAPP has been less reliant on foreign technologies since its inception. Instead, the company focused on building own capabilities in-house for what was initially a niche market. In the 1990s, all fuel tanks were made of steel. Even in the early 2000s plastic fuel tanks played a minor role in the auto industry and were the exception rather than the rule. But because fuel tanks offer a significant cost advantage compared to conventional steel fuel tanks, YAPP has become the largest producer of plastic fuel tanks in China. Moreover, ever stricter emission standards worldwide have given the plastic fuel tank a steep rise. Plastic fuel tanks weigh about two-thirds less than those made of steel, thereby lowering overall vehicle weight to help decrease CO2 emissions. Hence, plastic fuel tanks have emerged to play a critical role for assembly firms to meet ever tighter emission standards. They also have other advantages including cost-effectiveness, biofuel compatibility, and lower corrosion. Such characteristics helped plastic fuel tanks to displace steel fuel tanks in the past years. As of 2016, approximately 80% of all fuel tanks were made of plastic. In Europe, even close to 95% of fuel tanks are made of plastic.

As a market leader during the period of rapid market growth for plastic fuel tanks, YAPP was able to move into high end, five-layer plastic fuel tanks for the China market. YAPP was able to internationalize vie Greenfield investments to establish a global manufacturing footprint with new facilities. During the time of strong global market growth, YAPP established manufacturing locations in

Australia (2010), India (2010 and 2012), Russia (2011), and Czech Republic (2012). Furthermore, YAPP developed a strategic alliance partnership with ABC Corp Fuel Systems Inc., for the US market in 2010, a company that YAPP subsequently acquired and integrated in 2014. As the General Manager of the holding company, Lui Xuewu, explained:

> This acquisition is part of our strategy to support our customers on global platforms. Over the past few years automotive [assemblers] have been moving to global platforms and we have been working with ABC to support our customers in North America.
>
> (Miel 2014)

Through the acquisition, YAPP added an additional plant in Gallatin, Tennessee. Like Yanfeng, YAPP extended the relationships it had previously established to foreign customers in China (General Motors, Volkswagen, and Ford). Through a number of international investments, YAPP was able to comply with the requirements of its global clients, which require their supply firms to have a global footprint and supply to all production plants worldwide. Each of YAPP's investments was made to establish production sites in close proximity to the production plants of a particular customer, so as to enhance its position within these business networks.

As the management stressed, the strong relationships YAPP had established in China were vital in winning these overseas projects. Moreover, localizing its production in close proximity to its customers internationally was particularly important to further strengthen its network ties (Interviewee, YAPP case). The global footprint enabled YAPP to supply its products to all large automotive assembler and serve international customers abroad. In order to support the development of its products for the vehicles of international clients, YAPP also developed an international network of R&D centers comprised of four locations: Germany, India, Australia, and the former ABC R&D center in the US. An important factor driving the international co-location to its customers is the 'simultaneous engineering' process of the global assemblers. Co-operating in R&D has become central to modern day automotive competition that use global platform strategies. As a developing supplier, whose products require adaptation and customization to the vehicle, YAPP is involved in the R&D process early on. Through early involvement in the R&D process of its customer, YAPP ensured a deeper integration in the business network and further built strong inter-firm relational ties. The early integration in the R&D process of the customer opened further learning opportunities within the network and enabled YAPP to become an early adopter of changes in technology and vehicle designs owing to its position as an insider. Through the acquired knowledge as an insider of the business network, YAPP could thereby continuously upgrade its products and positioned itself at the cutting-edge of plastic fuel tank provision. YAPP had actively sought to become more actively involved in the R&D process of its customers: "We want to engage in the global platforms from an early stage on. But we have just started to do so" (Interviewee, YAPP case). In order to effectively learn from its network and to strengthen its position within the network, YAPP hired key engineers that were former employees of its customers: "We have to hire retired experts, maybe engineers from those OEMs because they have a very smooth communication with the system engineers in the technical center in the global OEM" (Interviewee, YAPP case). The primary function of the German and US centers is research and product development, to deepen the technological ties with innovation systems on site as well as enabling simultaneous engineering of products for local assemblers.

YAPP's position in the global automotive value chain

Even though YAPP has the same mother company (HASCO), its strategy differs significantly from that of Yanfeng. Unlike Yanfeng, YAPP relied much less on external available technology and alliances with foreign supply firms. Instead, the firm internally developed the capabilities and technology that eventually led to its successful rise in the global automotive industry. YAPP's trajectory is a case of 'the right idea at the right time.'. When YAPP developed its plastic fuel tank, such fuel tanks were a niche product in the global automotive market. Over 90% of fuel tanks used at that time were made of steel, and there were no signs indicating that this would change. Only through the rapid succession of ever stricter emission standards worldwide did the assemblers start to put emphasis on decreasing vehicle weight by reducing weight of components such as the fuel tank. The rise of the plastic fuel tank market put YAPP on the map as one of the leading fuel tank suppliers based on first mover advantages and leading technology in the formerly niche product. In 2016, YAPP had a global market share of 12% in the overall fuel tank market, which puts YAPP in the top four global fuel tank suppliers, together with Plastic Omnium, Kautex, and TI Automotive (see Table 5.6). Furthermore, with its strong focus on emerging markets, YAPP is well positioned to further benefit from the fast growing automotive markets in the emerging economies.

Table 5.6 Global market share of leading fuel tank manufacturers

Company	*Global market share*
Plastic Omnium S. A.	21%
Kautex	15%
YAPP	12%
TI Automotive	11%
Others (<5% market share)	20%
Steel fuel tanks	21%

Source: Author's own table, based on MarkLines industry data.

Fuyao

Fuyao has risen to become one of only a handful of major international auto glass suppliers that dominate the global market. Less than a decade ago, Fuyao was only a local supplier in China. Since then it has dramatically transformed itself from its former position as a loss-taking state owned plant that supplied glass for water meters. It has witnessed rapid expansion in the US and Europe through which it has become deeply embedded in the value chains of most major international assembly firms. In 2015, Fuyao supplied the world's largest auto groups (i.e., VW, General Motors, Toyota, Hyundai) on an international basis and has become a main supplier for numerous well recognized brands like Mercedes-Benz, AUDI, Bentley, Ford, Honda, Nissan, PSA, and Volvo (Sevestapulo 2014).

Fuyao's vice president of global sales related to us how Fuyao's rise had been significantly shaped by its relationship with VW and how the relationship was 'extremely important' to Fuyao (Interviewee, Fuyao Glass case). The network commitment building commenced in China. A lengthy gestation period, involving building successively higher levels of commitment, preceded the foreign investment. Prior to undertaking its first FDI project in 2007, Fuyao successively established production plants in close geographic proximity to all of VW's major operation sites in China: Changchun (2000), home to VW's major joint-venture with First Automotive Works (FAW) (in operation since 1991 and VW's second largest production plant in China, employing 15,991 people), Chongqing (2001), the third largest automotive center in China, to supply VW in Chengdu (VW's third largest production plants), and Shanghai (2002), the location of VW's second joint-venture, with the Shanghai Auto Industry Corporation (SAIC).

Through the domestic investments, Fuyao assiduously developed its relationship with VW. In 2007, Fuyao started supplying to the VW Group internationally for the first time. Because of its long-standing relationship domestically, Fuyao was 'requested' by AUDI, a subsidiary of VW, to supply windows for the AUDI A6 on a trial basis for their main production location in Ingolstadt, Germany. This first FDI project with AUDI can be directly traced to Fuyao's involvement in the VW value chain in China: "The contact to AUDI was established via FAW-VW [a VW joint-venture in China], ultimately via AUDI Changchun, and their global purchasing department approached us" (Interviewee, Fuyao Glass case).

During the trial project, Fuyao acquired a local German firm, FüMo Tec GmbH for US$ 1.5 million in 2007. While only a comparatively small FDI project, it proved an important first international commitment to VW. The acquisition provided Fuyao with two key assets for the future learning development within the business network: first, the services of the CEO of FüMo Tec, who used his long working relationship with VW in tandem with Fuyao's pre-existing knowledge of supplying to VW to help Fuyao work with AUDI in Europe. His help greatly accelerated Fuyao's learning of how to do business in Europe, eventually meeting the required technological and quality standards [interviewee, Fuyao Glass case]. Second, Fuyao obtained essential complementary technologies required to supply the European market. As a manager explained: "the automotive glass companies in Europe had more value-added activities than those provided by Fuyao in China" (Interviewee, Fuyao Glass case). Fuyao used the acquisition to upgrade its product offering by adding the chemical application for the glue between the glass and the chassis, which in China had previously been carried out by the assembler.

The pilot project was highly successful and Fuyao's engagement with VW expanded: "After the A6 project followed a project for the VW Passat, and then more others" (Interviewee, Fuyao Glass case). Eventually, Fuyao became the main supplier of automotive glass for the whole VW group, which included the brands such as AUDI, Seat, Skoda, Volkswagen, and later Porsche.

Larger commitments to VW's international business network followed. In September 2013, a US$ 375 million investment led to the opening of a production plant in Kaluga, Russia (Figure 5.1). Again, this was directly linked to VW: "[they] invited us to open this production plant in Russia because of our good relationship with VW here in China" (Interviewee, Fuyao Glass case). With a capacity of 1 million units, the new production plant will serve VW's newly established Kaluga manufacturing plant but also the European market, as Fuyao planned to increase its volume to 3 million units per annum.

The relationship Fuyao established with VW in China was considered 'path breaking' for Fuyao because it was to lead to further and closer interactions with AUDI, VW, and even other foreign assemblers outside of China (Interviewee, Fuyao Glass case). Successfully supplying to AUDI in Germany solidified Fuyao's reputation for quality, which, according to one interviewee "hugely improved our brand perception" (Interviewee, Fuyao Glass case). This led to

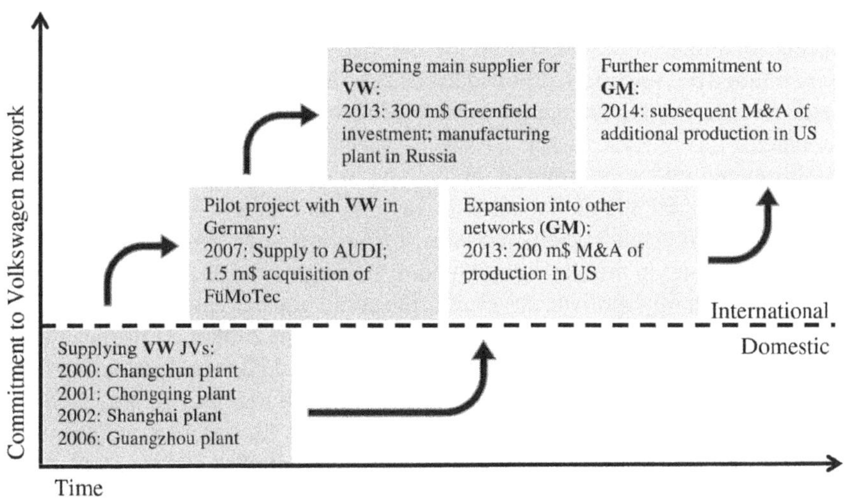

Figure 5.1 Fuyao building networks over time

Source: Hertenstein et al. (2017).

further supply chain involvement with other assemblers in different locations: "without the AUDI project, we would not have been considered an option for other [assemblers] in Europe" (Interviewee, Fuyao Glass case). This was partly because AUDI had a reputation for having the very highest quality standards, and partly because the particular windscreen for the AUDI A6 was considered to be the most complex and difficult to produce at that time (Interviewee, Fuyao Glass case). Successfully supplying this windscreen to German quality standards opened doors beyond the VW network: "After AUDI came VW, after VW came Volvo, then Jaguar and Land Rover, Bentley [which belongs to the VW Group], General Motors, BMW, Daimler and Fiat. Step by step they approached us" (Interviewee, Fuyao Glass case).

Subsequent commitments to business networks of other assemblers followed. In 2011, Fuyao made a number of smaller US investments in General Motors' network, and in 2013 bought a large former General Motors site in Dayton, Ohio. This US$ 200 million investment was at that time the largest Chinese investment in Ohio. In 2014, Fuyao acquired a US based glass production plant from PPG, a business partner it had been working with in China for 13 years and from which it had licensed technology and had a strong collaborative relationship. The acquired assets were in close geographic proximity to major US automotive manufacturers that Fuyao previously supplied in China. Through the investments, Fuyao further committed to its existing business networks and strengthened its international relationship ties with its major customers.

But it was especially the close relation established with Volkswagen in China that brought the breakthrough for Fuyao. As interviewees from Volkswagen confirmed, Volkswagen was interested in establishing a new global automotive glass manufacturer, and deliberately selected and nurtured Fuyao, supported and steered the company's internationalization and capability building, and selected projects for Fuyao that would help the company to build its capabilities. Such steps included the selection of Fuyao as the key supplier for specific windscreens, as well as encouraging the merger with FüMoTec and putting the two companies in contact.

Volkswagen had own strategic objectives in developing Fuyao. At the time Fuyao was selected, the global automotive glass market was highly consolidated and consisted of a few large companies. In Europe, four companies controlled 90% of the market in the EU: Saint Gobain, Pilkington, AGC Asahi, and Soliver. As often in such oligopolistic structures, the companies did not compete on price and enjoyed above normal profits for years. In fact, in 2008 the European Commission unveiled a glass cartel in the EU that included all four dominating firms. The fines totaled 1.384 million EUR, at that time the highest fine imposed on a cartel in Europe. In this market environment, prices for automotive glass were very high in Europe for years, and Volkswagen wanted to put pressure on the prices by establishing a new low-cost competitor in the EU. The low-cost producer Fuyao, with which Volkswagen had made positive experience in China, was selected for this purpose and gradually developed to be able to compete in the European market.

Fuyao's position in the global automotive value chain

Fuyao is one of the most impressive cases of a company that has been able to catch up with global competition in terms of technological and manufacturing capabilities, market share, global footprint, and involvement in the vehicle development process of its customers. After its rapid and aggressive internationalization, Fuyao has been able to develop a manufacturing footprint that enables the company to service its clients in all key automotive production hubs. Moreover, Fuyao has been able to break into the group of leading automotive glass companies in the world, despite its highly consolidated nature and high entry barriers. In 2016, Fuyao was among the largest four automotive glass manufacturers in terms of revenue, amidst the traditional firms such as Asahi Glass, Saint-Gobain, and Nippon Sheet Glass (see Table 5.7). While data for sales units is difficult to obtain, it can be expected that Fuyao exceeded the other producers, given its low cost advantage in recent years (Interview, Fuyao case and VW case).

Fuyao showcases a classical example of value chain product upgrading via the acquisition of products complementing the existing products in the portfolio, which enabled the company to play a more important role in the value chain. The case furthermore highlights the key role the automotive lead firms play in the development of the supply firms, in particular for latecomer firms from the emerging markets that have to fight their way into the global industry through the development of firm specific advantages in conjunction with its clients.

Even more importantly, however, Fuyao has been able to develop an R&D capability that is on par with its foreign rivals. Through its close ties to the assembly firms, in particular Volkswagen, Fuyao has been able to get involved in the vehicle development process of its clients. While car glass has little interdependencies with other components, and hence involvement is more one-directional and does not require heavy bi-directional knowledge and information exchange, it is still considered a key component of the vehicle, and suppliers are managed very carefully by the assembly firms. After all, the glass is one of the defining characteristics for customer perception of the final product. Despite this, Fuyao has been able to meet the quality and design requirements of its international clients and has

Table 5.7 Revenue of largest automotive glass manufacturers

Company	*Revenue mUS$*	*Origin*
Asahi Glass Co (AGC)	$3,681.1	Japan
Saint-Gobain S.A.	$3,128.0	France
Nippon Sheet Glass Company (NSG)	$2,676.0	Japan
Fuyao Glass Industry Group Co., Ltd.	$2,398.8	China
Xinyi Glass Holdings Limited	$484.2	China

Source: Author's own summary, based on company annual reports.

been able to establish itself as a trusted supplier even for the highest demands of luxury vehicles in the western markets.

Lawrence of the Huaxiang Group

Ningbo Huaxiang Electronic Co., Ltd. is a tier-2 supplier of electronic components and interior solutions. Its interior trim business unit illustrates the depth of value chain orchestration by lead firms in the automotive industry. The interior trim business unit was originally organized in an independent legal entity and marketed under the brand 'Lawrence Automotive.' The interior business produces door trims, door panels, wooden trims, center consoles, pillars, dashboards, grills, and provides instrument panel assembly services. The following case study solely focuses on the interior business of the Huaxiang Group.

The interior business was built through a number of cross-border acquisitions of established automotive suppliers in the advanced economies. The Huaxiang Group acquired Lawrence in the UK in 2007, a supplier of high-grade wooden interior panels for luxury vehicles. "The way we do things: we buy companies. . . . That is an easier and much faster way of doing it [than developing new technologies/products and related capabilities]" (Interviewee, Huaxiang case). Huaxiang relocated the operations to China, established manufacturing in the city of Ningbo but maintained the development and marketing capacities in Europe. This acquisition proved instrumental in building the necessary capabilities for Lawrence Automotive and the subsequent development of the interior business in the Huaxiang Group.

What followed was a number of additional cross-border acquisitions: Veneer Manufacturing Center in the UK in 2010, Northern Automotive Systems in the UK in 2011 and Northern Engraving Corp in the US in the same year. Through the subsequent acquisitions in the US and Europe, Lawrence Automotive extended its product portfolio with complementary products such as aluminum trims, door, and dashboard interior assembly and plastic molding. Finally, in 2016, the interior business under the 'Lawrence Automotive' brand was acquired and integrated into the Ningbo Huaxiang Electronic Co., Ltd. – a formerly independent company that is part of the Huaxiang Group belonging to the same owner.

What is most fascinating about this case is the level of influence the assembly groups, in particular Volkswagen, had over the Huaxiang Group during its time of capability building and reorganization of its business activities. In the interviews, the CEO of Lawrence Automotive emphasized the close relationship to Volkswagen, and how being part of Volkswagen's business network helped the company to build capabilities and elevate its position within the automotive value chain. This is odd, as Lawrence is a tier-2 company, supplying its components to tier-1 suppliers that then supply the assembly group with readily assembled doors or consoles. Lawrence automotive has no direct supply contract with Volkswagen. Yet Volkswagen had significant influence on Huaxiang. It appears Volkswagen exercised a level of control over Huaxiang that is unexpected for companies that have no direct supply contract.

Even though Lawrence is only a tier-2 supplier to the assembler, it has developed a very close relationship to Volkswagen. Volkswagen oversaw the reorganization of the production processes of Lawrence through regular company visits in the new manufacturing location in Ningbo to approve the production line and methods. Through its supplier development program, Volkswagen established a continuous support of Lawrence in China to develop its manufacturing capabilities to meet the requirements and standards of production for the German assembler. Its process optimization development program also included support and alignment regarding supply chain management, to ensure just-in-time and just-in-sequence delivery to the tier-1 supplier and assembler of panels and to mitigate potential disruptions in the supply chain. Even though Lawrence has no contract to supply directly to Volkswagen, as it suppliers to another tier-1 supplier, Lawrence had to be approved by Volkswagen as a tier-2 supply firm to the tier-1 supplier of doors and consoles.

Even long-term ties between Volkswagen and Lawrence that go beyond the initial operational reorganization and relocation of manufacturing to China were established. This includes simultaneous engineering process of vehicles in the Volkswagen group and Lawrence's interior products, which are important for customer perception of the final vehicle. Engineers from Lawrence and Volkswagen are in regular contact to fine-tune drawings, discuss finishes, and finalize production methods. Strategic decisions made by Lawrence are being influenced by Volkswagen, such as the expansion and development of complementary capabilities via mergers and acquisitions and the expansion of Lawrence to foreign locations via cross-border acquisitions.

But Volkswagen's influence and value chain governance did not end with the tier-2 supplier Lawrence. Volkswagen reached even deeper into the value chain to orchestrate the extended activities. For instance, supply firms to Lawrence, tier-3 suppliers in the Volkswagen value chain, had to be approved by Volkswagen. When Lawrence wanted to substitute the supplier for specialized glue between the wood trim and the plastic holder, Volkswagen insisted it would have to approve the supply firm. In the end, Volkswagen was not satisfied with the proposed new tier-3 supplier, and Lawrence had to keep using the special glue provided by BASF, which has previously been approved by Volkswagen. This illustrates how tightly Volkswagen is controlling its upstream value chain, and goes to show how far the orchestrating activities of lead firms can go in its GVC.

Huaxiang's position in the global automotive value chain

Huaxiang is a case with many similarities to Yanfeng but a very different trajectory. Like Yanfeng, Huaxiang entered the interior trim market. However, unlike Yanfeng, Huaxiang has used a different strategy and has seen very different results. While Yanfeng relied heavily on joint-ventures with leading foreign multinational suppliers, Huaxiang opted for M&A in order to acquire foreign technological capabilities, know-how, and access to a foreign client base. This somewhat limited Huaxiang's ability for rapid growth, as the company had to put a lot of effort into ramping up production in China, complying to quality standards set by international customers, maintaining the knowledge and development capabilities, while being constrained to its own financial resources with no external joint-venture partner. Even though the initial customer base from the acquired target Lawrence UK was based in Europe and in particular the UK, orders shifted with the production capacities to China. The same customers, most importantly Land Rover and Jaguar, shifted orders of wooden panel trims for European based production lines to its newly opened assembly line in the Chinese joint-venture Chery Jaguar Land Rover. While the Chinese automotive market has been the fastest growing market in the world, the market for luxury components such as wooden panels still lags behind the mature markets in Europe and North America. Lawrence put too much focus on the Chinese market, to some extend neglecting the European and North American market and thereby missed a chance to establish itself as a globally leading supplier of wooden panels. Therefore, Huaxiang has still a long way to go to become a truly global automotive supplier and is currently an insignificant player in the highly consolidated global automotive interiors industry.

ASIMCO

Founded in 1994 by an American citizen, ASIMCO is one of the largest, private-owned components manufacturers in China. Located in Beijing, the company supplies to both Chinese and global automotive markets. The company offers engine and chassis products: powertrain products, including fuel injection systems, piston rings and castings, rotating electrics, cylinder blocks and heads, camshafts, and aluminum castings. It also offers chassis products, including air compressors, brake drums, disc and slack adjustors, rubber products like engine mounts, isolations and dampers, seals for braking systems, semi-active suspension mounts, and plastic brackets. In addition, the company offers powdered metal products and starters and alternators. ASIMCO is a remarkable case study exemplifying the struggle of companies from emerging markets to upgrade within the global automotive value chain beyond a certain point.

Since its inception, it has been the strategy of ASIMCO to use capital and technology from the US and Europe to establish a leading automotive supply firm for the growing market in China. To this end, ASIMCO started off by establishing a number of joint-ventures for a wide variety of products. In 1994, two joint-ventures were founded: ASIMCO Meilian Braking Systems and ASIMCO Tianwei Fuel Injection Equipment Stock for diesel engines. Additionally, ASIMCO NVH Technologies was founded as a wholly-owned subsidiary. One year later, in 1995, three additional joint-ventures were created: Hubei Super-Elec Auto Electric Motor, with its daughter joint-venture Remy Electricals Hubei Company and Yizheng Shuanghuan Piston Ring. After initial struggles to fight corruption and establish a trusty relationship with the top management in its joint-ventures, ASIMCO established two additional business branches in 1997 and 1998: ASIMCO International Castings as a joint-venture, as well as an additional ASIMCO Castings company as a wholly-owned subsidiary.

Through the rapid successive creation of business units mostly with foreign partners, ASIMCO was able to quickly meet the product requirements of the local industry. However, to get to a new level and upgrade its quality, ASIMCO realized it had to start exporting its products and serve international clients in the high demanding advanced economies. This proved to be a major challenge for ASIMCO. As one interviewee put it:

> At first, we did not understand the clients at all. . . . For instance, one of our components was 2 grams too heavy. . . . This is a 2.5 kg component, and we were only 2 grams off! But they would not approve it this way. . . . It was a difficult learning experience. It took us weeks to manage and reduce [the weight]. . . . The international clients challenged us to achieve this, and we really learned a lot. Not how to manufacture lightweight components, but how western engineers think and how we had to adapt to meet their requirements.
>
> (Interview, ASIMCO case)

Despite the early difficulties, ASIMCO managed to raise its quality and become approved by multiple international clients. In 1999, ASIMCO exported components to advanced economies for the first time, to Delco Remy and BOSCH. Additional international clients followed, and more and more of ASIMCO's products were approved by global automotive suppliers and assemblers for use in advanced economies. After the increasing success, additional joint-ventures were established with the ASIMCO Foundry and ASIMCO Camshaft in 2003 and 2004 respectively.

In 2004, shortly after the initiation of its two new joint-ventures and its growing international success, ASIMCO started to transform its business. The focus shifted from an investment-oriented strategy to an industry-focused supplier that puts the specific needs of its clients first. The company was renamed 'ASIMCO Technologies Limited.' With its new strategy, ASIMCO initiated a new focus on building sustainable firm specific advantages through internal R&D and innovation.

To this end, ASIMCO set off to acquire foreign suppliers in order to obtain leading edge technology. In 2004, the company made its first notable cross-border acquisition of the camshaft plant of Federal-Mogul Corporation. In 2005, it acquired NVH Concepts LLC in the US. To utilize its cost advantage from China, operations were relocated to China. Additionally, ASIMCO started to build a number of R&D centers for its different business units. In 2006, ASIMCO Shuanghuan opened a Research and Development center for the development of piston rings. Two years later, in 2008, ASIMCO Shuanghuan created an alliance with the Chinese Academy of Sciences to further strengthen its piston research center. Later in the same year, ASIMCO Shendian launched the development of start-stop starters. In 2013, ASIMCO Shuanghuan established additional joint-ventures with the US and Japan based ASM and NPR supply firms, to further strengthen its technological know-how and R&D capabilities. Six independent new products were developed for international companies such as JMC, SFH, Cummins, and Weichai, marking the first success of its own R&D capabilities. A further R&D center was established by ASIMCO Shanxi in 2014, for the development of castings like cylinder blocks and cylinder heads.

Nevertheless, the company struggles in its efforts to upgrade from a 'produce per blueprint' supplier to a developing supplier. While continuous relationships in particular to international customers such as Volkswagen, Cummins, General Motors, or Daimler helped the company to upgrade its processes and be able to manufacturing contemporary products, the company made little progress to break into the category of developing or even better innovating supply firms. To this date, ASIMCO is essentially a 'produce per blueprint' sub-contractor that receives the drawings from its clients to manufacturing components to the requirements of the client. The development and design activities for each component are done by the assembler or tier-1 supplier. The strategy to build own R&D capabilities and become a developing supplier has not paid off as of 2016. The top management is acutely aware of the challenge to upgrade to the next level:

> We are only what we call a PPT ['produce per blueprint'] supplier. . . . We are like a service company with no own intellectual property. We provide manufacturing services. But the part designing is done by the client. This is where the real value is created. And we don't have this yet – and we don't know how to get there.
>
> (Interview, ASIMCO case)

Another interviewee made an example:

> Even though we produce the five C of an engine [key components of combustion engines: connecting rod, cylinder head, cylinder block, camshaft, and crankshaft], we are not able to upgrade and produce the entire engine like Cummins, let alone develop our own engine. We produce all parts, but don't have the assembly capabilities. But even more critical, we are not experts on how engines work – we don't know how to design the components.
>
> (Interview, ASIMCO case)

The assembly and developing of engines require a different set of capabilities than manufacturing components based on drawings received. Developing such skills in-house and from the ground up proved to be extremely difficult. Ten years after putting emphasis on the development of such capabilities, ASIMCO is still at the beginning and has made only little progress towards its goal to become a developing supplier for such complex systems as engines.

While the company has not been able to become an engine assembler, let alone developer, it has been able to successfully build up development and innovate capabilities in other categories, like NHV components.

> We build engine mounts. . . . Those have to absorb the vibrations from the engine for years. In the past, they used to be made from rubber. We developed own hydraulic engine mounts. . . . This is a better way to build them, with a fluid chamber insight to dampen the vibrations. But manufacturing is difficult.

> It requires top-notch technology – and we can now do so. We were the first [supplier] in China [to produce hydraulic engine mounts].
>
> (Interview, ASIMCO case)

Therefore, over 12 years after launching its initiative to build own development and innovative capabilities, ASIMCO has shown the ability to do so, albeit for relatively simple components and not entire systems.

ASIMCO's position in the global automotive value chain

While ASIMCO has been one of the most successful independent Chinese automotive supply firms and has become one of the largest automotive suppliers in China based on revenue, the company plays an insignificant role in the global automotive market outside China. In its main components, ASIMCO has not been able to establish a global footprint of any significance, despite recent capital injections of its new owner Bain Capital.

In the global disc brake market, ASIMCO has not been able to break into the leading group of global suppliers. The disc brake market is dominated by four large suppliers Nissinbo, Federal Mogul, Akebono, and ITT, each of which have a global market share of over 15% (see Table 5.8). The remaining 23% of the market constitutes of a multitude of smaller companies with regional or market niche focus, such as brake manufacturers for high performance vehicles, for specific commercial vehicles, or for companies with a strong regional focus like ASIMCO in China.

Similarly, in the global piston rings market, ASIMCO plays a minor role (Table 5.9). While ASIMCO has been able to solidify its position in the Chinese market, in particular for larger diesel engines used in commercial vehicles, it has not

Table 5.8 Global market share of disc brake suppliers

Company	*Global market share 2014*	*Origin*
Nissinbo/TDM	21%	Japan
Federal Mogul/Honeywell	21%	USA
Akebono	19%	Japan
ITT	16%	Italy
Other	23%	

Source: Author's own table, based on MarkLines data.

Table 5.9 Global market share of piston rings suppliers

Company	*Global market share*
Federal Mogul	60–70%
Mahle	10–20%
Reihnmetall Automotive	>5%

Source: Author's own table, based on report from European Commission.

been able to break free of its dependency on the Chinese market and into international waters.

References

Automotive News. 2015. "Top 100 Global OEM Parts Suppliers." *Supplement to Automotive News.*

Comission of the European Communities. 2007. "Case No COMP/M.4456 – MAHLE/DANA EPG." *Journal of the European Union* C (27): 25.

Hertenstein, P., D. Sutherland, and J. Anderson. 2017. "Internationalization Within Networks: Exploring the Relationship Between Inward and Outward FDI in China's Auto Components Industry." *Asia Pacific Journal of Management* 34(1): 69–96.

Miel, R. 2014. "China's Biggest Fuel Tank Maker Getting a US Foothold." *Plasticnews.*

Sevestapulo, D. 2014. "The Monday Interview: Cao Dewang, Chairman of Fuyao Glass." *Financial Times.*

6 Towards a theory of network orchestration

The GVC literature emphasizes the notion of power to explain how mostly large multinational firms can orchestrate the value chain (Dembinski 2009; Sturgeon 2008). Through consolidation of industries, large multinationals have been able to create global value chains in which power asymmetries enable the lead firms to govern and control the activities beyond the boundaries of the firm (Cantwell 2013; Nolan 2001; Sturgeon 2002). Through a new wave of globalization, the power asymmetries increased on a global level (Dembinski 2008; Milberg and Winkler 2013). Theories of the multinational firm also appreciate the role of the MNC as a powerful firm (Buckley and Casson 1976; Casson 1987). Yet, the notion of power has never been conceptualized for economic governance in the context of globalization and the role of the MNC as a lead firm in GVCs. So far, GVC scholars turned to the concept of governance in transaction cost theory to explain the mechanics of lead firm power and orchestrating activity (Gereffi, Humphrey, and Sturgeon 2005). While the transaction cost theory has greatly contributed to our understanding of the nature of the firm, the degree of internalization a firm chooses, and the mechanics of governance between firms, it appears to have only limited explanatory power to explain the influence and orchestrating activities of some powerful firms in the GVC.

This chapter lays out the contours for a theory of lead firm orchestration and inter-firm governance based on power asymmetries. The theory evolves from the research findings and reflects it in light of what has previously been developed in transaction cost theory, the GVC literature, and the literature on power in political science. The theory is based on the argument that the increased power asymmetries have altered the mechanics of governance. New forms of governance have emerged that cannot be explained by contemporary theory. Therefore, the theory of economic governance needs to be extended to be able to explain the observed phenomena.

The contemporary theory of governance

The leading theory on governance mechanics is based on transaction cost theory (Casson 1986b; Coase 1937; Williamson 1979). Ronald Coase ingeniously described the transaction cost principle, what became the basis model for modern transaction cost economics (Coase 1937, 1984). The concept of governance is a cornerstone in transaction cost theory and concerns itself with the questions how to control processes that lie outside the boundaries of the firm, i.e. are performed by another firm. In transaction cost theory, a firm either internalizes or externalizes processes of the overall value chain for a final product. For instance, it can be better for a firm to internalize a process in order to avoid the cost of transportation or the cost of information transfer. At the same time, a firm can externalize other processes to allow market forces to lower prices through the principle of supply and demand. A firm is assumed to always choose the setup with the least cost (Coase 1937).

The degree to which a company internalizes a process influences its level of control. In the neoclassic economic literature, governance structures are often simplified to distinguish between the two extremes of hierarchy and market structures (Casson 1987; Williamson 1998). In a hierarchy structure, the firm has fully internalized the processes in scope, i.e. owns the processes, even if they are embedded in a separate legal entity that is owned by the parent company. It is assumed that the parent company has full control over its internal processes and subsidiaries. In a market structure, the firm chooses to buy a good or service from an independent source in a free market. In this case, the firm is assumed to have little to no control over the processes involved in the creation of the good or service. For such simplification, neoclassic governance theory has received much criticism (Williamson 1996). Hybrid forms of governance are often ignored in the literature, despite being an integral part of the theory (Casson 1987; Gereffi et al. 2005; Williamson 1979, 1996). Transaction cost theory and the mechanics of governance explicitly outlined hybrid forms of governance in contract relations (Casson 1987; Williamson 1996). Yet, research on hybrid forms of governance has been relatively scarce. In such hybrid governance forms, firms can exert a certain degree of control over others, without the necessity of full ownership (Casson 1986b).

According transaction cost theory, hybrid forms of governance are based on and can be measured through contracts. Choosing contracts as unit of analysis to understand non-ownership governance mechanics has been practical as the act of enforcement can be observed in the court. As Hennart describes:

> Contracts are promises, enforceable in court and valid over a specific amount of time . . . contracts reduce enforcement costs by defining, for the life of the contract, actions that would breach the promise and the compensation to be paid to the damaged party.
>
> (Hennart 1982)

The written contracts clearly outline the incentives to keep the promise and consequences of breach. It is enforced by a functioning legal system that can inflict the consequences upon the firm that breaches the contract. But the understanding of hybrid governance forms has evolved over time and so has the role of contracts. There are principally two types of hybrid-forms of governance explored in the literature: (1) forms of mixed control, in which the focal firm has only partially internalized the subsidiary to gain partial control over the processes based either on partial ownership or based on contractual arrangements like alliances or licensing; and (2) forms of market-type buyer-supplier relations in think markets, which are based on neoclassic elastic contracts.

Casson developed a typology of hybrid forms of governance based on partial control of the processes (Casson 1987). In his typology, Casson distinguishes between six types of governance forms. The first is *outright control*, where the parent's equity stake needs to be high enough to give outright control. The second is *joint-venture*, which gives the parent less control, but in which the parent's equity stake is high enough to have some control over quality and price of product. The third type is an *industrial co-operation agreement*, which is a similar form to the joint-venture but set in a time limit. The fourth form is *subcontracting*, in which the parent retains all control over intellectual property but hands over control over production and quality to the sub-contractor. The fifth type is *sales franchising*, in which the partner purchases products from the parent for sale, mostly under the same brand name. The sixth and final type is *licensing and production franchising*, in which the parent receives a fixed fee for produced or sold units (see Table 6.1).

Table 6.1 Definitions of contractual arrangements

Arrangement	*Control allocated to*			
	Parent	*Partner*	*Other partner*	*Comment*
Main types				
Outright control	APM	–	–	Parent's equity stake need not be 100% but is sufficient to give outright control
Joint-venture	APM	PM	–	Parent's equity stake need not be 50%, but is sufficient to give some control over quality and price of product
Industrial co-operation agreement	APM	PM	–	Similar to joint-venture, but with time limit on equity holding
Subcontracting	AM	P	–	Partner receives mainly a fixed fee for each finished unit supplied to parent
Sales franchising	AP	M	–	Partner purchases product from parent mainly for a fixed fee
Licensing and product franchising	A	PM	–	Parent receives mainly a fixed fee for each unit produced (or sold)
Some other possibilities				
Chain management	A	P	M	
Interlocking joint-ventures	APM	P	M	

Source: Casson (1987).

A: advantage, P: production, M: marketing

As seen in the table, the parent firm is assumed to have advantages in each of the governance forms. Advantage refers to proprietary advantage that comes from superior technology, brand recognition, or cost efficiency (de Bretani, Kleinschmidt, and Salomo 2010; Scalera et al. 2014).

Williamson explored hybrid forms of governance in thin markets, made possible through elastic contract law, which allows the establishment of long-term contracting in the context of (bilateral) dependency of the involved parties (Williamson 1996). In classical contract law contracts are static, not elastic. Any deviation from the contract is a breach. Rules are strictly applied and in case of dispute, contracts are interpreted in a legalistic way (Williamson 1996). This is not always the preferred option. For instance, it may apply that despite breach of contract it is in the best interest to both parties to continue to uphold the agreement. Neoclassic contract law allows for elastic contracts that relieve the firm from strict legalistic enforcement (Williamson 1979, 2002). Elastic contracts contain special adaptation mechanisms to restore efficiency after unforeseen disturbances to facilitate long-term inter-firm relations. This is important if dependencies are involved in the relations. To enforce such elastic contracts the courts are not necessarily involved. Litigation is substituted by arbitration as the main forum to handle disputes (Williamson 1996). Through elastic mechanisms employed in the contract, the two parties can find a solution through mediation (Williamson 1979, 1985, 1998). Elastic mechanisms are such that allow the two parties to jointly find a solution of the lowest cost to both. Instead of hard and defined penalties, both parties have an interest in finding a suitable solution. An example of such an elastic mechanism in a contract is from the supply agreement between Northwest Trading Company and the Nevada Power Company, as quoted in Williamson's book:

> In the event an inequitable condition occurs which adversely affects one Party, it shall then be the joint and equal responsibility of both Parties to act promptly and in good faith to determine the action required to cure or adjust for the inequity and effectively to implement such action.
>
> (Williamson 1996: 96)

Elastic contracts therefore need to contemplate unanticipated disturbances, state tolerances for the disturbance, define information disclosure in the event of a disturbance and define escalation to arbitration if voluntary agreement fails (Williamson 1996). Even in the event of highly consequential disturbances, when the contract reverts back to a legalistic regime, "neoclassic contract law averts truly punitive consequences by permitting appeal to exceptions that qualify under some form of excuse doctrine" (Williamson 1996: 97). As Macneil argues, even the legal regime acts modest in enforcing the keeping of promises (Macneil 1974). The ability to legally enforce the keeping of promises is limited by the severity of the consequences – be it in the relation between firms or within the firm.

The limitations of a theory based on contracts

The mechanics of governance in transaction cost theory are based on contracts (Casson 1987; Coase 1984; Williamson 2002). As a theory of contractual relations, it is limited to explain the relationship between two or more parties that entered a contractual agreement. However, some of the cases described in this book indicate that lead firms can influence other firms without the basis of a contract. While a contract can also be an oral agreement, the contract as a unit of analysis in transaction cost theory is intended to be enforceable by law, which is often difficult with no written documentation. Yet, firms can influence each other. It appears that enforcing contracts is not the only basis to employ power, to influence other firms, or to control and govern a firm's value chain. This is best exemplified by the case of the Huaxiang Group, a tier-2 supplier with no direct supply relation to Volkswagen. Despite the absence of a supply contract, Volkswagen developed close ties to the supplier. Volkswagen made regular firm visits for the approval of the production setup and processes in China, a prerequisite to become an approved tier-2 supplier. Volkswagen furthermore required a quasi-open book relation to assess the capabilities and efficiency of the tier-2 supplier. Through the supplier development program, Volkswagen further helped to develop Huaxiang to become more productive. And the influence did not end at Huaxiang. The penetration of Volkswagen's governance went one level deeper. Core suppliers of Huaxiang, which are tier-3 suppliers to Volkswagen, had to be approved by Volkswagen before supplying to Huaxiang. In the case described by interviews from Huaxiang, the selected supplier for a glue was not approved by Volkswagen, and Volkswagen demanded that BASF would supply the glue in the manufacturing of components that would eventually go into Volkswagen vehicles.

How can firms exert control over suppliers in the second tier? One option that can be explained by contemporary governance theory is to gain control over lower tier suppliers is by establishing direct contractual relations with the supply firms. In this case, the value-adding activities are sequentially spread out among multiple supply firms – all of which have direct contractual relations to the lead firm. The lead firm owns and provides the technical drawings to all firms. As studies in the 1980s have shown (Casson 1986b, 1986a), the extended supply base can indeed be part of the contractual realm, when the materials or blueprints for production are owned by the parent firm and undergo several processing steps in the value chain, each by independent firms. For efficiency purposes, logistic flows are established directly between the involved supply firms without the lead firm in between. But the parent firm maintains control over the production or process steps by owning either the material or the intellectual property such as technical drawings required for the process steps. Blue prints, technical drawings, materials, and tooling are provided by the lead firm, and only manpower, machinery, and processing capability is provided by the sub-contractor (Casson 2013).

Such arrangements involve contracts, to define ownership, license agreements, and such arrangements between the parties, regardless of the logistical process and

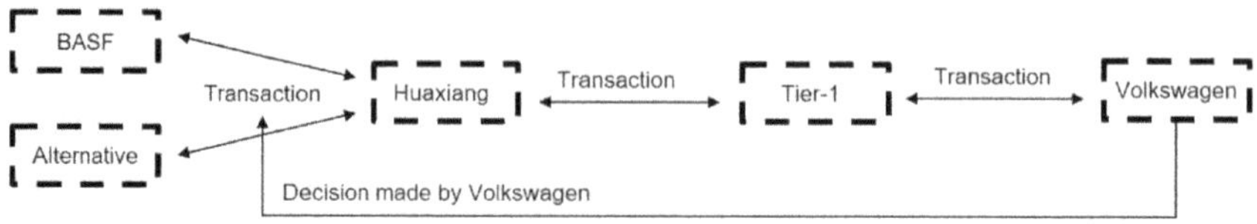

Figure 6.1 Governance and influence beyond direct suppliers
Source: Author's own figure, based on field research.

the question where the component is shipped to for further processing. However, such a contractual setup has not been the case with Huaxiang, which had no supply contracts with Volkswagen. In the observed setup Huaxiang has a contract with a tier-1 supplier that assembles the side panels for vehicle doors. The transaction is between Huaxiang and the tier-1 supplier. There is no direct supply contract between Huaxiang and Volkswagen and no direct transaction between the two firms. Yet, Volkswagen influences Huaxiang by not approving Huaxiang's choice for a new tier-3 glue supplier. Thereby, Volkswagen established a degree of control over Huaxiang, which shows the depth of value chain orchestration of Volkswagen and calls into question contemporary governance theory. The setup is not a unique phenomenon. Other research has found similar setups of lead firm influence on non-direct suppliers (e.g. Dembinski 2008).

The general literature on economic governance cannot explain the influence Volkswagen has over Huaxiang. As a theory of contracts, its explanatory power is limited to that of contractual arrangements, intended to be enforced by law. The theory is inherently unable to explain inter-firm relations and governance mechanics that have no (written) contract as a basis and are not enforced by law. The general assumption would have to be that Volkswagen has no degree of control over Huaxiang, as influence is created and enforced via contracts. Yet, multiple interviews of people involved in such setups revealed that there is very direct contact between the two firms, that Volkswagen influences decisions of Huaxiang and exerts a certain degree of control over processes and decisions made at the company, and that Volkswagen has a governance approach in place that includes non-direct suppliers in the second and third tier of the value chain (Interviews with Lawrence, Volkswagen, BOSCH, and Witzemann). By controlling transactions along the value chain the lead firm can influence transactions, even if not directly involved (see Figure 6.1). Therefore, the theory of governance needs to be adapted to explain such phenomena.

The limitations of contract enforcement as a source of power

The source of power as a base for contemporary governance theory is the law and the enforceability of a contract. This limits the source of power a firm has over another. Enforcing a contract is not the only way or preferred option to exercise power. In the case studies, the globally aligned product architecture changed the quality requirements and thereby the consequentiality of the contracts between firms. Consequentiality refers to the consequences from a breach of contract in the context of thin markets in which the involved firms are interdependent on one another. The breach of contract can either be a conscious decision by one party or a result from (operational) issues that prohibit the company to comply with the contract. Such instances can be accidents, like a fire at the production site, accidental errors or flaws in the product.

Williamson refers to instances as 'disturbances' of the contract (Williamson 1996: 96). He differentiates between three kinds of disturbances: inconsequential, consequential, and highly consequential. Inconsequential disturbances do not justify any mitigation, as the associated costs would exceed that of the disturbance. Consequential disturbances on the other hand can require mitigation. Highly consequential disturbances are such, in which the cost of terminating the contract is lower than mitigating the issue that has caused the disturbance. Hence, in the case of highly consequential disturbances, handling reverts back to classic contract enforcement.

Through several changes in the production and value chain setup, Volkswagen has become dependent on its suppliers to a degree that distorts the consequentiality of contracts. First, through the reduction of globally available supply firms for specific components, Volkswagen has become dependent on the few supply firms available in the market. Second, through lean production with zero stock practices, Volkswagen has to rely on timely deliveries. And third, by increasing the use of common parts in global vehicle platforms, Volkswagen relies on the same supply firm for very large volumes and on multiple production sites, increasing the cost associated with any disturbance. Such components can be used across multiple vehicles and in a variety of markets across multiple countries. This leads to a much wider use of components from the same design drawings and from a few production lines, which increases the risk associated with design flaws or production process errors. The wide use of a component enhances the cost associated with malfunctions based on design or production flaws. Where in the past such errors would impact only few vehicles that used the component in some countries, it now impacts many different vehicles types produced and sold around the world. A disturbance for one component can lead to recalls of large magnitudes and with very significant cost implications. The effect of such recalls can be observed in the automotive industry that has been plagued with increasingly large and widespread recalls in recent years. In the case of a malfunctioning component, the firm closest to the customer (i.e. assembler) suffers the most direct consequences of loss of quality and brand perception by the customer.

Even though some of the costs can be passed on to the supply firm that caused the issue, it is not always a feasible option for the assembler. The burden of the recall might cause additional disturbances with greater costs for the buyer, like the insolvency of Takata during the 2017 airbag recall. The cost of such an insolvency of a rare supplier in the supply base forced the assembler to switch supplier at a cost that can exceed the cost of the disturbance. Because of the oligopolistic structure of the value chain in combination with zero stock, dependencies have increased to an extent that additional disruptions in the supply chain can lead to even higher disturbances. Additionally, the assembler can be confronted with further opportunity costs in case the number of supply firms for a certain component drop below a certain level, at which the prices for the component increase. As there are typically only a handful of alternative supply firms, additional disturbances like insolvency of single firms can have an unwanted impact on the global supply base structure.

In the oligopolistic market environment, with high interdependencies between the firms involved in the value chain, it appears there can be a point at which the total cost of terminating a contract increases so drastically, that it exceeds the cost of mitigation (Figure 6.2). Drastic measures like termination of a contract are only viable under the assumption that alternative sources for the product are readily

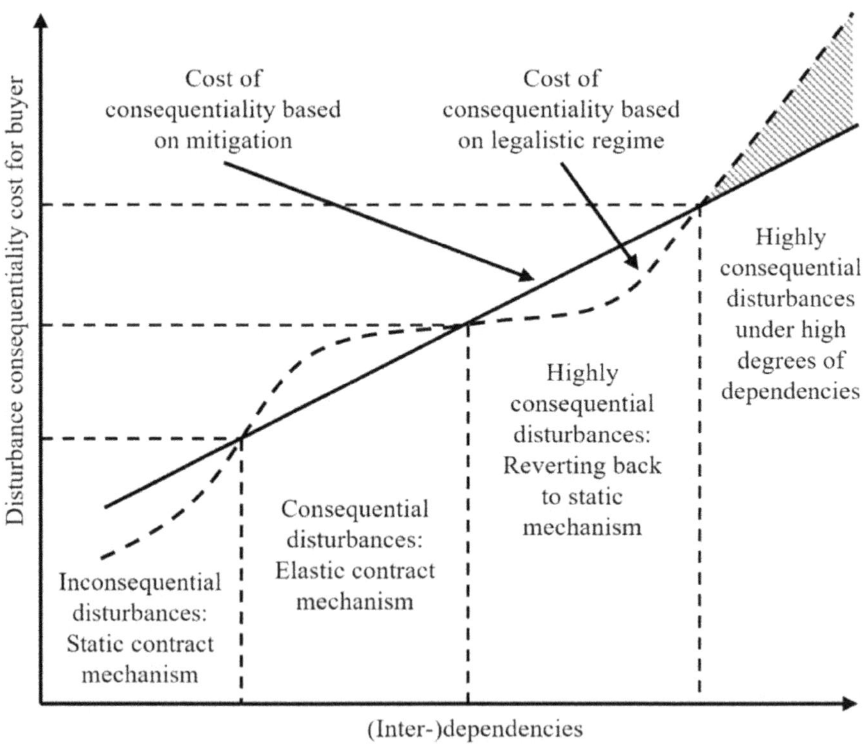

Figure 6.2 Consequentiality costs in highly interdependent environments

Source: Author's own figure.

available, as in the case for some but by far not all components. The product architecture and value chain setup of Volkswagen has drastically increased the company's dependency on key supply firms to the degree that even highly consequential disturbances have to be handled via mitigation, with no alternatives for immediate drastic measures. In such instances, reverting back to enforcing the law is not the optimum solution. The law, as a mechanism of power and control through enforement of the contracts, has become a toothless tiger. Yet, companies establish long-term relations, and lead firms can influence their suppliers, showcasing their increasingly powerful position in the value chain. Consequently, the law cannot be the sole basis of power for the lead firm. If the enforcement of the law is not the only source of power to influence other firms, other sources must exist.

A theory of orchestration based on power

In this chapter, a new theory is proposed to explore the inter-firm dynamics of value chain orchestration in a globalized economy. The new theory is not based on contracts but on power asymmetries between two or more parties. It is argued that *power* enables a firm to exert a degree of control over other firms. While the source of power can stem from the law, it is not the only source of power. The unit of analysis is not the contract between two firms but the power asymmetries in inter-firm relations.

In the proposed theory, power asymmetries between firms substitute the regime of external arbitrage, litigation, and the enforcement of the law. Rather than a contract enforced by law as its source of power, each party can have a number of means to execute power. For instance, the threat to cease the supply relation beyond the current contract duration in the context of thin markets with high interdependencies results in opportunity cost for the supply firm. Such a threat can be greater than the legalistic consequences of a breach of contract during its term. In an environment of great inter-firm dependencies such as in the oligopolistic automotive industry, the consequences that derive from the opportunity cost from a damaged long-term inter-firm relation can be more severe than the consequences of the law. Such long-term inter-firm relations are formed around common objectives and are based on trust that is carefully built over time, and they include joint planning, strategizing, and managing and controlling of activities (McDermott and Corredoira 2010; Park and Hong 2012).

This is a progression from the governance theory based on neoclassic contract law. In classic contract law, the ability to enforce the keeping of promises was based on consequences of the law. In neoclassic contract law, it is based on two instances: first, arbitration, so that the involved parties can find the common ground of least cost for all involved parties, and second, the law, if arbitration fails to solve the dispute. The consequences of breach of contract are therefore defined through negotiations in arbitration and the law. In the cases of highly interdependent relations legal consequences can be fully replaced by arbitration. This can only function if the consequence by arbitration are more severe than the legal consequences (Figure 6.3). Inter-firm relations, then, are not based on contracts but on the power to inflict changes.

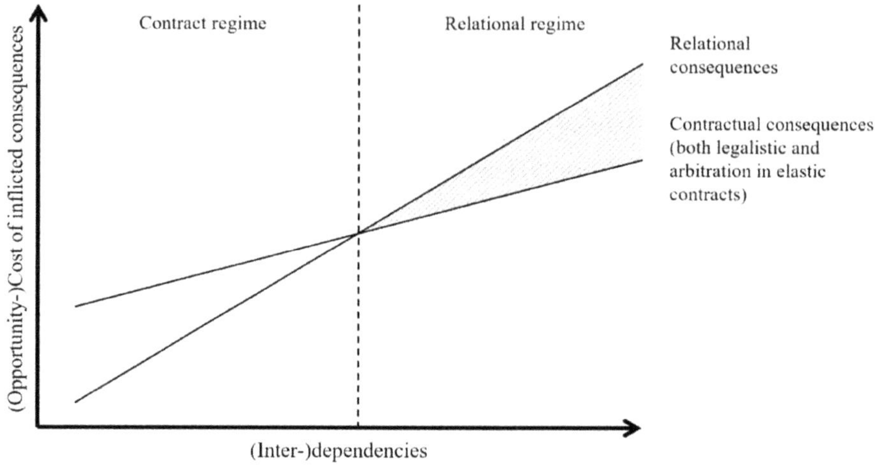

Figure 6.3 From classic contract law to non-contractual governance
Source: Author's own figure.

Definition of power

For the development of the theory, earlier conceptualizations of power from political science were used, in particular from Dahl and Galbraith (Dahl 1957; Galbraith 1983). Dahl defines power as "A has power over B to the extent that he can get B to do something that B would not otherwise do" (Dahl 1957: 202f). Power is thereby a relational value between two (or more) parties. The parties involved can be individuals, groups of people, organizations, institutions, or in this case firms. For simplicity reasons, the theory outlined here concerns itself with the power-delta between just *two* parties, even though in reality it is often the case that multiple actors are involved in any given decision and oftentimes with conflicting propositions and reactions to the outcome. The two parties will be called *influencer* and *reactor*. In some instances in the literature terms like "submissive" are used for the reactor (e.g. Dahl 1957; Galbraith 1983), but it is important to note that the *reacting* party may not necessarily be found to be the weaker of the two – it is simply the party that reacts on the proposition of the *influencer*, i.e. does something it would otherwise not do. Moreover, the power asymmetries between the two actors are not static but dynamic in nature. One firm does not have a given amount of power over another. Instead, the power asymmetries appear to be spontaneous and bound to a decision in the context of a specific situation. Furthermore, in many instances, both parties may play both roles of influencer and reactor simultaneously. Such is the case in any win-win scenario, in which both parties were able to assert what is important to them – and compromise in what is important to the other party. In such scenarios both parties can be equally seen as influencer and reactor.

The source of power

The power to influence the reactor is based on different sources. The theories of the MNC have taken 'powerful' positions in the form of its monopolistic position of a firm as a prerequisite condition for its internationalization (Buckley and Casson 1976; Casson 1987; Johanson and Vahlne 1977), and it is quite tempting to accept such a position as a prerequisite for power. However, it is necessary to be cautious not to oversimplify the potential sources of power, else the explanatory power of the theory is limited to mostly large firms with monopolistic positions. While a monopolistic position in the market can be a source of power, it is by no means the only source.

In his study about politicians, Galbraith identified three sources of power: *Personality*, *property*, and *organization* (Galbraith 1983). *Personality power* in the context of Galbraith's research about politicians is described to derive from personal attributes, such as great appearance and strength, ability to produce clear and resounding speeches, and power exertion and the like, which can create loyalty and trust in the ability to inflict either coercive or compensatory measures. In the context of inter-firm relations, similar properties can be said to derive from corporate brands, charismatic individuals representing companies, or marketing efforts by the company. *Property* as a source of power provides the influencer with the ability to compensate the reactors, e.g. by paying a premium in a transaction, offering long-term contracts or other benefits to the reactor. *Organization*, sometimes called legitimate or positional power (Pierro, Cicero, and Raven 2008), is the power given by a position held by the influencer.

The instruments of power

The influencer can make use of several instruments to wield power. In his work on the 'Anatomy of Power,' Galbraith identified three types of instruments to exert power: *Condign* power, *compensatory* power, and *conditioned* power (Galbraith 1983). *Condign* power is often called coercive power and is based on the ability to inflict or threaten adverse consequences sufficiently high so that the reactor abandons his or her preferred alternative (Raven 1992). Conversely, *compensatory* power works with the offer of affirmative reward that gives value to the reactor upon the reactor's compliance. Finally, *conditioned* power targets at changing the reactors belief through persuasion, education, and reasoning so as to influence the decision "to what seems natural, proper or right" (Galbraith 1983: 6). The decision of the reactor thereby reflects his own preferred alternative, with no promise of incentive or threat from the influencer. While the first two types of power are easy to understand from the point of view of profit maximization for the reactor, the third type is more subtle and may not be found in the context of transactions. Nevertheless, firms can use conditioned power as a means to orchestrate their value chains and to achieve their strategic objectives. And indeed, all three types have been observed in the case studies summarized in the table as follows (Table 6.2).

Table 6.2 Examples of exerted power instruments

Situation	*Power-delta in situation*	*Strategic objective of influencer*	*Instruments*	*Base*
Situation: HuaXiang wants to change its glue supplier, but Volkswagen does not approve the new supplier	**Influencer:** Volkswagen **Reactor:** HuaXiang	Maintain quality standards, by not approving the new tier-3 supplier	Condign	Threat of losing future business, if HuaXiang does not comply
Situation: Volkswagen invites supply firm (Fuyao) to collocate production in Europe	**Influencer:** Volkswagen **Reactor:** Fuyao	Lower cost of components (wind screen glass) in particular location (Europe)	Compensatory	Incentivization, by providing security of revenue through long-term supply contract
Situation: BOSCH encourages the merger of two supply firms (A and B)	**Influencer:** BOSCH **Reactor:** Supplier A and supplier B	Consolidate supply base to strengthen suppliers and decrease complexity	Conditional	BOSCH proposes a favorable alternative scenario to the supply firms; no threat or incentive necessary

Source: Author's own table, based on case studies.

Combining the sources and the instruments of power

The instruments of power can be linked to the sources of power they rely on. For an organization to exercise *compensatory* power, the most prevalent source of power stems from *property*, so that the influencer can incentivize the reactor. The core mechanism for compensatory power is to make one alternative the most attractive from two or more alternatives. In most cases, influence through compensatory power will lead to a transaction of the two parties involved. However, the transaction does not have to take the form of a sale. The resources a company can offer can vary, from monetary incentives like offering long-term contracts to access to goods, knowledge, networks, processes, or other rewards. Access to goods can include access to new technologies, to manufactured goods, or to particular raw materials. Access to knowledge can be granted through licensing of intellectual property rights, exchange of tacit knowledge through meetings or joint projects, or information exchange for consulting services. Access to networks can include access to a particular network of other powerful players such as organizations or individuals, or to the network of potential buyers. Access to processes can refer to access to service offerings a firm provides, e.g. by providing access to all established distribution system to the final customer. Intangible rewards can include prestige from membership to certain organizations, or from receiving awards or certificates that add to the value of the brand.

For an organization to wield *conditional* power the influencer needs superior or additional knowledge vis-a-vis the reactor. Since convincing the other party occurs without the promise of compensation or the threat of penalty from either of the two parties, the source for the change of mind comes from somewhere else. In the case of conditioned power, this stems from a knowledge gap between the two parties. The influencer has additional or superior knowledge that the reactor does not have and shares it with the reactor to influence the decision of the reactor in a way that is favorable for the influencer. This mechanism works under the assumption that once the information has been shared, both parties will come to the same conclusion as to what is the favorable alternative. It furthermore requires imperfect knowledge distribution between the two parties, as the two parties need to have either incomplete information regarding the alternative or incomplete information for the interpretation of the alternative options. The knowledge advantage can stem from the influencer's position and embeddedness in the value chain that grants the firm superior access to gain new knowledge, which can be described as a form of *organizational* source of power. Alternatively, superior knowledge can stem from the creation of new knowledge through R&D, a form *property* source of power. Note that there are two states of mind between the two parties, with a time lapse between the two states. At first, the two parties do not agree upon the favorable alternative. Once one party has convinced the other, both agree and have the same understanding. This form of power does not require a transaction or investment from the influencer, yet the influencer can gain from influencing the reactor by sharing (selected) information. This form of power can thereby easily be misused in a manipulative way. In order to establish a power delta and wield power over the reactor, it thereby requires the reactor to trust the influencer that the influencer is honest about his own interest in the matter and does not give false or incomplete information in a way that is not in the interest of the reactor. This form of power thereby builds on trust an organization has established over time, which gives the organization its authority and the information its legitimacy (Dietz and Gillespie 2011).

Condign power can utilize the sources of *personal*, *property*, and *organizational* power. For instance, personal power can be utilized by threatening the influence of external third parties in a way that negatively impacts the reactor (e.g. through disclosure of specific information to the public). This source of power can be used to enforce corporate social responsibility policies to combat child labor in the extended value chain. Condign power can be based on organization power, for instance in the context of public monopolies, in which a government corporation is the sole provider of a good or service. But mostly, condign power is based on property, with the threat of withdrawing from a relation and not renewing supply contracts. The effect of condign power based on property is especially increased in the context of dependencies of the involved parties because it increases the effect of the inflicted adverse consequences on the other party. Dependency arises when there is a lack of attractive alternatives for a given decision.

Dependency can arise from a multiple of sources. The most obvious form is the enforcement of the law, in particular if the two parties have entered a contractual agreement. In this case, the organization has the power to force the other party to uphold the agreed terms and conditions in the contract or else to inflict the consequences for a breach as outline in the contract. Both parties depend on the contract, as long as the alternative to breach the contract is less attractive. As in transaction theory, firms can obtain power by capturing a monopolistic position in the market (Bain 1956; Chamberlin 1933; Robinson 1933). A high degree of consolidates means that fewer alternatives are available, leading to higher dependencies. If the market shows oligopolistic features along the value chain, key firms along the entire value chain are difficult to substitute. If a firm is difficult to substitute, other firms become dependent on it – be it as a buyer of components from a non-substitutional supplier or as a supplier to a large firm in an oligopsonic market. If firms can control bottlenecks in the value chain that are crucial for the entire value chain, they can become the sole influencer and controller of the bottleneck (Ponte et al. 2014). Such a crucial link or position in the value chain can be established through superior product knowledge of essential components, systems integration capabilities required and owned by just one firm, or unique access to the market (Gibbon, Bair, and Ponte 2008; Nolan 2001; Teece 2014). A third source of dependency comes from asset-specificity. Asset specificity increases the dependency of one firm to another – the higher the asset-specificity, the higher the degree of dependency (Williamson 1979, 1981). Asset specificity describes "the degree to which an asset can be redeployed to alternative uses and by alternative users without sacrifice of productive value" (Williamson 1996: 59). This means investments of a high asset specific nature only have value for the particular transaction or customer to which they were made for. If the transaction is not concluded, the investing firm would have to depreciate its investment at great loss. Hence, the investing firm is dependent on the realization of the transaction. Transactions that involve high degree of asset specificity are often remunerated by long-term relations (Carney 2005). The literature distinguishes between several kinds of asset specificity, of which five are commonly used (Williamson 1996). The first type is *site specificity* – if one firm commits to invest into a particular site for a specific customer, for instance by collocating production to a particular customer. The second type is *physical asset specificity*, such as customized tooling or dies that can only be used for a particular customer. The third type is *human asset specificity*, by which a particular skillset is embedded in certain employees that have been fired for a particular transaction. The fourth type is *brand name specificity* – if a brand has value for a particular use or purpose, to which it is attached. The fifth type is *dedicated assets*, which are discrete investments that are made at the behest of a particular customer. The higher the asset specificity of a transaction, the higher the dependency between the two firms.

A fourth source of dependency stems from the product architecture and features, in particular the relevance of a component for the final product. Gereffi et al. argued that the degree of required knowledge-transfer in a transaction, together with the ability to codify such knowledge, is a source of interdependencies (Gereffi et al. 2005). Furthermore, if the product architecture is integral, the companies involved have a higher need for knowledge sharing compared to an open architecture. Open architecture is given when the interfaces are known and standardized beyond the boundaries of the firm or firms involved in the production of the final product. For instance, industry norms define interfaces for open architectures. A closed architecture, on the other hand, is given when products information, technical drawings, and interfaces between components are customized for a particular final product of a firm, and the information is handled as proprietary information of the firm. Only the firms directly involved in the production receive the required information from the lead firm that owns the technical information. Detailed designs are only known to the firm and can be subcontracted to an outside firm, but the basic design of the tool system is contained within one company (Fujimoto 2007). Moreover, if the component is highly relevant, e.g. for a key function of the final product or because it is important for the product perception of the end-user, the buyer is dependent on the supplier's quality (Park and Ro 2013).

A fifth type of dependency derives from the capability delta between buyer and supplier, which is reflected in the supply-setup of the two firms. For instance, 'produce per blueprint' suppliers depend on the R&D capability of the buyer. Reversely, the buyer depends on the R&D capability of innovating and developing suppliers, which develop their own parts and components.

Power delta

The power delta describes the degree to which one firm can influence the other. It is often, but not always, based on dependency as a source of condign power. Dependency can be unilateral, if one party is dependent on another. It can also be bilateral, if both parties depend on one another. For unilateral or asymmetric bilateral dependency, the hypothesis is that the higher the dependency of organization A is on organization B, the larger the potential power delta between A and B, with B having power over A. If dependency is bilateral, and both parties are interdependent on one another, then the organizations will develop long-term relations based on trust. But a power delta can also be based on the sources of power that are available to the influencer for compensatory power – without the mechanism of dependency. For instance, Volkswagen and Schaeffler used the same instrument of power (i.e. compensatory power) to incentivize suppliers to collocate to their new production sites, but Volkswagen appeared to have more sources of power at its disposal than Schaeffler. Both companies used long-term contracts as an incentive to collocate. But while Volkswagen showed great success in collocating its suppliers, Schaeffler's attempt to collocate its suppliers during its own expansion to Slovakia failed. Hence, Schaeffler appears to have less resources available to incentivize its supply firms to collocate.

For a holistic understanding of the power delta it is important to consider both sides, influencer and reactor. The sources and instruments of power mentioned earlier are concerned with the influencer. Equally important are the scope and the extent to which the reactor reacts on the influencer. Following Dahl's concept of power, *scope* describes the type of response evoked, while the *extent* describes the number of comparable respondents (Dahl 1957). The reactors response is required to describe the amount of power a company has. For instance, while Volkswagen is able to enforce open book relations with its small supply firms, Volkswagen is unable to enforce the same on large supply firms such as BOSCH. While Volkswagen uses the same sources and instruments of power, it is the difference in the reactors response that is needed to fully understand the power delta between the two actors.

Developing orchestration capabilities

Owning the sources of power are an important prerequisite, but a firm must be able to utilize its sources to effectively wield the instruments of power. While the power enables the firm to enforce its strategies, the orchestration capabilities are required to effectively wield the instruments of power to manage, control, and steer the value chain in the desired direction.

Key activities for building effective orchestration capabilities include the ability to develop a deep understanding of the value chain by identifying key activities, and knowing and understanding the processes, value-adding activities, core products, and roles of different participants in the value chain. By understanding the different participants, it is possible to assess their strategic relevance and their potential power within the value chain by mapping the players on a competency-role matrix. This enables the influencer to assess its own dependency on specific participants in the value chain and thereby identify and determine the power delta between the players. Furthermore, this knowledge enables the influencer to identify capability or power gaps in the value chain, which helps identifying opportunities to further strengthen the overall value chain. The ability to develop a deeper understanding of the supply firms' processes and activities enables the lead firm to benchmark and identify capability gaps in the value chain.

A key element for the influencer is to develop strategies to build knowledge and utilize the knowledge for orchestration of the value chain. Elements of an orchestration strategy can include the reduction of supply firms to reduce overall value chain complexity, the identification of opportunities to increase efficiency of interfaces between companies, or to develop and strengthen capabilities through supplier development programs or induced M&A of two or more players in the value chain. A value chain development program, such as supplier development programs, can be useful tool to advance capabilities in the extended value chain, thereby building trust over time and advancing inter-firm ties with other players, which increases the interdependencies and builds an important source of power. A necessary requirement is to generate transparency and gain deeper knowledge of the value chain. Knowledge can be developed through open book relations, which offers deep insights into the processes of the participant and might offer insights into the extended value chain, beyond the immediate realm of the direct suppliers (Womack, Jones, and Roos 1990). Such knowledge can be acquired through supplier development programs, which can go beyond the first tier of supply firms.

The ability to orchestrate the extended value chain is increasingly important in volatile markets or converging industries that undergo rapid technological changes through disruptive innovations (Christensen 2006; Christensen, Verlinden, and Westerman 2002; Markides 2012). In the automotive industry, the large players are challenged by disruptive technological changes that require the firms to judge the viability of such new technologies and the role such technologies may or may not play in the future. Such new technologies are inherently uncertain (Christensen and Raynor 2003; Utterback 1994); yet the expertise of the industry, combined with expertise of new technologies and a high absorptive capacity and high degree of dynamic capabilities at the lead firm can enable big businesses to adapt to disruptive technologies (Eisenhardt and Martin 2000; Teece 2014; Teece, Pisano, and Shuen 1997). Capabilities to orchestrate the value chain beyond the direct suppliers will enhance the firm's ability to identify key future technologies and key firms for potential strategic alliances (Fine 1998).

Developing orchestrating capabilities is possible at different positions in the value chain and for firms with different functions within the value chain. Different industries have shown to bring forth different powerful lead firms, from large firms in the primary sector over large technology firms focusing on R&D, to large manufacturers and large retailers focusing on marketing and distribution. A key element to establish a powerful position and orchestrate the value chain is to build advantages from occupying a crucial link or position in the value chain through superior product knowledge of essential components, systems integration capabilities, or unique access to the market or resources (Gibbon et al. 2008; Nolan 2001; Teece 2014). To establish a sustainable powerful position, a firm must have competitive advantages that are valuable, rare, inimitable, non-substitutable, and exploitable (Barney 1991; Fine 1998; Porter 1987).

The mechanism of value chain orchestration beyond the first tier

The cases indicate that the lead firms have two ways to influence and control firms beyond the first tier. First, by exercising condign power and enforcing tier-1 suppliers to pass on requirements to the second tier. Such requirements can be materials to be used, the choice of supply firms, definition of processing steps, etc. In case the specifications include steps that are not performed by the direct supplier, these are passed on from the direct supplier in its contracts and technical documents to the upstream supplier, and from there to the next supplier, and so on (see Figures 6.4 and 6.5). Such practices are supported by open book relations, when the supplier

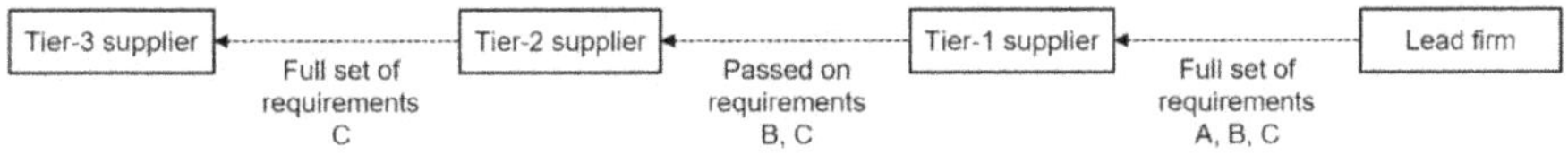

Figure 6.4 Passing on requirements in deep value chain orchestration

Source: Author's own figure.

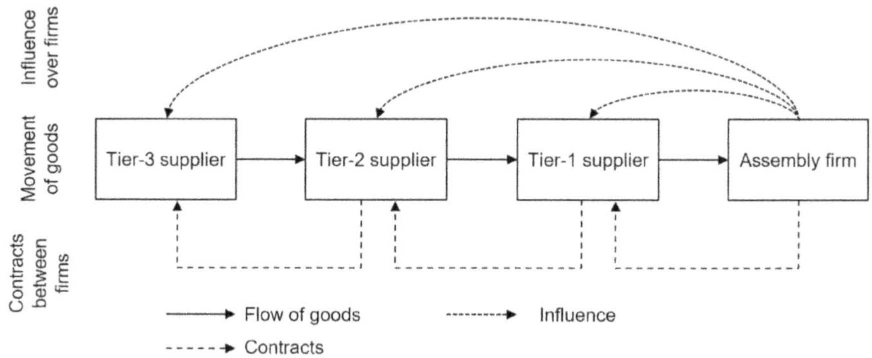

Figure 6.5 Influence beyond the supply contracts

Source: Author's own figure.

has to provide the customer a list of suppliers (Womack et al. 1990). Volkswagen exercised a form of condign power, as it threatened the supplier with adverse consequences in case of non-compliance. In the case of Huaxiang, if Huaxiang did not comply, Volkswagen would force the tier-1 door supplier to substitute Huaxiang with an alternative supplier. Given Volkswagen's size and market share in the global automotive industry, this is a serious threat, as many suppliers are at least partially dependent on doing business with Volkswagen.

Second, Volkswagen can use compensatory power and incentivize suppliers to align their strategies. For instance, Volkswagen can provide its supply firms assistance for performance improvement and process optimization through its supplier development program (including, in this example, the tier-2 firm Huaxiang). Through such services, the supplier can become more profitable, and Volkswagen gains deep insights into its value chain. Other incentives observed are extending the role of the supply firm in the value chain, e.g. by offering to collocate production in additional markets or assigning the supplier to other tier-1 firms as core supplier. For large commitments of the supply firm, such as high investments to collocate to a Volkswagen production site, Volkswagen offers long-term relationships and involvement in large projects.

Linking the theory of orchestration to the GVC framework

The theory of orchestration can be linked to the concepts of the GVC to offer new insights and deepen our understanding of inter-firm dynamics in such value chains. Power appears to be distributed asymmetrically in the GVC, enabling the more powerful firms to exert control over less powerful firms (Rugman and D'Cruz 2000). The automotive value chain resembles that of a multipolar value chain, with multiple powerful actors along the value chain, since key activities that can be dominated by one firm are spread out along the value chain

(Ponte 2014). While large assembly firms, such as Volkswagen, act as the most powerful firm and systems integrator, large sub-system suppliers such as BOSCH take on the role as systems integrator for their particular sub-system (Humphrey and Memedovic 2003; Pavitt 2003). In the past, small supply firms of niche products have been assumed to have little power and have often been neglected in the research. As shown in the case studies and developed in the theory, even small supply firms of niche products can develop powerful positions. For small firms to become powerful requires them to build resources as sources of power, such as proprietary knowledge acquired through extensive innovation or development capabilities to enable the firm to control the market for their niche product. Through such firm specific advantages, relatively small firms can gain considerable bargaining power towards the assembler. This can be illustrated with small niche producers that have their own technology and expert knowledge. One example that illustrates the important role of niche suppliers in the value chain is that of Merck KGaA, a Japan based producer of aluminum-flaked Xirallic pigments that are used in automotive paints to make the car sparkle. The company came to fame after the 2011 earthquake destroyed the company's factory in Onahama, and the entire automobile industry worldwide had to stop producing vehicles of certain colors that needed the specific pigment that was produced only by this particular company in this particular location. There was no alternative supplier available for such pigments, and it took months to reopen the production plant and start production again. Such a niche firm, little known even to industry experts, has the ability to control the bottleneck for its niche product worldwide, as no alternatives are available. This unique position in the value chain lends the firm considerable bargaining power towards its customers – so long as it can protect and sustain the firm specific advantage of a non-substitutable product.

Firms with no non-substitutional resources for power will not be able to build powerful positions. Such firms include firms with undifferentiated products, such as bulk material like nuts and bolts, or producers of mechanical parts that are subcontractor firms to which the assembler provides the blueprint. These firms have little to no ownership advantages and are interchangeable for the assembler. Because they can establish no dependency, such firms are loosely integrated in the value chain and are governed by market mechanisms, as they can be interchanged or substituted at relative low cost.

The multiple facets of power in a GVC

The concept of power in the GVC literature can be extended by introducing two sides of power. In the extant literature, the power of a firm in a specific value chain is assumed as one value for a company. A firm is assumed to either have power, or not to have power (Gereffi and Korzeniewicz 1994; Ponte 2014). This concept of power needs to be extended to enable more precise analysis of inter-firm relations based on the power dynamics between the actors in the value chain. The power of a firm is always relative in relation to its counterparts in a specific situation. In the most simplistic aggregation, the power of a firm needs to be viewed at the interface of the input-output structure, as the firm acts as buyer and supplier and has at least two facets for power: first, as buyer towards its suppliers, and second, its power as a supplier towards its customers. To illustrate why a more faceted view is required, let's assume the two sides of power as buyer power and supplier power: the producer for specialized exhaust pipes, Witzenmann, has some degree of power as supplier towards its buyers, but little power as buyer. While there are many steel pipe manufacturers available, producing pipes for exhaust systems requires expertise and knowledge in exhaust flow dynamics, heat development, and vibrant tolerance, to produce an exhaust system that can support strict emission standards, support complex in-take pressure management for turbo-charged engines, and ensure quality and durability despite extreme temperature development and constant vibrations. Such a firm offers a valuable contribution to the assembler and has unique knowledge and experience, which are of strategic importance to the assembler or the tier-1 systems integrator supply firm of exhaust systems. Only a few companies are able to produce such pipes, which lends the company a strong position towards its customers. Due to its relatively small purchasing volume, however, the firm is an insignificant buyer of steel and materials and possesses little power towards its suppliers. The 'power' of the company in the value chain can therefore differ for its two roles as buyer and supplier. Quite the opposite is true for CIE. As a large global metal processing firm, the company has developed relatively strong buyer power. As a 'produce per blueprint' manufacturer, however, it is an interchangeable supplier to the assembler and therefore has little power towards its customers.

Product architecture, value chain position and the nature of the market

Through the ongoing globalization and especially the centralization and consolidation of activities within the multinational firm, the nature of the market for intermediate goods has changed. As the MNC harmonizes its product architecture globally and centralizes its global purchasing activities, formerly separated markets become merged into a single, homogenized and global market. Through its globally centralized procurement the MNC can control a global market for intermediary goods. This is particularly the case for intermediary goods that have a high degree of asset-specificity.

Such globally harmonized markets, dominated by powerful lead firms and orchestrated as discrete value chains, have other properties compared to what is normally seen as a market. In the contemporary understanding of a market the market is defined by product type and geographic determinants such as national borders (Coase 1990). Take the market for apple juice in Germany. This market is defined by the product, apple juice, and the geographic boundaries of Germany. Both determinants, the geographic scope and definition of a product scope, are defined by the viewer. A different scope could be beverages in the European Union. The market for apple juice in Germany is a subset of the beverage market in the

European Union. Geographic boundaries are typically selected to resemble areas of a harmonized market, like similar trade legislation as found in nations, subnational economic zones, or supranational free-trade areas (Rugman and Doh 2008). Product determinants are selected by clustering similar products (ideally products that can substitute each other), into one type, regardless of the characteristics such as asset-specificity.

In the case studies presented in this thesis, markets appear to be shaped by a different set of properties. In the modern, globalized economy, for many intermediary goods markets appear to be organized in global value chains. By selecting different determinants to define a market, we can create a different view and gain a better understanding of the dynamics of such market structures. As previously discussed, value chains with hierarchical structures defined by strong inter-firm ties are often the structure of choice for products with closed-integral product architecture, i.e. high interdependencies. In such value chains, the goods are highly customized and have highly specialized properties and a high asset-specificity. The effort and costs for customization can be larger than the cost and effort for core development. The market for such highly customized intermediary goods is very narrow, as the specialized components can only be sold to a specific buyer (Williamson 1996). How narrow the market for goods with a high degree of asset-specificity is depends on the form of asset-specificity.

Two factors determine the asset-specificity: the scope of the market for the specific component and the cost of customization and the cost of redeploying the asset to a different customer. The scope of the market can be industry-wide (e.g. similar components used across all passenger cars from various assembly firms, but not used in commercial vehicles, agricultural machinery, heavy machinery, or shipbuilding), or singular to a specific buyer as in closed-integral systems (Fujimoto 2007). In the case of closed-integral products with high customization cost in relation to core development, like in the automotive industry, the market for highly asset-specific intermediary goods can be as narrow as one customer. If, in such narrow cases, the cost of customization in the relation to the cost for core development is high, so that any adaptation to other customers is as expensive as developing a new product, the market for any particular finalized product is effectively limited to the specific buyer.

The trend of increased asset-specificity falls together with the globalization of the assemblers and the global harmonization of the platform. As a consequence, value chains have become global, duplicating the buyer-supplier relations made at home in the target markets (Anderson, Håkansson, and Johanson 1994; Ge and Wang 2013). In our sample, the lead firm harmonized its product to use one globalized platform across national borders. When previously different vehicles in two countries needed different designed and manufactured components, now they require identical ones. As a result, purchasing has been globalized, and one company can be selected to supply a specific component to all production locations worldwide. For the chosen supply firm, formerly separated national markets have been merged into one harmonized global market. In such global value chains, geographic perimeters of the market are no longer primarily shaped by political borders such as national, sub-, or super-national economies are. Instead, the market is shaped by the footprint of the global buyer, i.e. the lead firm and system-integrators in the value chain (Johanson and Vahlne 2011). The global value chain with its product architecture, governance structure, and geographic expansion determines the borders and properties of the market. In cases where lead firms occupy large shares of the market, and components have a high degree of buyer specific asset-specificity, the role of a single buyer becomes disproportionately large for the supply firms. The notion of 'key accounts' has a widespread use among the supply firms, and sales managers are measured and often structured around key customers rather than countries or regions. The sales force targets particular customers across all national borders and is measured by sales to the customer, not sales by region. The focus for growing future sales is put on the 'key accounts,' i.e. 'developing key customers,' rather than generating sales in a particular country. As business networks are considered to be 'borderless,' once embedded in a value chain in one country the relationship may be replicated elsewhere. Consequently, the distinctions between international and domestic expansion diminishes in the global value chain (see Figure 6.6). 'Distance,' that played a key role in the theory of the MNC (Dikova 2009; Ghemawat 2001; Sousa and Bradley 2005), plays a less significant role, owing to the ability of inter-firm relations in GVC to bridge distances and reduce the liabilities of foreignness when entering new markets (Hertenstein, Sutherland, and Anderson 2017; Johanson and Vahlne 2009, 2011).

Moreover, production has become 'unbundled' from consumption in the modern GVC (Baldwin 2014; Milberg and Winkler 2013; OECD 2013). This is

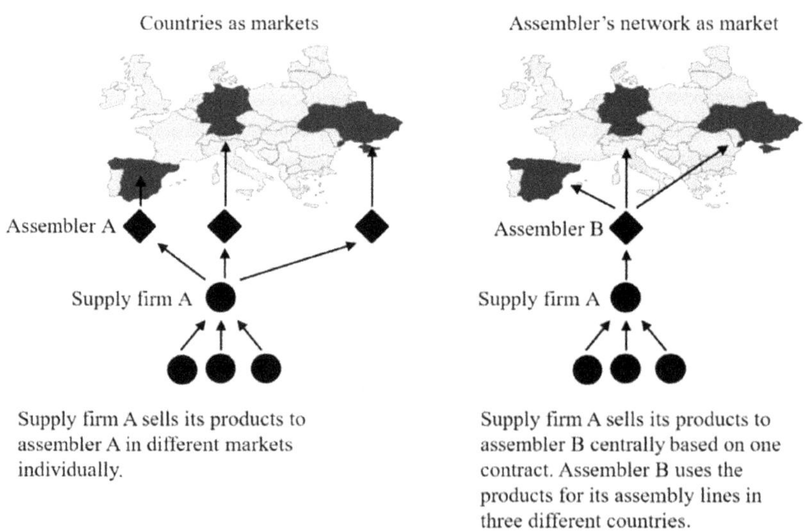

Figure 6.6 The GVC as a market

Source: Author's own figure.

particularly the case of goods with a high value over shipping cost ratio. Even though the firms in the study employed local-to-local strategies in which production is in close proximity to the final market, some components are not produced locally. Examples are electric components, such as semiconductors, or entire entertainment systems. For such components the country of origin of the supplier and the location of production has become detached from where the component is used by the buyer in the final product. Firms involved in the production of intermediary goods may not even have transparency in which country its products end up being used by the final customer.

Conclusion and outlook

This research has shown how the ongoing global business revolution has changed the organization of economic activity and the nature of the firm (Chandler 1977; Coase 1937, 1990; Nolan 2001). The global business revolution entails the restructuring of economic activities through fine-slicing of tasks, the reconfiguration of production the globalization of economic activity, including the internationalization of big business, and the liberalization of trade and capital flows and the privatization of industries. This converged with the evolution of product architecture that increased interdependencies between firms and requires new forms of cooperation in simultaneous development processes. These trends have triggered a reorganization of the firm, with new approaches to governance emerging. The 'visible hand' as postulated by Chandler (1977) has globalized through the internationalization of big business and the emergence of the MNC as a dominant force in shaping international economic activity (Milberg and Winkler 2013; OECD 2013; UNCTAD 2013). The dynamics of inter-firm relations between large and powerful MNCs and participants in their value chains have changed (Gibbon et al. 2008; Milberg and Winkler 2013; WTO 2013). The observed value chain orchestration beyond the realm of direct suppliers requires a new theoretical approach to understand the orchestration activities of lead firms. This chapter proposed a new theory, based on power asymmetries between firms.

Outlook

This research project was conducted at a pivotal moment in the development of the automotive industry. After over 100 years of dominance of the internal combustion engine as the industry's core technology, unprecedented technological changes lie ahead. This book encapsulates the competitive dynamics, the structure of the value chain, and the governance mechanics that matured over time and were developed and refined in more than 100 years of the industry. As the automotive industry is often at the forefront of developments in the economy, its current state may very well represent a peak in the development of conscious industrial restructuring and the evolving forms of governance.

In the upcoming years, the automotive industry will be shaken and changed by rapid technological changes. New technologies like the electrification of the powertrain or the advancements in autonomous driving based on intelligent systems with self-learning algorithms revolutionize the automobile and disrupt the industry. Some of the highest value-adding components of the past may be rendered obsolete if future technologies replace current technology. Some of the industry's most dominant and successful firms that owe their success to technologies relevant for the internal combustion engine may vanish, while new entrants with capabilities relevant for the new technologies will emerge to claim powerful positions in the automotive value chain. Formerly unrelated industries will converge with the automotive industry. This can already be seen, as large players from the ICT sector such as Alphabet or Amazon make advances into the automotive sector, by developing systems for automated driving, connected vehicles, and future entertainment systems. New ventures are rapidly emerging to create new technologies, like Tesla revolutionizing the powertrain, or Uber, which collects key data relevant for driverless vehicles. Existing firms, like BOSCH, react by reorganizing their business to focus on future technologies, carving out old technologies like the starter motor business that BOSCH sold in 2017. But the prevalence of new technologies is uncertain, and the future of the industry is unknown.

While the structure of the industry, its key players, and the structure of the global value chain may change, the underlying principles and theory developed in this chapter are likely to be unaffected. The theory of orchestration based on power, as developed in this chapter, is based on the literature on global value chains, product architecture, transaction cost theory, and power in political science, four streams of literature that have been used to explain dynamics observed in many different industries. The insights from this book may even become more relevant for the turbulent time that lies ahead. Understanding and effectively implementing orchestration capabilities is arguably even more critical in times of uncertainty, as conscious value chain orchestration can be a source for stability to reduce uncertainty. Recognizing the relationship between product architecture (including the characteristics of components and systems) and dynamics of inter-firm relations help opt for optimum governance. This can enable firms to efficiently select the right strategic partners for joint R&D and strategic alignment, to gain insights and learn from the developed business networks, and become more agile and resilient against disruptive technologies. Lead firms that are effective orchestrators have developed the ability to identify core components, technologies, and firms in the vast outstretches of the automotive value chain – a capability that can be transferred to identify future technologies and opportunities at an early stage and react appropriately.

References

Anderson, J., H. Håkansson, and J. Johanson. 1994. "Dyadic Business Relationships Within a Business Network Context." *Journal of Marketing* 58(4).

Bain, J. S. 1956. *Barriers to New Competition*. Cambridge, MA: Harvard University Press.

Baldwin, R. 2014. "Trade and Industrialization after Globalization's Second Unbundling: How Building and Joining a Supply Chain Are Different and Why It Matters." In *Globalization in an Age of Crisis: Multilateral Economic Cooperation in the Twenty-First Century*, edited by R. C. F. Feenstra and A. M. Taylor. Chicago: University of Chicago Press.

Barney, J. B. 1991. "Firm Resources and Sustained Competitive Advantages." *Journal of Management* 17(99–120).

Buckley, P. J. and M. C. Casson. 1976. *The Future of the Multinational Enterprise*. London: Macmillan.

Cantwell, J. 2013. "Blurred Boundaries Between Firms, and New Boundaries Within (Large Multinational) Firms: The Impact of Decentralized Networks for Innovation." *Seoul Journal of Economics* 26(1): 1–32.

Carney, M. 2005. "Globalization and the Renewal of Asian Business Networks." *Asia Pacific Journal of Management* 23: 337–54.

Casson, M. 1986a. "Contractual Arrangements for Technology Transfer: New Evidence From Business History." *Business History* 28(4): 5–35.

Casson, M. 1986b. *Multinationals and World Trade: Vertical Integration and the Division of Labour in World Industries*, edited by M. Casson. London: Allen & Unwin.

Casson, M. 1987. *The Firm and the Market: Studies on Multinational Enterprise and the Scope of the Firm*. Cambridge, MA: MIT Press.

Casson, M. 2013. "Economic Analysis of International Supply Chains: An Internalization Perspective." *Journal of Supply Chain Management* 49(2): 8–13.

Chamberlin, E. H. 1933. *The Theory of Monopolistic Competition: A Reorientation of the Theory of Value*. Cambridge, MA: Harvard University Press.

Chandler, A. D. 1977. *The Visible Hand: Managerial Revolution in American Business*. Cambridge, MA: Harvard University Press.

Christensen, C. M. 2006. "The Onging Process of Building a Theory of Disruption." *Journal of Product Innonovation Management* 23: 39–55.

Christensen, C. M. and M. Raynor. 2003. *The Innovator's Solution: Creating and Sustaining Successful Growth*. Boston, MA: Harvard Business School Press.

Christensen, C. M., M. Verlinden, and G. Westerman. 2002. "Disruption, Disintegration and the Dissipation of Differentiability." *Industrial and Corporate Change* 11: 955–93.

Coase, R. H. 1937. "The Nature of the Firm." *Economica*: 386–405.

Coase, R. H. 1984. "The New Institutional Economics." *Journal of Institutional and Theoretical Economics* 140(March): 229–31.

Coase, R. H. 1990. *The Firm, the Market, and the Law*. Chicago: University of Chicago Press.

Dahl, R. A. 1957. "The Concept of Power." *Systems Research and Behavioral Science* 2(3): 201–15.

de Bretani, U., E. Kleinschmidt, and S. Salomo. 2010. "Success in Global New Product Development: Impact of Strategy and the Behavioral Environment of the Firm." *Journal of Product Innonovation Management* 27(2): 143–60.

Dembinski, P. H. 2008. *Enhancing the Role of SMEs in Global Value Chains*. Paris: OECD Publishing.

Dembinski, P. H. 2009. "Very Large Enterprises, Focal Firms and Global Value Chains." *Revista de Economia Mundial* 23: 107–30.

Dietz, G. and N. Gillespie. 2011. *Building and Restoring Organisational Trust*. London: The Institute of Business Ethics.

Dikova, D. 2009. "Performance of Foreign Subsidiaries: Does Psychic Distance Matter?" *International Business Review* 18: 38–49.

Eisenhardt, K. M. and J. A. Martin. 2000. "Dynamic Capabilities: What Are They?" *Strategic Management Journal* 21(10–11): 1105–21.

Fine, C. H. 1998. *Clockspeed: Winning Industry Control in the Age of Temporary Advantage*. London: Little, Brown and Company.

Fujimoto, T. 2007. "Architecture-Based Comparative Advantage – A Design Information View of Manufacturing." *Evolutionary and Institutional Economics Review* 4(1): 55–112.

Galbraith, J. K. 1983. *The Anatomy of Power*. Boston, MA: Houghton Mifflin Company.

Ge, G. L. and H. Q. Wang. 2013. "The Impact of Network Relationships on Internationalization Process: An Empirical Study of Chinese Private Enterprises." *Asia Pacific Journal of Management* 30: 1169–89.

Gereffi, G., J. Humphrey, and T. J. Sturgeon. 2005. "The Governance of Global Value Chains." *Review of International Political Economy* 12(1): 78–104.

Gereffi, G. and M. Korzeniewicz. 1994. *Commodity Chains and Global Capitalism*. London: Greenwood Press.

Ghemawat, P. 2001. "Distance Still Matters: The Hard Reality of Global Expansion." *Harvard Business Review* 79(8): 137–47.

Gibbon, P., J. Bair, and S. Ponte. 2008. "Governing Global Value Chains: An Introduction." *Economy and Society* 37(3): 315–38.

Hennart, J.-F.. 1982. *A Theory of the Multinational Enterprise*. Ann Arbor: University of Michigan Press.

Hertenstein, P., D. Sutherland, and J. Anderson. 2017. "Internationalization Within Networks: Exploring the Relationship Between Inward and Outward FDI in China's Auto Components Industry." *Asia Pacific Journal of Management* 34(1): 69–96.

Humphrey, J. and O. Memedovic. 2003. "The Global Automotive Industry Value Chain: What Prospects for Upgrading by Developing Countries." UNIDO Sectorial Studies Series Working Paper, Vienna: UNIDO.

Johanson, J. and J.-E. Vahlne. 1977. "The Internationalization Process of the Firm – A Model of Knowledge Development and Increasing Foreign Market Commitments." *Journal of International Business Studies* 8(1): 23–32.

Johanson, J. and J.-E. Vahlne. 2009. "The Uppsala Internationalization Process Model Revisited: From Liability of Foreignness to Liability of Outsidership." *Journal of International Business Studies* 40(9): 1411–31.

Johanson, J. and J.-E. Vahlne. 2011. "Markets as Networks: Implications for Strategy-Making." *Journal of The Academy Of Marketing Science* 39(4): 484–91.

Macneil, I. R. 1974. "The Many Futures of Contracts." *Southern California Law Review* 47(May): 691–816.

Markides, C. 2012. "How Disruptive Will Innovation From Emerging Markets Be?" *Sloan Management Review* 54(1): 22–5.

McDermott, G. A. and R. A. Corredoira. 2010. "Network Composition, Collaborative Ties, and Upgrading in Emerging-Market Firms: Lessons From the Argentine Autoparts Sector." *Journal of International Business Studies* 31(2): 308–29.

Milberg, W. and D. Winkler. 2013. *Outsourcing Economics: Global Value Chains in Capitalist Development*. New York: Cambridge University Press.

Nolan, P. 2001. *China and the Global Business Revolution*. Basingstoke: Palgrave Macmillan.

OECD. 2013. *Interconnected Economies: Benefiting From Global Value Chains*. Paris: OECD Publishing.

Park, J.-K. and Y. K. Ro. 2013. "Product Architectures and Sourcing Decisions: Their Impact on Performance." *Journal of Management* 39(3): 814–46.

Park, Y. W. and P. Hong. 2012. *Building Network Capabilities in Turbulent Competitive Environments: Practices of Global Firms From Korea and Japan*. Boca Raton, FL: CRC Press.

Pavitt, K. 2003. "Specialization and Systems Integration: Where Manufacture and Service Still Meet." In *The Business of Systems Integration*, pp. 78–91. Oxford: Oxford University Press.

Pierro, A., L. Cicero, and B. H. Raven. 2008. "Motivated Compliance With Bases of Social Power." *Journal of Applied Social Psychology* 38(7): 1921–44.

Ponte, S. 2014. "The Evolutionary Dynamics of Biofuel Value Chains: From Unipolar and Government-Driven to Multipolar Governance." *Environment and Planning* 46(2): 353–72.

Ponte, S., I. Kelling, K. S. Jaspersen, and F. Kruijssen. 2014. "The Blue Revolution in Asia: Upgrading and Governance in Aquaculture Value Chains." *World Development* 64(12): 52–64.

Porter, M. E. 1987. "Changing Patterns of International Competition." In *The Competitive Challenge: Strategies for Industrial Innovation and Renewal*, edited by D. J. Teece, pp. 27–57. Cambridge, MA: Ballinger.

Raven, B. H. 1992. "A Power Interaction Model on Interpersonal Influence: French and Raven Thirty Years Later." *Journal of Social Behavior and Personality* 7(2): 217–44.

Robinson, J. V. 1933. *The Economics of Imperfect Competition*. London: Macmillan.

Rugman, S. M. and J. R. D'Cruz. 2000. *Multinationals as Flagship Firms: Regional Business Networks*. New York: Oxford University Press.

Rugman, A. M. and J. P. Doh. 2008. *Multinationals and Development*. New Haven: Yale University Press.

Scalera, V. G., D. Mukherjee, A. Perri, and R. Mudambi. 2014. "A Longitudinal Study of MNE Innovation: The Case of Goodyear." *Review, Multinational Business* 22(3): 270–93.

Sousa, C. and F. Bradley. 2005. "Global Markets: Does Psychic Distance Matter?" *Journal of Strategic Marketing* 13(1): 43–59.

Sturgeon, T. J. 2002. "Modular Production Networks: A New American Model of Industrial Organization." *Industrial and Corporate Change* 11(3): 451–96.

Sturgeon, T. J. 2008. "From Commodity Chains to Value Chains : Interdisciplinary Theory Building in an Age of Globalization Those of the MIT Industrial Performance Center or the Massachusetts Institute of. Technology." Working Paper, Industrial Performance Center, MIT.

Teece, D. J. 2014. "The Foundations of Enterprise Performance: Dynamic and Ordinary Capabilities in an (Economic) Theory of Firms." *Academy of Management Perspectives* 28(4): 328–52.

Teece, D. J., G. Pisano, and A. Shuen. 1997. "Dynamic Capabilities and Strategic Management." *Strategic Management Journal* 18(7): 509–33.

UNCTAD. 2013. *World Investment Report 2013: Global Value Chains: Investment and Trade for Development*. Geneva: UNCTAD.

Utterback, J. M. 1994. *Mastering the Dynamics of Innovation*. Boston, MA: Harvard Business School Press.

Williamson, O. E. 1979. "Transaction-Cost Economics: The Governance of Contractual Relations." *Journal of Law and Economics* 22(2): 233–61.

Williamson, O. E. 1981. "The Economics of Organization: The Transaction Cost Approach." *The American Journal of Sociology* 87(3): 548–77.

Williamson, O. E. 1985. *The Economic Institutions of Capitalism*. New York: The Free Press.

Williamson, O. E. 1996. *The Mechanics of Governance*. Oxford: Oxford University Press.

Williamson, O. E. 1998. "Transaction Cost Economics: How It Works; Where It Is Headed." *De Economist* 146(1): 23–58.

Williamson, O. E. 2002. "The Theory of the Firm as Governance Structure: From Choice to Contract." *The Journal of Economic Perspectives* 16(3): 171–95.

Womack, J. P., D. T. Jones, and D. Roos. 1990. *The Machine That Changed the World*. New York: Rawson Associates.

WTO. 2013. *Global Value Chains in a Changing World*, edited by D. K. Elms and P. Low. Geneva: WTO Publications.

7 Globalization and the challenge for development

Globalization and the emergence of coordinated global value chains has implications for supply firms from the emerging economies. The lead firms have globalized their procurement efforts, leading to globally harmonized markets for intermediate components and modules. Well established and technologically leading supply firms from the advanced economies have benefited from the changing environment. Their close interaction with the assembly firms helped them to rapidly develop an international footprint and gain access to new markets. Moreover, through deep involvement in the vehicle development process of the assembly firm, years before start of production, supply firms of technologically demanding integral components are constantly at the forefront of technological developments and gain insights into future demands that help them adapt their business models in a timely manner and maintain their leading-edge position in the market. The close relations to the assembler further helps the firms to embraced new responsibilities and activities in the value chain, and some were able to upgrade from component producer to systems integrator, as in the case of Brose. Firms from the emerging markets, on the other hand, saw themselves confronted with increased competition with supply firms from the advanced economies. While some were able to enter the GVC of leading western assemblers, and upgrade over time to slowly catch-up with the industry leaders from the advanced economy, others were squeezed out of the value chain.

While the case study approach can only shed light into few individual cases, the general trend seems to be supported by industry-wide data. As evident from the top 100 automotive supplier list of 2015, the global automotive components industry is dominated by firms from the advanced economies (Table 7.1). The companies from the advanced economies are firmly occupying the highest value-adding and revenue generating activities in the global automotive value chain. Only very few companies from the emerging economies partake in the global supply industry, despite the size and relevance of their markets for the global automotive industry.

Data on company R&D expenses indicates that supply firms from the advanced economies are better placed for future positioning of the companies in the industry (European Commission 2016, summarized in Table 7.2). Automotive supply firms from the advanced economies have increased their R&D expenses in recent years, which helps them to solidify their position in the global industry. On the other hand, as indicated in the case study and supported by the data on R&D

Table 7.1 Countries of origin of top 100 global automotive suppliers by revenue

Country of origin	*Sales revenue (US$ billions) in 2015*		*Number of top 100 suppliers*
	Sum of revenues	*Share of overall revenues in top 100*	
Japan	213.7	28%	30
Germany	190.2	25%	18
USA	136.5	18%	25
South Korea	47.1	6%	5
France	46.9	6%	4
Canada	39.9	5%	3
Spain	14.8	2%	3
China	13.7	2%	2
Sweden	11.1	1%	2
Italy	7.4	1%	1
India	7.2	1%	1
United Kingdom	6.5	1%	1
Luxembourg	5.9	1%	1
Mexico	4.5	1%	1
Switzerland	2.0	0%	1
Singapore	2.0	0%	1
Netherlands	2.0	0%	1

Source: Author's own table, based on Top 100 Automotive Supplier List, 2015.

Table 7.2 Top 20 automotive suppliers in R&D spending

World rank	*Company name*	*Country of origin*	*R&D spending 2015 (€million)*	*R&D intensity (% of revenue)*	*R&D 3 years growth (CAGR-3y, %)*
1	ROBERT BOSCH	Germany	5,202.0	7.4	1.8
2	DENSO	Japan	3,041.5	8.8	5.9
3	CONTINENTAL	Germany	2,528.3	6.4	11.4
4	ZF	Germany	1,350.0	4.6	17.9
5	AISIN SEIKI	Japan	1,239.7	5.0	6.4
6	DELPHI	UK	1,102.2	7.5	0.0
7	VALEO	France	954.0	6.6	10.6
8	FUJI HEAVY INDUSTRIES	Japan	780.4	3.2	27.5
9	BRIDGESTONE	Japan	724.0	2.5	4.7
10	MICHELIN	France	689.0	3.3	3.5
11	HELLA	Germany	662.5	10.4	9.3

World rank	*Company name*	*Country of origin*	*R&D spending 2015 (€million)*	*R&D intensity (% of revenue)*	*R&D 3 years growth (CAGR-3y, %)*
12	MAHLE	Germany	657.0	5.7	31.4
13	SCHAEFFLER	Germany	647.0	4.9	4.7
14	AUTOLIV	US	459.7	5.5	4.7
15	HYUNDAI MOBIS	South Korea	454.6	1.6	17.3
16	TOYOTA INDUSTRIES	Japan	419.0	2.5	12.1
17	GOODYEAR	US	350.9	2.3	1.1
18	JOHNSON CONTROLS	US	338.9	1.0	−10.2
19	GKN	UK	303.5	3.1	7.4
20	TOYOTA BOSHOKU	Japan	293.1	2.7	1.9

Source: Based on European Commission (2016).

spending, supply firms from the emerging economies do not seem to be so deeply involved in the R&D process of vehicles. Apart from a few examples, such as Yanfeng, the supply firms from the emerging markets are mostly limited to manufacturing of 'produce per blueprint' components. In the top 2500 R&D companies worldwide, 113 are automotive supply firms, of which 23 firms originate from the emerging markets (European Commission 2016). However, the top 20 automotive companies in R&D spending is firmly in the hands of firms from the advanced economies (Table 7.2).

The 23 supply firms from the emerging markets occupy the bottom half of the list, with the highest ranking company ranked 36th in R&D spending (Table 7.3).

Finally, the harmonization of vehicle platforms globally and the increased use of common parts across national borders intensifies competition between companies from advanced and emerging markets, as it effectively merges the formerly separated markets into one global automotive supply market. As Volkswagen wants to have two to three suppliers per components *globally*, supply firms from all countries compete for the position to become the lead firm's main supplier. The bleak position of the supply firms from the emerging markets can be observed from the top 100 global supply firms by revenue. Only four supply firms from the emerging markets managed to enter the list in 2015 (Table 7.4).

The prospects of participating in the GVC

In a globalized economy of coordinated and orchestrated GVCs, the prospects for new entrants from the emerging markets have changed. Lead firms with considerable power influence their supply base and shape the development of participating

Table 7.3 Top automotive suppliers from emerging markets in R&D spending

world rank	*Company name*	*Country of origin*	*R&D spending 2015 (€million)*	*R&D intensity (% of revenue)*	*R&D 3 years growth (CAGR-3y, %)*
36	CHENG SHIN RUBBER INDUSTRY	Taiwan	120.5	3.7	23.6
44	XIAMEN JINGLONG MOTOR	China	88.3	2.4	15.2
46	WEICHAI POWER	China	82.8	0.8	−14.2
53	NINGBO JOYSON ELECTRONIC	China	75.1	6.8	60.3
57	CHINA MOTOR	Taiwan	68.1	6.6	5.9
61	WANXIANG QIANCHAO	China	56.2	4.1	7.6
73	MINTH	China	46.8	4.3	12.6
74	ASHOK LEYLAND	India	45.3	1.7	−4.1
75	LINGYUN INDUSTRIAL	China	42.1	4.2	39.6
77	BEIJINGWEST INDUSTRIES INT'L	China	41.2	11.8	n/a
80	NINGBO HUAXIANG ELECTRONIC	China	39.3	3.0	18.1
81	WULING MOTORS	China	38.0	2.0	32.4
86	ANHUI ZHONGDING SEALING PARTS	China	35.3	4:0	34.6
87	ZHEJIANG WANFENG AUTO WHEEL	China	34.1	2.9	14.9
93	T V S MOTOR COMPANY	India	31.4	2.0	21.2
94	APOLLO TYRES	India	31.0	1:9	24.3
95	KENDA RUBBER INDUSTRIAL	Taiwan	29.3	3.4	37.5
97	AEOLUS TYRE	China	28.6	3.3	−15.2
102	LIFAN INDUSTRY	China	26.3	1.6	−25.1
107	SAILUN	China	24.0	2.0	89.9
109	DEPO AUTO PARTS INDUSTRIAL	Taiwan	23.1	5.5	4.0
112	DONGFENG ELECTRONIC TECH.	China	22.4	3.5	27.5
113	GUIZHOU TYRE	China	22.2	3.9	−10.1

Source: Author's own summary, based on European Commission (2016).

Table 7.4 Emerging market firms in the top 100 supplier list

2015 rank	*Company*	*Country of origin*	*Revenue in million US$*	*Products*
18	Yanfeng Automotive Trim Systems Co.	China	11,242	Interiors, exteriors, electronics, seating, safety
31	Samvardhana Motherson Group	India	7,245	Rearview mirrors, plastic modules cockpits/IPs, door trims & bumpers, wiring harnesses, molded plastic parts and assemblies, molded and extruded rubber components, lighting systems, air intake manifolds, pedal assemblies, shock absorbers, HVAC systems, roof hatches
51	Nemak	Mexico	4,482	Aluminum cylinder heads, engine blocks, transmissions, structural components and other components
77	CITIC Dicastal Co.	China	2,429	Aluminum alloy wheels, aluminum casting parts

Source: Author's own summary, based on Top 100 Automotive Supplier List, 2015.

*Companies from Singapore and South Korea were excluded from this list, following the IMF definition that sees both countries as advanced economies.

firms in the value chain. In the following, a number of factors that changed the barriers of entry and the nature of competition in the industry are discussed.

Explicit restructuring of the supply base by the lead firm

Lead firms such as Volkswagen have centralized their global purchasing, increasing its bargaining power and ability to coordinate and restructure their supply base. Through a number of explicit policies, Volkswagen has shaped the automotive supply base in the past decades. In particular the objective to reduce the number of supply firms, and the strategy to localize production of components in close proximity to the assembly lines erect barriers of entries for firms from the emerging markets. The policy to reduce the number of supply firms involved in the value chain accelerates the consolidation of the supply base. In the consolidation of supply firms, leading firms from the advanced economies can strengthen their position and often acquire the competition from the emerging markets. Volkswagen actively encourages and steers the restructuring of the supply base, for instance by initiating M&A between different supply firms or by modularizing components to reduce the number of direct suppliers to Volkswagen. For both, induced M&A or the selection of supply firms for sub-assembly, Volkswagen chooses the most capable and trusted supply firms. With the exception of few cases, like Fuyao, the majority of selected supply firms are from the advanced markets, which can thereby fortify their position in the value chain. The local-to-local policy forces supply firms to internationalize and collocate with Volkswagen's largest production hubs. This has several effects on the supply base. First, it pressures the existing supply firms to rapidly internationalize and become MNCs, creating a supply base of large, transnational firms. Second, it harmonizes the supply base of Volkswagen in the different regions and countries. Third, Volkswagen can strategically restructure its supply base in any given region, by introducing new entrants to the market and nurturing them in a way that they can become fully competitive. This way, Volkswagen can break up the competitive dynamics in a place. Volkswagen can ensure capabilities are available in key regions, prices are acceptable, and quality standards are met.

The pressure to internationalize and restructure the global value chain goes beyond the first tier of suppliers. Large suppliers at all tiers along the value chain, like BOSCH, Continental, ZF, or BASF, adapted their strategies to match these of the lead firm, passing on the pressure to internationalize and consolidate to their supply firms (Nolan, Zhang, and Liu 2007). Like the assemblers, large tier-1 suppliers act as systems integrators and actively steer and control this process, taking the initiative to invite suppliers to collocate, or else to merge with other suppliers. Nolan coined the term 'cascade effect,' which describes the process of passing down the pressure for concentration at multiple levels of the value chain (Nolan 2001, 2014). Nolan observed that lead firms pass on the pressure for consolidation to their supply base, leading to international and large supply firms with similar market shares as the lead firm (Nolan, Zhang, and Chunhang 2007). The pressure is further passed on by the tier-1 supplier to tier-2 supply firms, as tier-1 supply firms adapted their strategies accordingly. What has been conceptualized to describe how the pressure for consolidation is passed on along the value chain can be further extended to describe how different strategic objectives set by the lead firm are passed on along the value chain. Such objectives include setting of quality standards, standardization of management techniques, establishing of worldwide logistics standards such as just-in-time or just-in-sequence delivery, and also strategic objectives such as the internationalization of supply firms and the reduction of suppliers globally through mergers and acquisitions. As shown in the case of BOSCH, large supply firms have adapted their sourcing strategy to mirror the purchasing strategy of Volkswagen. This way BOSCH can accommodate the requirements set by Volkswagen and simultaneously further increase efficiency in its own value chain. By behaving in such a way, the system integrator passes on the strategic objective set by the assembler and sets the cascade effect in motion.

The explicit restructuring of the supply base favors the established companies in the field and increases the barriers of entry. Through the reduction of supply firms, the best performing supply firms are selected to increase their activities and responsibilities within the value chain, squeezing out smaller firms and firms with lower capabilities. Firms with good relationships to Volkswagen are asked to collocate to new production locations, expanding their business with the lead firm, while new entrants are faced with additional requirements for participation in the value chain.

The oligopolistic equilibrium along the value chain

Through the cascade effect and the consolidation of the supply base at several levels of the value chain, the component supply industry has developed oligopolistic features. One strategic objective of Volkswagen is to decrease the complexity of their supply chain by decreasing the total number of suppliers for their global production network. Volkswagen seeks to have the same supplier for any given component for every location globally. This has created a situation in which only few supply firms have developed into multinational suppliers for each component.

The number of supply firms for strategically important components tends to be lower, while the number of suppliers for non-strategic components, such as mechanical parts produced per blueprint by local sub-contractors, is significantly larger. Unfortunately, no detailed data for strategically important components was disclosed, but according to interviews, the number of supply firms for such components is mostly below four. Moreover, interviews with managers from other large assemblers such as General Motors have confirmed that there are "essentially just two to three international supply firms for any component . . . [and that these] supply all large [assembly firms]. We all have the same suppliers." (Interview, General Motors). The picture was further confirmed by interviews with the supply firms in the case study. Through its policies and active restructuring of the supply base, Volkswagen encourages the global consolidation of the supply base for strategically relevant components to the point that the market for each component has turned into an oligopoly.

Eventually, the consolidation would lead to monopolies in the value chain. To prevent this, Volkswagen has another set of policies that effectively creates an oligopolistic equilibrium in the supply base. To maintain independence from any given supplier and to ensure a certain degree of competition in the supply base, Volkswagen implemented a strict multiple supplier strategy. This means that no supplier can become the exclusive supplier for any particular component. This strategy counters the abovementioned reduction of supply firms to a certain degree, preventing the emergence of pure monopolies for any component, thereby creating an oligopolistic equilibrium for the supply base. Interestingly, the largest automotive supplier, BOSCH, has enforced the exact same procurement policies, thereby creating the same structure for its key suppliers. Through such strategies, an oligopolistic equilibrium is created for core companies along the value chain.

The oligopolistic structure of the value chain increases the barriers of entry to the industry. With the exception of 'produce per blueprint' suppliers, it brings forth large and powerful supply firms along the entire value chain, which have been able to build close ties to assemblers. New entrants are being faced with strong and deeply integrated competition that has first mover advantages at several fronts, from a globally developed manufacturing footprint to closely developed relationships with the customer.

Approaches of lead firms to build a local supply base

With the local-to-local strategy in place, Volkswagen aims to increase the localization rate for production of components to its assembly lines around the world. If capabilities are lacking in a specific region or for a specific component, Volkswagen can effectively build up the capabilities in its supply base through the continuous support of selected supply firms. Interviewees from Volkswagen described two potential ways to build a local supply industry when entering a new market: either by developing and nurturing local supply firms, so that the required capabilities are being built over time, or by collocating existing supply firms from other locations. As several interviewees from Volkswagen, BOSCH, and Continental expressed, the option to collocate existing supply firms is mostly preferred, as it brings several advantages. First, the number of global suppliers is kept low – one of the objectives of the global purchasing strategies. Second, by collocating existing supply firms, most of the responsibility to meet the requirements of the assembler lies with the supply firm. The existing supplier is aware and experienced in achieving quality standards, knows the required management, production and supply chain standards, and has an experienced team that can ensure the standards are met in the new location. When nurturing new supply firms, on the other hand, the assembler is involved in lengthy supplier development programs to reach the necessary requirements. And finally, the process of collocating existing suppliers is significantly faster than nurturing new supply firms.

> Collocating supply firms takes one to two years to reach the full volume. If we help local supply firms, it takes years to develop them. . . . Based on our experience, it is usually between six and eight years, until the supplier finally meets our requirements. And then we still need to build up capacity.
>
> (Interview, Volkswagen case)

Consequently, when firms like Volkswagen open new production locations in the fast growing emerging markets they bring along established suppliers from their existing supply base rather than nurturing local indigenous supply firms. By collocating the supply firms, competition for existing local suppliers increases even for their existing local customer base.

Globalization and changing prerequisites for participation

Volkswagen sets high standards to its supply firms – which even increased as Volkswagen first globalized its operations, later its vehicle platform, and finally its central procurement strategy and approach. All supply firms must be able to integrate into Volkswagen's management and production system, which includes harmonization of software interfaces, participation in regular meetings, and ensuring logistic interfaces and supply chain planning to allow just-in-time and just-in-sequence delivery. Furthermore, Volkswagen requires its innovating and developing supply firms to have a global footprint. Production of customized components should be collocated to key production hubs of Volkswagen, with a minimum distance of 300 km to enable seamless just-in-time delivery. Only standardized components, which are mostly low value-adding parts, or non-customized and low-weight high-value components like control units can be produced at greater distances. To facilitate the knowledge transfer with development and innovation suppliers during the vehicle development process, R&D centers of supply firms should be located in close proximity of Volkswagen's core development center in Wolfsburg, Germany. And last, supply firms must meet the increased quality demand to mitigate risks from increased volume production of common parts. Supply firms must submit to stricter controls, including annual audits, participating in the supplier development program if necessary, and often open book relations. The requirements increased over time, as Volkswagen globalized its operations, in particular with the introduction of the new vehicle platform. The increased requirements increase the barriers of entry, in particular for suppliers of high value-adding components.

Role of the supply firm in the value chain

The role of the supply firm changed over time, as Volkswagen adapted its product architecture to a modular system in which supply firms play a key role for sub-assembly, product development, and innovations. In the majority of the supply chain management literature, the role of a supplier is defined by its position in a tiered supply chain structure (McCann and Kim 2008; Womack, Jones, and Roos 1990). In the globalized production network of the automotive industry, the tiered structure is becoming increasingly complex and differentiated and has lost its meaning as a defining category for the role of the supply firm. The supply chain tier in which a firm is situated does no longer indicate its role and importance to the value chain. Most of the supply firms in the case study were situated at different tiers of the supply chain, depending on the product and at times on the customer. For instance, BOSCH is a tier-1 supplier of engine injection systems to Volkswagen for their production in Germany, but at the same time they can be a tier-2 supplier for the same component in a different location, for instance if the assembler buys externally assembled engines (Figure 7.1). Supply firms supplying the same component to multiple production lines of the same customer can be situated at different tiers in the supply chain, depending on the particular setup of the assembly line.

Supply chains can also vary in length, depending on the number of sub-assembly steps. For more modularized value chain setups, with multiple sub-assembly steps, the supply chain becomes longer as fewer components are directly supplied to the final assembly line, but they are bundled and assembled into modules at sub-assembly lines of the system integrators. However, the particular organizational setup of such production lines differs from location to location depending on the level of in-house

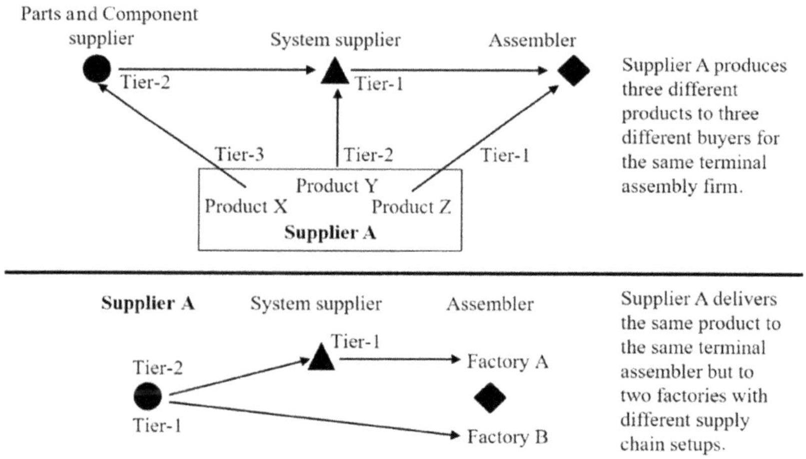

Figure 7.1 Potential positions of a supply firm in a value chain
Source: Author's own figure.

assembly activities of the final assembler and the localization of (sub-assembly) competencies of the supply firms in the geographic proximity to the final assembly line. Additionally, the geography of activities can vary, in particular for components that require little effort and cost for transportation. While the production of customized components or the sub-assembly of modules should ideally be close to the final assembly line to ensure just-in-time and just-in-sequence delivery, some standardized components can be manufactured in entirely different continents.

Consequently, the descriptive consideration of the position in a tiered structure becomes increasingly blurred and does not indicate the role or relationship of a supply firm to the final assembler. Instead of a tiered structure to differentiate the position and importance of supply firms in the value chain, supply firms can be differentiated by strategic relevance to the assembler and its role in the value chain. Volkswagen differentiated between four groups of supply firms: innovating, developing, 'produce per blueprint' and commodity supply firms, with each having a different strategic relevance to the assembler. Highly relevant components are key for the vehicle's performance, safety, or design. Additionally, highly relevant firms can provide their own innovations and inventions and have superior knowledge for key components in the vehicle. Relevant suppliers have development capabilities for key components but develop the components as per the requirements of the assembler. Non-relevant supply firms produce commodities or components per blueprint that is provided by the assembler (Table 7.5). The following table summarized the categories of supply firm relevance to the assembler.

Innovating suppliers have developed their own market research capabilities to identify consumer trends, enabling them to generate innovation based on future

Table 7.5 Types of suppliers by strategic relevance to buyer

	Strategic relevance	*Involved in R&D*	*Barriers of entry*	*Value-added*	*Technical drawings*	*Aspects of buyer-supplier relationship*
Innovating	very high	4–6 years before SOP	very high	very high	approved by assembler	• Supplier proposes innovations to buyer • Supplier has superior knowledge about product • Supplier makes own market research • Supplier defines specifications and performance requirements
Developing	high	2–4 years before SOP	high	high	approved by assembler	• Buyer 'pulls' R&D capabilities and knowledge from supplier • Supplier has specialized knowledge and R&D expertise • Specifications and performance requirements are set by the buyer
'Produce per blueprint' and commodity supplier	low	1/2–2 years before SOP	low	low	provided by assembler or industry-wide standard	• Buyer utilizes production capabilities of supplier • Buyer has R&D capability, supplier not • Tooling is provided by the buyer • Specifications and performance requirements are set by the buyer

Source: Author's own table.

demand. The innovating suppliers are thereby ahead of the buyer in terms of innovation and the development of new functionalities. It is involved in the vehicle development process at the earliest stage, approximately four to six years before start of production.

Developing supply firms have their own development capabilities but no innovation capabilities. The assembler sets the specifications and requirements for the component, and the supplier develops the component to meet the buyer's specifications. The developing supply firms are involved in the vehicle development process about four years before start of production. Because of their R&D capabilities, developing suppliers are of strategic relevance to the buyer.

Supply firms in the commodity and 'produce per blueprint category,' on the other hand, have neither innovation nor development capabilities. They have production capabilities and produce components that have been developed by the buyer or for which industry standards have been defined. Firms in this group have little ownership advantage and are of little strategic relevance to the buyer. Firms in this group mostly have sub-contracts from the buyer and are governed by hands-off market-type price mechanisms. These firms are only loosely integrated into the value chain, are interchangeable, and thereby mostly not coordinated by the lead firm.

The barriers of entry differ for the three categories of suppliers. For innovative suppliers, barriers of entry are very high. The supply firm has to develop superior innovation and development capabilities (Guo, Jiang, and Yang 2014; Lall 1990; Teece 2014). Furthermore, it has to develop a high level of trust with the buyer to be seen as a competent firm that is on par with the buyer (Johanson and Vahlne 2009; Menkhoff 1992). Similarly, barriers of entry are high for developing supply firms, as the supply firms have to own development capabilities and develop trust with the buyer (Argyres and Silverman 2004). Only the most competent firms are selected by the lead firm, as the buyer depends on the development capability of the supply firm. Barriers of entry for 'produce per blueprint' suppliers are relatively low. Such firms are easily interchangeable.

Because of the high barriers of entry for developing and innovating supply firms, such firms from the emerging markets have difficulties breaking into the value chain. Firms from the advanced markets, on the other hand, have advantages from their close ties to the assembler. By building trusting relationships over years, the firms from the advanced markets are more likely to be selected as suppliers going forward. Trust based on previous experience plays an increasing role in the buyer-supplier relationship. For innovating and developing supply firms, developing engineers of Volkswagen have a significant influence on supplier selection. Personal relationships built over time between engineers from Volkswagen and the supply firm are often the decisive factor. Only the most capable supply firms are selected to support Volkswagen's internationalization of production and globalization of the new platform strategy, while local firms are squeezed out of the value chain. This gives an advantage to supply firms from the advanced markets that have more time to develop close relationships, have less distance to the assembler so that developing future relationships is easier, and have further advantages from cultural conformities. Overall, suppliers from the advanced markets are more likely to meet the requirements of assembly firms, while supply firms from the emerging markets are more likely to be squeezed out of the GVC. 'Produce per blueprint' supply firms from the emerging markets, on the other hand, often have a cost advantage and are therefore able to enter the value global automotive value chain.

Additionally, geographic proximity and close interaction of R&D activity has become a major competitive advantage for firms from the advanced markets. Supply firms that are developing integral components need to have R&D centers close to the assembler (Hertenstein and Williamson 2018). These trends put supply firms from the emerging markets at a disadvantage, which have geographic distance to the R&D centers of the leading assembly firms in the global auto industry.

The role of national champions

Large developing economies have long used the automotive industry as a driver for economic and industrial development. Brazil and China are no exception to that (Shapiro 1994; Thun 2006). The automotive industry acts as a pillar industry that can transform a nation's economy. Not only does it create rents and direct jobs in the industry but also spillover effects to other industries, from a trained manufacturing workforce, increased knowledge base, and industrial base, to large demands in steel, rubber, and oil, to mention just some of the spillover effects a working car industry can have on an economy (Shapiro 1994).

Brazil and China have taken different routes to industrial development, and the case studies indicate different results. While Brazil has not been able to bring forth strong and technologically leading supply firms, some of the Chinese firms have been able to catch-up with their competitors from the advanced markets. Why have some firms from China been able to succeed while the majority of the Brazilian firms have not? The case studies indicate that the two different approaches to industrial development plays a role for the different trajectories. The case studies highlight the importance of 'national champions' at the assembly level and their joint-ventures with western assemblers for the development of an indigenous supply base. The most successful cases in this study, Yanfeng, YAPP, and Fuyao, all had close ties to the indigenous assemblers at the early stages of their development. The ties to the assemblers helped the firms to build up capabilities, develop ties with foreign assemblers through the joint-ventures, and eventually utilize the established network relations to internationalize and become globally competitive through the support of the foreign assembler. In the absence of the national champions and their close relation to leading western assemblers, foreign assemblers are inclined to develop a local supply base by collocating existing supply firms from their home markets. As seen in the Brazilian market, this can lead to an eradication of the local indigenous industry. From the perspective of developing a strong indigenous supply base, it appears the 'national champions' at the assembly level play a key role in providing a gateway of entry into the global value chain of foreign assemblers for the indigenous supply firms.

Conclusion: gateways of entry to GVC

The findings of the research indicate that participation of supply firms from the emerging markets in the global value chains of the lead firm is often limited to relatively low value-added component supply firms. Only few supply firms from the emerging markets break into the group of high value-adding global supply firms, by entering the GVC through their indigenous assemblers that established network ties with foreign assemblers (Hertenstein, Sutherland, and Anderson 2017).

In the case of the Brazilian firms, the intensified competition among developing and innovating supply firms in the emerging markets squeezed the local supply firms out of the market. From the cases of Brazilian firms, only the 'produce per blueprint' firms have been able to maintain their position in the value chain. Moreover, none of the Brazilian firms in the initial selection of case studies produces components that require very strong technological and R&D capabilities. The products with the highest technological demands are produced by international supply firms from the developed economies, such as BOSCH, Delphi, or Continental. The highest technological demanding products by a Brazilian firm in our sample are engine cooling and air conditioning systems by Metal Leve – a company that is now owned by a foreign competitor. Only the firms with very simple products were able to maintain full control and independence. Maxion-Iochpe even actively downgraded its product portfolio to less value-added products to stay competitive and to provide simpler products, so as to maintain its position in the value chain.

For the supply firms from China, the picture is slightly different. Some of the firms are in the group of developing supply firms. These firms have been able to maintain the position in the value chain by developing close relations with the western assemblers, often by utilizing the joint-ventures. For instance, both Yanfeng and YAPP are subsidiaries of HASCO, which in turn is controlled by SAIC, one of the joint-venture partners of Volkswagen in China. The selection of suppliers has to be aligned between the joint-venture partners Volkswagen and SAIC. Yet for the highest value-adding components, such as airbags, safety relevant components, or sub-systems, western supply firms dominate the market in China. Their key advantage is long-term relationships and trust with the western assemblers, superior technology and intellectual property, and close proximity of R&D centers to those of western assemblers, which enables a close interaction during the simultaneous development process that further strengthens the ties between the two firms. Nevertheless, based on the good experience made with Chinese supply firms in China and their price advantage, some Chinese firms have been able to develop close relations to Volkswagen and expand their role in the GVC.

In summary, there appears to be a separation of highly capable high-tech suppliers with high value-added activities and companies with relatively low value-added activities. While the high value-added positions are occupied by western supply firms such as BOSCH, Delphi, ZF, Infineon, DuPont, or BASF, participation of supply firms from the emerging markets seems to be limited to a relatively low value-added position within the value chain (Figure 7.2). Entering the GVC of western assembly firms such as Volkswagen seems to be restricted to the 'produce per blueprint' group of supply firms. Even the most capable supply firms of this study, such as Yanfeng, began by supplying relatively simple components to the assembler and only gradually upgraded to become a developing supplier with

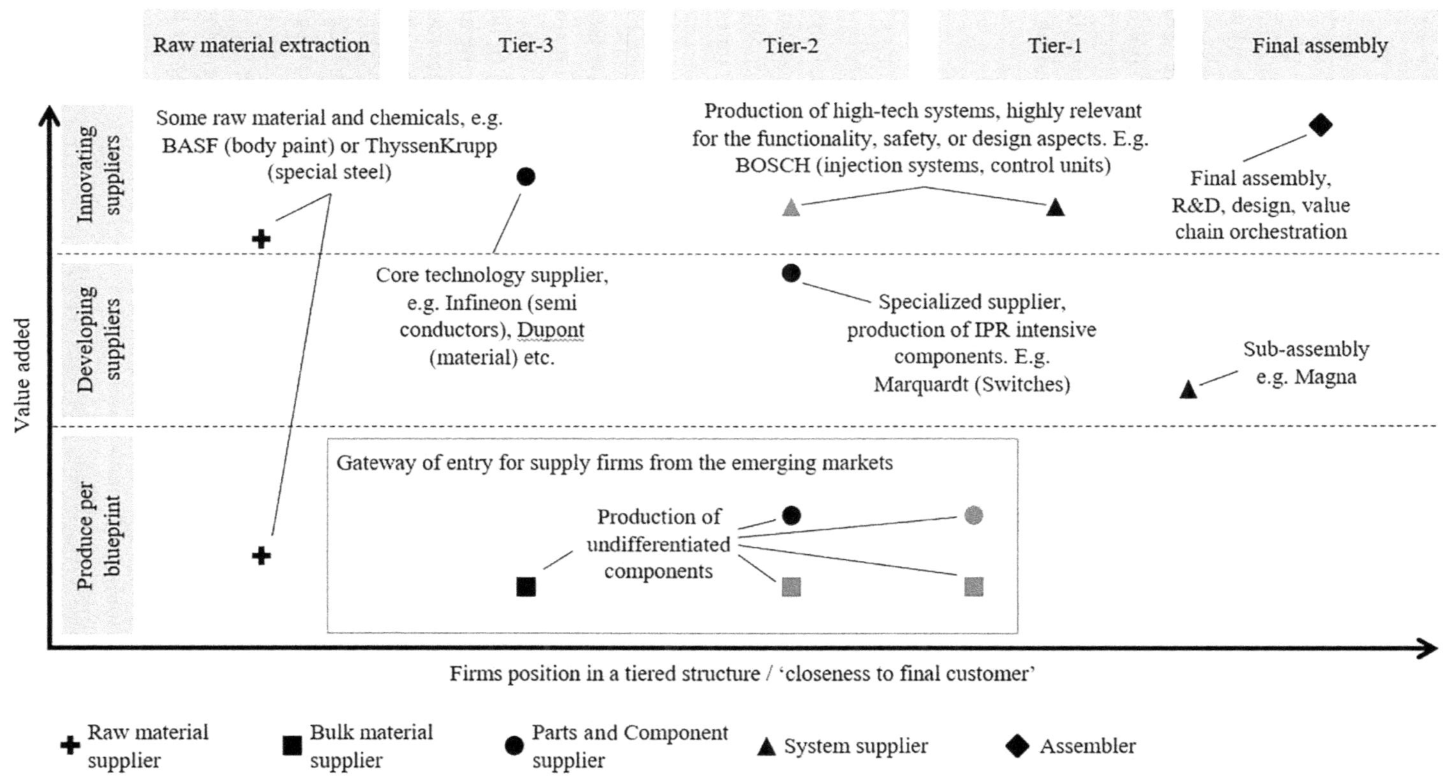

Figure 7.2 Participation of emerging market firms in GVCs

Source: Author’s own figure, based on field research.

strong R&D capabilities. The following figure summarizes the concept and highlights the prospects for participation and gateways of entry for supply firms from the emerging markets (Figure 7.2).

Prospects of upgrading in global value chains

Once a firm has entered the network of a lead firm and participates in the value chain, it can upgrade to higher value-adding activities in the value chain (Humphrey and Memedovic 2003; McDermott and Corredoira 2010; Mei 2008). For firms from the emerging markets that enter the value chain at a relatively low value-added position, upgrading is an opportunity to establish a sustainable long-term relation to the assembler and capture higher value-added activities by becoming a developing or innovating firm (Ponte et al. 2014). In the following the role of the lead firm in facilitating the process of upgrading is explored.

The role of lead firms for upgrading: supplier development programs

It has been observed that large global buyers facilitate the upgrading process of local firms in the emerging markets in the manufacturing industries (Bair and Gereffi 2001; Bazan and Navas-Aleman 2004; Gereffi 1999; Giuliani, Pietrobelli, and Rabellotti 2005; Schmitz and Humphrey 2000). Lead firms may choose to assist the supply firm because they rely on the competencies of their suppliers and feel "obliged to assist them in improving products and processes" (Giuliani et al. 2005: 562). Multiple studies have documented links between value chain governance and upgrading, arguing that closer inter-firm ties lead to stronger lead firm involvement for upgrading supply firms (Gereffi 1999; Giuliani et al. 2005; Schmitz and Humphrey 2000). Lead firm facilitated upgrading includes the allocation of activities within the value chain (i.e. selecting and allocating activities to capable supply firms), developing and enabling supply firms for technological upgrades (Giuliani et al. 2005), collaborative expansion to new (international) production hubs (Hertenstein et al. 2017), and restructuring and consolidating the supply chain (Nolan et al. 2007). Consequently, the upgrading prospects of participating supply firms in the automotive industry depends to a large extent on the lead firms' orchestrating activities. Supply firm development often occurs in the emerging markets, in which some of the supply firms lack in quality controls and production process standards to ensure that quality standards are met.

The case studies suggest that lead firm facilitated upgrading plays an important role for process upgrading, product upgrading, and functional upgrading. Both the assembler as well as large turn-key suppliers are found to support the supply firms to increase process efficiency. Process upgrading was also widely observed in the case studies. Through Volkswagen's supplier development program, Volkswagen installed efficient logistics, supply chain, and management capabilities within the supply firms, and offered production process consultancy to the supply firms, in order to increase efficiency. Through the joint development process with developing supply firms, Volkswagen promotes knowledge exchange and creation between the assembler and the supply firm, thereby facilitating the product development of the supply firm. Moreover, by nurturing the supply firm to achieve better quality standards, or by orchestrating M&A for complementary products, the lead firm further facilitates product upgrading of the supply firm. Product upgrading was observed in the case of Fuyao, a Chinese glass manufacturer. Volkswagen encouraged the merger with a German specialized firm that provides the glue between the glass and the vehicle body. Through the merger, Fuyao was able to apply the glue on the windows before delivery, thereby upgrading its product and performing a sub-assembly activity. By increasing the number of modules used for automobile production, Volkswagen allocates additional sub-system assembly and orchestrating activities of the upstream value chain to a systems-integrating supply firm, facilitating their functional upgrading. Additionally, the majority of the case firms were actively incentivized by Volkswagen to expand their activities within the GVC by collocating new production locations in additional markets and globalize production to become a global supplier for their respective component. This is a form of functional upgrading that was facilitated by Volkswagen. See Hertenstein et al. for a deeper analysis (Hertenstein et al. 2017). Facilitation of chain- or inter-sectorial upgrading, on the other hand, has not been observed. Chain- and inter-sectorial upgrading occurs outside the lead firm's value chain, where the lead firm's influence is limited.

Limitations of lead firm facilitated upgrading

While lead firm facilitation can support the development of supply firms from the emerging markets, the effect for the development of emerging markets is limited by a number of factors. First, facilitation for supply firms is not limited to firms from the emerging markets. As a result, multiple competitive firms from the advanced markets experienced facilitation, further increasing their competitiveness vis-à-vis the firms from the emerging markets. Due to efforts to reduce the number of supply firms, only a few supply firms are nominated to create intensified ties with the assembly firm through assistance and co-development programs. In many cases, firms from the advanced markets were selected, rather than assisting a multitude of local supply firms. Incentivizing strong and efficient supply firms with superior capabilities to collocate in the emerging markets intensifies the local competition for the local indigenous firms, often squeezing the local firms out of the global value chain.

Second, the strong role of the lead firm in the supply firm's upgrading limits the ability of independent upgrading of the supply firm. The process of upgrading is a capability building process and in itself a capability. Traditionally, research emphasized capabilities such as leading-edge technology or better access to the market through superior marketing and branding. Traditional capabilities are an important source for competitive advantage. However, for firms to sustain their competitive advantage, dynamic capabilities are required (Teece and Pisano 1994). Dynamic capabilities can be understood as a higher order of capabilities, or as dynamic capabilities enabling firms to create new traditional capabilities through adaptation and innovation (Collis 1994; Teece 2014; Zollo and Winter 2002). This is necessary to ensure sustainable superior performance, especially in changing environments with constant technological updates (Teece 2014). When lead firms facilitate upgrading, the innovation and new technologies that lead to the upgrading are based on the dynamic capabilities embedded in the lead firm, not the supply firm. Hence, while technology is updated, the process of innovating to upgrade, a second order capability, lies outside the firm. The workforce may be trained in understanding and using the new technology and processes, but it is not trained to detect inefficiencies or to further develop new technology or processes. This is critical, as it leaves the 'upgraded' firm dependent on the innovating lead firm. Similar to the situation in Technical Assistance Agreements, the firm is able to increase its productivity (process upgrading), or introduce new products based on leading-edge technologies (product upgrading), but the firm remains dependent on the partner firm and is not able to create long-term sustainable advantages through upgrading.

Even though these firms were able to maintain ownership, such agreements limit their future development in several ways. Through such co-competitive relationships, the indigenous Brazilian firms are limited in their regional reach and internationalization aspirations to the Latin American market, serving as production service providers for their international competitors and paying high licensing fees for the technology of the foreign partner. Moreover, as evident in the case of Arteb and Hella, such relationships are asymmetric and often unstable, ending either in a takeover by the foreign partner or by terminating the licensing agreement, after which the local supply firm is left where it was before.

Conclusion

The new structure of economic activity in orchestrated value chains further influences the integration of emerging markets into the world economy and the prospects of firms from the emerging markets for participating and upgrading in such value chains (Buckley 2009; Morris and Barnes 2008; Rugman and Doh 2008).

Can firms from the emerging markets catch-up?

Due to the orchestrating activities of global lead firms, entrants from the emerging markets face a new set of challenges to catch up with leading western firms. Despite the increased outward FDI from emerging markets since the early 2000s, which indicates a rapid catch-up of firms from the emerging markets and the theories that support the assumed rapid catch-up via cross-border asset-seeking M&A (Luo and Tung 2007), the evidence from this study suggests that the prospect of firms from the emerging markets face a unique set of challenges to catch-up with the advanced market competitors. While participating in GVC promises potential for upgrading and growth, entry to the established value chains is limited to products with relatively low technological requirements that require little R&D capabilities. The ability to establish close ties with the lead firm and become deeply integrated into the GVC is limited because of the low requirements for knowledge exchange and low interdependencies of the two firms for such products. This limits the potential for lead firm facilitated upgrading and instead intensifies competition with firms from the advanced economies. From the case studies in this study, some of the firms that had become international had previously downgraded their value chain position, reacting to the intensified competition from the supply firms. Yet some firms have been able to successfully enter the GVC of a western lead firm and establish close ties with the firms. In such cases, further capability building is facilitated by the lead firm, leading to additional opportunities to further upgrade and often to rapidly internationalize within the GVC, catch up with western counterparts, and establish a strong and competitive position in the GVC (Hertenstein et al. 2017).

References

Argyres, N. S. and B. S. Silverman. 2004. "R&D, Organization Structure and the Development of Corporate Technological Knowledge." *Strategic Management Journal* 25: 929–58.

Bair, J. and G. Gereffi. 2001. "Local Clusters in Global Chains: The Causes and Consequences of Export Dynamism in Torreon's Blue Jeans Industry'." *World Development* 28(11): 1885–903.

Bazan, L. and L. Navas-Aleman. 2004. "The Underground Revolution in the Sinos Valley: A Comparison of Upgrading in Global and National Value Chain." In *Local Enterprises in the Global Economy: Issues of Governance and Upgrading*, edited by H. Schmitz. Cheltenham: Edward Elgar.

Buckley, P. J. 2009. "The Impact of the Global Factory on Economic Development." *Journal of World Business* 44(2): 131–43.

Collis, D. J. 1994. "Research Note: How Valuable Are Organizational Capabilities?" *Strategic Management Journal* 15(1): 143–52.

European Commission. 2016. *The 2016 EU Industrial R&D Investment Scoreboard.*

Gereffi, G. 1999. "A Commodity Chains Framework for Analyzing Global Industries." Working Paper, Duke University: Center on Globalization Governance and Competitiveness.

Giuliani, E., C. Pietrobelli, and R. Rabellotti. 2005. "Upgrading in Global Value Chains: Lessons From Latin American Clusters." *World Development* 33(4): 549–73.

Guo, C., C. X. Jiang, and Q. Yang. 2014. "The Development of Organizational Capabilities and Corporate Entrepreneurial Processes: The Case of Chinese Automobile Firms." *Thunderbird International Business Review* 56(6): 483–500.

Hertenstein, P., D. Sutherland, and J. Anderson. 2017. "Internationalization Within Networks: Exploring the Relationship Between Inward and Outward FDI in China's Auto Components Industry." *Asia Pacific Journal of Management* 34(1).

Hertenstein, P. and P. J. Williamson. 2018. "The Role of Suppliers in Enabling Differing Innovation Strategies of Competing Multinationals From Emerging and Advanced

Economies: German and Chinese Automotive Firms Compared." *Technovation* 70–71: 46–58.

Humphrey, J. and O. Memedovic. 2003. "The Global Automotive Industry Value Chain: What Prospects for Upgrading by Developing Countries." UNIDO Sectorial Studies Series Working Paper, Vienna: UNIDO.

Johanson, J. and J.-E. Vahlne. 2009. "The Uppsala Internationalization Process Model Revisited: From Liability of Foreignness to Liability of Outsidership." *Journal of International Business Studies* 40(9): 1411–31.

Lall, S. 1990. "Technological Capabilities and Industrialization." *World Development* 20(2): 165–86.

Luo, Y. and R. L. Tung. 2007. "International Expansion of Emerging Market Enterprises: A Springboard Perspective." *Journal of International Business Studies* 38(4): 481–98.

McCann, P. and H. Y. Kim. 2008. "Supply Chains and Locational Adjustment in the Global Automotive Industry." *Policy Studies* 29(3): 255–66.

McDermott, G. A. and R. A. Corredoira. 2010. "Network Composition, Collaborative Ties, and Upgrading in Emerging-Market Firms: Lessons From the Argentine Autoparts Sector." *Journal of International Business Studies* 31(2): 308–29.

Mei, L. M. L. 2008. *Study on the Automotive Industrial Upgrading in China Based on Global Value Chain*. 2008 4th International Conference on Wireless Communications, Networking and Mobile Computing.

Menkhoff, T. 1992. "Xinyongor How to Trust Trust? Chinese Non-Contractual Business Relations and Social Structure: The Singapore Case." *Internationales Asien Forum 23*: 26–288.

Morris, M. and J. Barnes. 2008. "Staying Alive in the Global Automotive Industry: What Can Developing Economies Learn From South Africa About Linking Into Global Automotive Value Chains?" *The European Journal of Development Research* 20(1): 31–55.

Nolan, P. 2001. *China and the Global Business Revolution*. Basingstoke: Palgrave Macmillan.

Nolan, P. 2014. "Globalisation and Industrial Policy: The Case of China." *The World Economy* 37(6): 747–64.

Nolan, P., J. Zhang, and C. Liu. 2007. *The Global Business Revolution and the Cascade Effect*. Basingstoke: Palgrave.

Nolan, P., J. Zhang, and C. Liu. 2007. "The Global Business Revolution, the Cascade Effect, and the Challenge for Firms From Developing Countries." *Cambridge Journal of Economics* 32(1): 29–47.

Ponte, S., Ingrid K., K. S. Jaspersen, and F. Kruijssen. 2014. "The Blue Revolution in Asia: Upgrading and Governance in Aquaculture Value Chains." *World Development* 64(12): 52–64.

Rugman, S. M. and J. P. Doh. 2008. *Multinationals and Development*. New Haven: Yale University Press.

Schmitz, H. and J. Humphrey. 2000. *Governance and Upgrading: Linking Industrial Cluster and Global Value Chain Research*. IDS Working Paper 120.

Shapiro, H. 1994. *Engines of Growth: The State and Transnational Auto Companies in Brazil*. Cambridge: Cambridge University Press.

Teece, D. J. 2014. "The Foundations of Enterprise Performance: Dynamic and Ordinary Capabilities in an (Economic) Theory of Firms." *Academy of Management Perspectives* 28(4): 328–52.

Teece, D. J. and G. Pisano. 1994. "The Dynamic Capabilities of Firms: An Introduction." *Industrial and Corporate Change* 3(3): 537–56.

Thun, E. 2006. *Changing Lanes in China: Foreign Direct Investment, Local Governments, and Auto Sector Development*. Cambridge: Cambridge University Press.

Womack, J. P., D. T. Jones, and D. Roos. 1990. *The Machine That Changed the World*. New York: Rawson Associates.

Zollo, M. and S. G. Winter. 2002. "Deliberate Learning and the Evolution of Dynamic Capabilities." *Organization Science* 13: 339–51.

Index

For Product Safety Concerns and Information please contact our EU
representative GPSR@taylorandfrancis.com
Taylor & Francis Verlag GmbH, Kaufingerstraße 24, 80331 München, Germany

www.ingramcontent.com/pod-product-compliance
Ingram Content Group UK Ltd.
Pitfield, Milton Keynes, MK11 3LW, UK
UKHW022123190926
475702UK00013B/1618
9780367784423